Latinos and the 2012 Election

Latinos and the 2012 Election

THE NEW FACE OF THE AMERICAN VOTER

Edited by GABRIEL R. SANCHEZ

Michigan State University Press • East Lansing

Copyright © 2015 by Michigan State University

♾ The paper used in this publication meets the minimum requirements
of ANSI/NISO Z39.48-1992 (R 1997) (Permanence of Paper).

Michigan State University Press
East Lansing, Michigan 48823-5245

Printed and bound in the United States of America.

21 20 19 18 17 16 15   1 2 3 4 5 6 7 8 9 10

Library of Congress Control Number: 2014951527
ISBN: 978-1-61186-160-0 (pbk.)
ISBN: 978-1-60917-448-4 (ebook: PDF)
ISBN: 978-1-62895-171-4 (ebook: ePub)
ISBN: 978-1-62896-171-3 (ebook: Kindle)

Cover and book design by Charlie Sharp, Sharp Designs, Lansing, Michigan

g green press Michigan State University Press is a member of the Green Press
INITIATIVE Initiative and is committed to developing and encouraging
ecologically responsible publishing practices. For more information about
the Green Press Initiative and the use of recycled paper in book publishing,
please visit *www.greenpressinitiative.org*.

Visit Michigan State University Press at *www.msupress.org*

Contents

RUBÉN O. MARTINEZ

Foreword

MEXICAN AMERICANS BROUGHT NEW ENERGY AND VISION TO ELECTORAL politics in the decade of the 1960s, when they redefined their ethnic identity as Chicanos. In 1963, the Political Association of Spanish-Speaking Organizations led a campaign in Crystal City, Texas, to register Mexican Americans to vote, getting them to pay the poll tax and then vote on Election Day. The result was the election of Los Cinco, five Mexican American candidates, to city council despite the efforts of local Texans to suppress voting among Mexican Americans. These included intimidation by the local political establishment, job dismissals of workers at the local Del Monte plant for wearing campaign buttons, increased surveillance by the notorious Texas Rangers, and overtime production at the Del Monte plant. Mexican Americans had not been elected to local office since the city's incorporation in 1910. Once in office, however, the Texan response was to undermine the governing capacity of the new council members by using numerous tactics. This is best symbolized by the refusal of Texas Ranger captain A. Y. Allee to turn over the keys to City Hall, doing so only after a telephone call by Governor John Connally, and by local businesses that fired some of new council members and decreased the pay of others.

In response, the Mexican American Youth Organization, formed in 1967, led successful Chicano electoral campaigns in municipalities in South Texas and gave rise to the formation of the Raza Unida Party in 1970. Dramatic, successful campaigns in 1970 in Crystal City, Cotulla, and Carrizo Springs gave Chicanos fifteen seats, including two city-council majorities, two school board majorities, and two mayoralties. The challenge to the political power of white Texans engendered a white backlash that again undermined the newly elected and diminished their capacity to carry out their responsibilities as elected officials. The Raza Unida Party had support among young Chicanos in Colorado and California as well. The Chicano struggle for political power would lead to the establishment of the Southwest Voter Registration Education Project and the registration of millions of Latinos. It would also lead to the election of thousands of Latinos to public offices across the country, but especially in the Southwest, in the following decades. Increased political representation, however, would not necessarily lead to improved socioeconomic conditions for Latinos, as the political climate across the country would turn extremely conservative and anti-Latino.

The backlash in Texas was not unlike that which occurred in Boston and other cities across the country against school busing and other civil rights gains. White Americans took to the streets to oppose busing and in many instances resorted to covert acts of violence against minorities. Despite the long history of white violence against Native Americans, blacks, Latinos, and Asian Americans, white Americans responded negatively to the dismantling of white racism and the integration of racial and ethnic minorities into the nation's institutions, claiming they were the victims of racism by minorities—an incredible assertion given their historical role as the dominant group. Over the next several decades, Chicanos, Puerto Ricans, and Cuban Americans would be joined by millions of immigrants from Mexico, Central America, and South America, making Latinos the second largest ethnic group in the country at the turn of the twenty-first century.

The backlash to the civil rights movement and the struggle for political power by Latinos would bring together different groups of white Americans to create a neoconservative movement that seeks to restore a mythical moral and social order that maintains a racial order where whites remain at the pinnacle of the hierarchy. At the same time, a stealth, free-market, fundamentalist movement that has come to be known as neoliberalism has been underway to roll back the components of the welfare state that promoted equality and social support for those in need. In short, neoliberalism represents a revolt by the ruling class to Keynesian economics, which promoted active government intervention in the economy through fiscal policies to stabilize output through the business cycle. The welfare state also promoted tax-and-transfer policies that ameliorated the condition of the poor in society.

Today, neoconservatism and neoliberalism combine to maintain a tense relationship that mobilizes negative sentiments against Latinos, other minority groups, and the poor. With Latinos having become the largest ethnic minority group in this country soon after the turn of the century, and with the demographic shift continuing to change the composition of the student population, the work force, and the electorate, white Americans are more and more willing to take negative stances toward Latinos. The increase in transnational workers, millions of whom are undocumented Latinos, has made immigration a controversial political issue among voters, and one that has been used by conservatives to promote policies and practices that racially profile Latinos. White Americans have been mobilized by the media and well-heeled politicians in efforts to promote policies intended to limit, if not diminish, the electoral influence of Latinos. In other words, they promote voter-suppression policies. While the white response is predictable, at least among some, what is most distressing is the willingness to undermine the most basic right citizens have in a representative democracy.

The current volume is the first to examine in depth the influence of the Latino electorate, and demonstrates its increasing influence even if Latinos are less likely to vote than white and black Americans. That pattern is changing, however, and we can expect that the repressive policies of conservatives will mobilize Latino voters in the coming years. In the 2012 general election, the Latino vote was instrumental in determining the outcomes of many campaigns, including that for the president of the country. Acceptance of this fact, however, is distressing to white Americans, who turn to politically conservative ideologies as a result (Craig and Richeson 2014). The threat to their dominant position in society leads them to accept retrenchment tactics even if it means the undermining of democracy. As we move into the future, it may be the case that the demographic shift and the increasing electoral influence of Latinos will lead to increased political polarization across the country. As more people become disaffected with neoliberal policies, however, white Americans may become aware that the class war launched against them by the ruling class is actually a greater threat to them than the rising numbers of Latinos, and that preserving democracy is critical to improving the well-being of all citizens. After all, no group has a monopoly on democracy, even if those with wealth have a disproportionate influence irrespective of the color of their skin.

REFERENCE

Craig, M. A., and J. A. Richeson. 2014. "On the Precipice of a 'Majority-Minority' America: Perceived Status Threat from the Racial Demographic Shift Affects White Americans' Political Ideology." *Psychological Science*. Doi: 10.1177/0956797614527113.

Preface

IN MARCH 2013, A GROUP OF SCHOLARS OF LATINO POLITICAL BEHAVIOR IN THE United States met in Los Angeles for the Western Political Science Association's (WPSA) yearly conference. This group had been heavily involved in tracking the influence of Latino voters in the 2012 presidential election, and the conference was our chance to come together to present our findings after a momentous year. The result was a panel of conference papers exploring themes related to Latinos and the election that all relied on the best data available to examine Latino political behavior during the 2012 election. After receiving positive feedback at the conference, we decided that the time was ripe for an examination of Latino voter influence by many of the leading experts on Latino politics in this country. The resulting book is the product of decades of expertise in the field of Latino participation applied to the question of just how influential Latino voters were during the 2012 presidential election. The purpose of this book is to evaluate this question retrospectively through analyses of the various ways the Latino vote may have been felt in what we now know was a pivotal moment in the history of our nation.

The political landscape of the United States is undergoing an important transformation being driven by major demographic changes, mostly attributable to the growth of the Latino population. Although these trends have been underway for some time now, the implications of these changes seemed to become visible to the wider public during and after the 2012 election season. The 2012 campaign was a tense and exciting time for scholars and observers of Latino voter influence in United States politics, but professionals from all fields were paying close attention to Latino voters during the election, generating a wide and often heated debate among journalists, scholars, and pundits as to what role Latino voters would play in the outcome of the race. The stakes of this debate were set high early on, as interested parties and political pundits began wrangling over whether Latino voters would determine the outcome of the presidential race early in 2012.

The Latino political-opinion research firm Latino Decisions, in partnership with America's Voice, an immigrant-rights lobbying organization, conducted a series of surveys of Latino likely voters throughout the 2012 election season, culminating in the widely cited "2012 Latino Election Eve Poll." This research provided the definitive data on the Latino electorate throughout the country and supplied the foundation for the authors featured here to explore the nuances of the campaign within their state and relevant to the Latino community, first in a series of blog posts on the Latino Decisions website, then as conference papers at the WPSA meeting, and finally as chapters in this book. What emerged from this collaboration is a picture of the election from the perspective of unprecedented Latino voter influence.

We have organized the chapters to best represent the compelling aspects of our topic, starting with a methodological approach to evaluate Latino influence within the context of the Electoral College, followed by a discussion of how different forms of mobilization contributed to Latino voter turnout in 2012. As the politics of immigration policy emerged as a driving force in Latino mobilization, we next explore how the salience of immigration policy to the campaign was driven largely by the Latino electorate. Since voting preference is closely tied to the context of where voters live, the bulk of this book is devoted to a state-by-state discussion of Latino voters in 2012 by scholars of Latino politics currently working within the states that proved to be critical to the election outcome.

What we hope to reveal here is a compelling picture of just how and why Latinos turned out in record numbers for the 2012 election. Additionally, and perhaps even more importantly, the analysis presented here can be used to project how influential Latino voters could be in future electoral races, both in numbers and in helping to define the policy agendas that motivate people to vote. These topics are critical in a country where electoral preferences are an ever-shifting tide, and where representative democracy is an ever-changing game.

Acknowledgments

AS WITH ANY PROJECT OF THIS NATURE, THIS BOOK IS THE PRODUCT OF CONTRI-butions from a wide set of people who were instrumental in seeing this volume come to fruition. Of course, a special debt of gratitude goes to the staff of Michigan State University Press, and particularly Rubén Martinez, who as the series editor of *Latinos in the United States* worked closely with our team to move the project forward. We also want to thank the reviewers who provided very helpful feedback on our draft manuscript, as well as a host of colleagues who attended our session at the Western Political Science Association and provided useful suggestions that helped us improve our individual chapters. The staff of the Robert Wood Johnson Foundation Center for Health Policy at the University of New Mexico was very helpful in this effort, with particular recognition going to Jee Hwang, our Center statistician, and Morgan Sims, our Center technical writing expert, who devoted hours to ensuring that the book was ready for publication.

Introduction

THE 2012 ELECTION WAS A WATERSHED MOMENT FOR THE LATINO ELECTORATE in many respects.[1] As early as March 2012, *Time* magazine announced loudly that Latino voters would determine the outcome of the presidential race (Scherer 2012). This set the stage for what proved to be a hot debate regarding just how influential Latino voters would be in 2012. For example, the Pew Hispanic Center cautioned that Latino voters were less certain about voting than other segments of the electorate (Lopez and Gonzalez-Barrera 2012), which fueled widespread discussion of an enthusiasm gap among Latino voters in 2012.

In giving President Obama a record level of support (75 percent), Latinos proved to be decisive to the election outcome—an unprecedented mark of influence for this segment of the wider electorate. Prior to Election Day, both parties went out of their way to include more Latinos in marquee roles at their convention than seen before. This included Mayor Castro from San Antonio providing a primetime speech at the Democratic Convention, and Governor Martinez from New Mexico speaking on the national stage on the Republican side. The undeniable influence of the Latino electorate continued after the election, as Latinos remained at the center of national discussions regarding a potentially enduring coalition of minority voters, the future of the Republican party, and the prospect of the passage of immigration reform. In short, 2012 was undoubtedly big for Latinos.

Our volume intends to provide a comprehensive overview of the 2012 election as it pertained to the Latino electorate. This includes a discussion of the prominent role of immigration policy in the election and of the factors that explain a record level of support for President Obama across key states and nationally, as well as an analysis of the impact the Latino electorate had on election outcomes in several key states across the nation in 2012. The chapters are structured to provide a balanced mixture of rigorous analysis of Latino political behavior conducted by experts in Latino politics who drew from the best data available for their chapters, along with commentary from organizations that were directly engaged with the mobilization of Latinos and advocacy for immigration reform. The end result is a must-read book, not only for scholars of Latino and electoral politics, but for anyone interested in learning more about the factors that led 2012 to be the year of the Latino electorate.

The power of this book is driven largely by the combination of the first-rate set of scholars recruited to participate in this project along with the rich data they were provided with to complete their individual chapters. In partnership with America's Voice, Latino Decisions conducted a series of surveys of Latino likely voters in battleground states during the 2012 election season, culminating in the widely cited impreMedia/Latino Decisions 2012 Latino Election Eve Poll, which provided the definitive data on the Latino electorate during an election where in many ways, Latinos were the story. Building on a series of blog posts featured on the Latino Decisions website during the 2012 election, and a panel at the 2013 meeting of the Western Political Science Association, this volume features many of the leading experts of Latino politics and draws from the exclusive survey data provided to the authors from Latino Decisions. The appendix provides a detailed description of the methodology for these surveys, along with links to additional content and analytical tools available through Latino Decisions. Therefore, while each substantive chapter may provide some discussion of the specific measures the authors used in their analyses, the appendix is essentially the data and methods section for the entire volume.

In the wake of the 2012 presidential election, many interest groups and advocacy organizations made claims that their constituencies, including the Latino electorate, were influential to the election outcome. Furthermore, scholars and journalists were hungry to know whether Latino voters ended up having as large an impact on the outcome as was widely speculated throughout the campaign season. Latino Decisions, among others, stated emphatically that 2012 was the first election cycle where Latino voters were decisive to the election outcome. The question addressed in the first substantive chapter essentially focuses on just how influential Latino voters actually were in the election. The authors, Matt Barreto (professor of political science at the University of Washington and cofounder of Latino Decisions) and Justin Gross (assistant professor of political science at the University of North Carolina, Chapel Hill and senior statistician at Latino Decisions), review several approaches to determining group influence, with a critical assessment of conventional wisdom in this area. The authors then utilize the best available data and their original methodology to assess the degree to which Latinos and African Americans collectively influenced the outcome of the 2012 election. Barreto and Gross conclude with a discussion of how their innovative approach can be applied to future races.

One of the valuable aspects of the approach Barreto and Gross provide in assessing Latino influence on electoral outcomes is that it directly accounts for the nature of the Electoral College system in presidential elections. It is not solely the rise in the Latino population that has led to an increased electoral influence, but also that Latino population growth has taken place in states that are electorally relevant. State context matters, as Latinos are having an impact on the politics within an increasing number of states across the nation. This book accounts for this context by having a number of authors discuss the nature of Latino influence within several states vital to the 2012 election. The quality of these discussions benefits from having authors who are uniquely positioned to conduct this analysis, as each of these state-focused chapters is authored by an expert in Latino politics who is also connected to the state they analyze. This has led to a set of chapters that provide the reader with a bird's-eye view of what occurred within several states during the election season, including the way in which the hugely salient issue of immigration played out differently within the context of each state covered.

The book moves from the big-picture assessment provided by Barreto and Gross to two critically important discussions: the effect of strategic mobilization of Latino voters in 2012, and the wide impact that immigration politics had on Latino voters in 2012. These discussions benefit from the inclusion of organizations that were vital to these two aspects of the election: the National Association of Latino Elected Officials (NALEO) and America's Voice. The chapter focused on the mobilization of Latino voters in 2012 combines the well-recognized expertise of Ricardo Ramírez (associate professor of political science at the University of Notre Dame) and the collective applied expertise of the NALEO Educational Fund. This collaboration has yielded a discussion of what we know about the success of approaches to the mobilization of Latino voters generally, and how these approaches operated specifically in the 2012 election. The authors here note that while the innovations in tactical mobilization techniques of the Obama campaign were important, they alone did not account for the record turnout of Latino voters in 2012. The authors also find that the nature of contact varied significantly among specific segments of the Latino population (native vs. foreign-born Latinos, for example). This chapter is an incredibly rich highlight within the collectively strong book.

Immigration was the backdrop of the 2012 election and the central focus of post-election discussions concerning the Latino electorate. Consequently, the role of immigration was woven into all of the chapters in this volume, and it is the direct focus of the next substantive chapter, authored by Maribel Hastings, senior advisor to America's Voice. To assess the role of immigration in the 2012 election, this chapter takes us back to 2008 when immigration emerged as a key issue following Senator McCain's decision to appeal to the far right of his party by campaigning against his own immigration-reform-focused past. The chapter then reminds us of the contradictory approach of the president on immigration—promises of immigration reform in speeches, but a record number of deportations during his first term. With this context in mind, Hastings takes us through the key themes of the 2012 race, ranging from self-deportation to deferred action policy, and eventually to the post-election immigration reform debates. The chapter leaves us with the question of whether or not the Republican Party will learn from its past missteps on this issue and seize an opportunity to make inroads with Latino voters by helping to pass comprehensive immigration reform.

With respect to the state-focused chapters, this volume includes analysis of a mixture of states traditionally associated with Latino influence (New Mexico, Florida, and California), states with a recent surge in the viability of the Latino electorate driven by demographic shifts over the last decade (Colorado and Nevada), as well as key battleground states that at first glance do not seem to be relevant to Latino politics, but where Latino voters are becoming, and will continue to be, highly influential (Ohio, North Carolina, and Virginia).

The section of state-focused chapters opens with the Rocky Mountain states of Colorado and New Mexico, two locales where growth in the Latino electorate is having marked yet divergent impacts on each state's national profile. In 2012, Colorado once again lived up to its status as a swing state and emerged as one of the key battleground states in the general election. Democrat Barack Obama won the presidential election with 51.5 percent of the popular vote, due largely to the surge in Latino voting power, which has resulted in what Professor Robert Preuhs (Metropolitan State University of Denver) notes as a shifting political tide in Colorado, a state that formerly had produced victories for Democratic presidential candidates only twice since 1948 (Clinton in 1992 and Johnson in 1964).

The continued increase in Hispanic voting strength, coupled with a shift in preference to Democratic candidates among this population, has moved New Mexico away from the status of key battleground state they have enjoyed in recent memory. The symbolic shift in Electoral College saliency between these two states is examined by Gabriel Sanchez (associate professor of political science at the University of New Mexico and director of research for Latino Decisions) and Shannon Sanchez-Youngman (PhD candidate in political science at UNM) in their discussion of the relocation of Latino campaign outreach specialists from New Mexico to Colorado when an Obama victory in the Land of Enchantment became evident rather early in the election season. The commonalities between Colorado and New Mexico also extend to the surprising emergence of immigration as a key policy issue for Hispanic voters in both states where immigration has not had a significant influence on electoral politics. The authors from both states draw from Latino Decisions data to examine why immigration policy became a central theme in the 2012 race, and what implications this may have for the future of Latino politics in these locales.

California remained a Democratic stronghold in 2012 and a state where Latino voters were largely ignored by both parties (only 31 percent of respondents to the 2012 Latino Election Eve Poll in California reported that they were contacted during the 2012 race). Jason Morin (assistant professor of political science at California State University, Northridge) and Adrian Pantoja (professor of political science and Chicano studies at Pitzer College) provide an excellent historical narrative of California politics to explain the vital role that Latinos have played in the transition of California to a solidly blue state, as well as the consequences associated with a lack of mobilization and outreach from the Republican party to Latino voters out west. Morin and Pantoja note that despite the lack of mobilization, California Latinos remained surprisingly enthusiastic in 2012, largely due to the national debates surrounding immigration policy. The politics of using immigrants as a scapegoat is not new to Latino voters in California, which makes the analysis of how Latino voters in California reacted to this GOP strategy in 2012 extremely interesting.

The volume strategically moves from California to Ohio to provide a stark contrast in political context. Unlike California, the Buckeye state continued to be the battleground of battleground states, and a state where Latino voters are not generally part of the electoral discussion. However, as Tehama Lopez Bunyasi (assistant professor in the School for Conflict Analysis and Resolution at George Mason University, formerly assistant professor of political science at Ohio University) details in her chapter, Latinos in Ohio are becoming a key constituency that may have a direct say in whether the state remains a vital swing state into the future. This increased salience for Latinos is driven by their large growth patterns in a state whose overall population is stagnant—Latinos accounted for 75 percent of full growth of the Ohio population from 2000 to 2010—as well as the incredibly competitive electoral environment where every vote counts. This chapter provides a rich discussion of the demographic profile of the Latino population across the state of Ohio, as well as analysis of how Latino voters influenced not only the presidential race, but one of the most competitive U.S. Senate races in 2012.

The volume moves next to the South, a region where an explosion of Latino population growth has had a marked impact on all aspects of life in states like Virginia and North Carolina. Much attention was paid to these two states in 2012, after a 2008 race that found these two electoral prizes landing surprisingly in the hands of President Obama. Reflective of the migration patterns across the entire region, the Latino populations in Virginia and North Carolina are very diverse and growing at an amazing rate. D. Xavier Medina Vidal (assistant professor of political science at Virginia Tech University) notes that the Latino population in Virginia increased by 92 percent from 2000 to 2010, a rate ten times greater than non-Latinos, but one that trails the even greater 111 percent increase in North Carolina. Furthermore, only 26 percent of Latinos in Virginia are of Mexican origin, with no single national-origin group dominating the political landscape (as is generally the case elsewhere). Latino voters in Virginia were more likely to be mobilized by the Republican Party than Latino voters elsewhere, yet these efforts were offset by a strong anti-immigrant climate in the state. The interesting context of Virginia politics allows Medina Vidal to provide several lessons learned in Virginia that can be applied to effective outreach efforts for Latinos more broadly.

The Latino population in North Carolina has been one of the more closely followed in the nation. While the electoral context in North Carolina is very similar to that of Virginia, and despite large support for President Obama among Latino voters, this did not translate into overall success for the president or Democrats more broadly in North Carolina. Betina Cutaia Wilkinson (assistant professor of political science at Wake Forest University) notes in this chapter that the 2012 race in North Carolina was influenced by several down-the-ballot races and the Democratic National Convention being located in North Carolina, adding to the mobilization of Latino voters. While the strong showing of Latino voters in 2012 did not yield victory for Democratic candidates in that year, Wilkinson projects that the continued growth of the Latino electorate and their interest in immigration policy will be vital.

In the next chapter, Casey Klofstad (associate professor of political science at the University of Miami) persuasively contends that the state of Florida is an outlier in Latino politics for two important reasons: the Latino population tends to lean more to the right than Latinos more broadly, and Latinos in Florida are somewhat removed from the national immigration debate. Despite these caveats, Klofstad finds that (in 2012 at least) Latino voters in Florida are not all that different from their co-ethnics in other areas of the country. While Cuban Americans continue to have stronger ties to the GOP than non-Cubans, the Latino electorate in Florida proved to be heavily Democratic. This trend is driven largely by the significant increase in the Puerto Rican population in Florida, resulting in this state having the greatest number of Puerto Ricans of any state other than New York. Furthermore, although Latinos in Florida were less likely to report a personal connection to undocumented immigrants, they strongly favored the policy approach of Democrats, in line with Latinos nationally. Drawing from extensive analysis, Klofstad contends that due to the more moderate ideology of Cuban American voters over time coupled with the continued growth of the highly Democratic Puerto Rican population in Florida, the Latino population may push the state toward Democratic status down the line. He concludes by considering how the emerging national profile of native son and Republican Marco Rubio could influence Latino political behavior in the near future.

Nevada provides an extremely interesting perspective from which to analyze Latino voting influence, as this state was hit hard during the economic recession, which could have paved the way for Romney's success in a traditionally right-leaning state. However, fueled by an incredible 80 percent support from Latino voters, President Obama was able to become the first Democratic candidate to carry Nevada in a successive election in half a century. As in other states, immigration proved to be a major story line in Latino politics in Nevada in 2012.

However, arguably more than presidential rhetoric driving immigration-policy salience, a tough Senate race, featuring highly charged immigrant-focused rhetoric from Sharron Angle two years previously, primed Latino voters to consider immigration policy stances between the two parties in 2012. David Damore (associate professor of political science at the University of Nevada, Las Vegas) draws from multiple data sets to explore internal variation in vote choice among Latinos in Nevada in 2012, finding little prospect of a silver lining for Republicans. For example, a whopping 90 percent of first-time Latino voters supported the president in Nevada, with young Latino voters having the least support for Romney among all age groups. While these trends strongly suggest that the Latino population could push Nevada into becoming a blue-leaning state once and for all, Damore examines factors that could soften the Latino attachment to the Democratic Party in a state that in many ways reflects the overall influence of the Latino electorate more than any other.

The volume closes with a projection into the future of Latino electoral politics from three of the premier authorities on Latino politics: Dr. Gary Segura, Dr. Matt Barreto, and Dr. Sylvia Manzano, all from Latino Decisions. After providing some summative commentary on the major themes raised in the volume, the authors use two important states that were not covered in the volume to discuss the future influence of Latino politics: Arizona and Texas. This fascinating discussion provides demographic projections for both states, emphasizing the tremendous growth of the Latino electorate and how that growth could lead to significant changes in political outcomes if Latino mobilization rates were to increase. Given that there were not specific chapters on the states of Texas and Arizona, the authors' focus on these two important locales in their narrative makes the concluding chapter a must read, and it rounds out the overall discussion of Latino influence on the 2012 election.

NOTE

1. The authors use the pan-ethnic identification terms Latino and Hispanic interchangeably throughout the book, with no preference given to one term over the other.

REFERENCES

Lopez, Mark Hugo, and Ana Gonzalez-Barrera. 2012. "Latino Voters Support Obama by 3-1 Ratio, but Are Less Certain Than Others about Voting." Washington, DC: Pew Research Center's Hispanic Trends Project, October.

Scherer, Michael. 2012. "Yo Decido: Why Latino Voters Will Pick the Next President." *Time magazine*, March 5.

JUSTIN H. GROSS and MATT A. BARRETO

Latino Influence and the Electoral College

Assessing the Probability of Group Relevance

As long as journalists and scholars have been paying attention to Latinos as a potential voting bloc in the United States, they have debated the degree to which Latinos are influential and speculated on when they might finally gain their anticipated influence. Each new election season brings with it predictions of Latino electoral-power ascendance, as well as the requisite rebuttals insisting that Latinos remain a "slumbering giant." It was no different in 2012, as dueling headlines late in the election season proclaimed, "Latino vote may be subdued in 2012," and on the other hand, "Latino vote critical to Obama election." While the journalists interviewed various "experts," it was clear that no systematic analysis of Latino influence was present in these news accounts of Latino voters.

In 2012, pundits were once again trading post-election analyses of Latinos' role in national elections, this time amid broad consensus in conventional wisdom that Latinos were indeed a critical electoral group. But as scholars, we should stop to clarify this claim. What does it mean to declare that a group of voters will be decisive or superfluous? That is, what would Latino voting power look like, and how would we know it if we saw it?

We first briefly review some of the ways that group voting influence (Latino influence in particular) has been defined. We note a few aspects of voting influence that are not typically considered in such discussions, highlighting the counterintuitive nature of some of these. Having endorsed a multidimensional approach to understanding group-based electoral influence more broadly, we then focus on a particular notion of electoral power that, while narrowly defined, merits special attention during the periods just before and just after each presidential election. It is natural for journalists, pundits, and voters themselves to wonder: "What are the chances that Latinos (or single women, white evangelicals, NASCAR dads, etc.) will 'decide' the election?" And once the votes are counted: "Did this group of voters make the difference?" These questions are not only interesting, but they carry real political significance. In 2012, after it seemed clear that the Republican Party had witnessed a historic low in its Latino support, Republican senator John McCain took to CNN, where he quite clearly drew the connection between group influence and government responsiveness when he stated, "If we continue to polarize the Latino/Hispanic vote . . . our chances for being in the majority are minimal. . . . This issue of illegal immigration has obviously been a major driving factor in the decision-making of the Hispanic voter. We need to pass comprehensive immigration reform" (McCain 2013).

The seemingly straightforward questions of whether Latino voters "made a difference" in an election, or how likely it is that they "will have an impact" in an upcoming election are reasonable ones to ask, but surprisingly difficult to operationalize and measure.[1] We consider the usual way of answering these questions and suggest an alternative approach. We offer an evidence-based assessment of the probability that there will exist some set of states pivotal to the outcome, with each state in turn decided by a margin lying within a range of *plausible Latino variability* (based on current polling or estimates of actual Election Day turnout and vote choice, together with historical fluctuation of these two numbers). We use simulation, with hierarchical random effects, to capture the interdependence of outcomes across the states. We make the case that, once election results are known, the appropriate post facto measurement of influence is still probabilistic in nature. Using this measurement approach, we demonstrate the surprisingly synergistic potential of minority voting, showing that the electoral influence of Latinos and African Americans, taken together, in fact outweighed the sum of their individual components considered separately in the 2012 presidential election. Finally, we take a brief look forward to 2016 and the opportunities for expanded Latino influence.

Multiple Visions of Latino Voting Influence

As Barreto, Collingwood, and Manzano (2010) point out, asking whether Latinos "singlehandedly determined" an electoral outcome is too stringent a definition of influence. They instead recommend the consideration of three dimensions in measuring Latino electoral influence: state-specific demographics (including group size and growth rate); "electoral volatility" with respect to registration, partisanship, and turnout; and degree of resource mobilization. Among the variables they consider relevant are rates of party registration, pre-election polls of vote intention, targeted Latino campaign spending, media coverage of Latino voters within a state, estimated turnout rates, overall size of the Latino population, and the group's growth rate. The authors argue that "considering multiple aspects of political influence opens up avenues to investigate the extent to which different groups' influence in politics is conditioned on the combination and variation in group demographics, voting behavior, and mobilization" (2010).

Ricardo Ramírez, in his recent book *Mobilizing Opportunities* (2013), also takes a holistic approach to analyzing the power of the Latino electorate, focusing on state-level mobilization efforts of various sorts and asking about the nature of their influence in different states. He distinguishes this from what he sees as the three currently dominant approaches: the "ethnic approach" (e.g., Beltrán 2010; DeSipio 1996; Oboler 1995), the "demography is destiny" approach (e.g., Bowler and Segura 2012), and the "pivotal vote thesis" (de la Garza and DeSipio 1992, 1996, 1999, 2005; de la Garza, DeSipio, and Leal 2010). The first of these emphasizes heterogeneity by national origin and ancestry, and the second stresses large-scale demographic shifts as the key to racial and ethnic minorities' eventual place of power in winning electoral coalitions of a new "multiracial era of American politics." It is the pivotal vote thesis that we address most directly here, in order to challenge some aspects of it while retaining its spirit within the narrow confines of presidential pre- and post-election analysis. Our view is that, although this may be but one among several important ways to understand group-based political power, the search for pivotal blocs will continue to have an outsized appeal in popular accounts of elections as well as within campaigns themselves; we should thus help ensure that any such analysis is done thoughtfully and in a manner that does not emphasize random idiosyncrasies of electoral outcomes, but instead focuses on accurate assessment of uncertainty.

In considering group voter influence from a broad view, it is worth briefly noting a few underappreciated sources of tension that make it difficult to neatly operationalize the concept. First, the tension between group cohesion and heterogeneity is especially important to making sense of group influence. While we tend to think of group cohesion as a key requirement of bloc voting, too much uniformity can paradoxically weaken voting influence in some regards. While shared and recognizable interests make it possible—and potentially rewarding—for candidates to appeal to a given group, the perception of group homogeneity may lead the party not favored by the group to write these voters off, and the party favored by the group to take them for granted. A hidden benefit of group-targeted appeals, either symbolic or substantive, is that getting a toehold in a community may allow a candidate's message to spread via social networks. If, however, a candidate or party sees no realistic hope of gaining much support in a community, they will likely see no way to take advantage of this cohesion. This has been the case with African American voters, who have overwhelmingly supported Democratic candidates for decades, raising the potential danger of being viewed as too reliable a voting bloc for one party, and demonstrating the advantage of having some diversity of opinion in the quest for group voting influence. That said, a highly cohesive bloc that shows nearly uniform support for a party's candidates can have a special sort of influence that is itself sometimes underappreciated. Such a bloc realizes all its power through degree of turnout; the expected value of each additional vote from this group is extremely high for the favored candidate (and low for other candidates). The two fundamental ways that a campaign can help its candidate are through getting potential voters to actually vote, and convincing voters to cast votes for the candidate (or against her opponents). The relative appeals of each are not equivalent, nor do they remain constant throughout a campaign or among different candidates. While a group of actual voters perceived as giving nearly unanimous support to one side may attract little effort to convert them or maintain their favor, potential voters of this group will be enormously valuable in terms of turnout strategy, and not just to one side. This brings us to a second, counterintuitive point: negative attention is an indication of group influence. When a group's members are seen as strong and unwavering partisans, are easily identifiable, and tend to cluster geographically, they may attract not only their favored candidate's GOTV (get out the vote) efforts but also attempts, overt or subtle, to suppress their turnout. From this perspective, efforts at making voting less appealing or more difficult for a group may in fact be seen as an indication of that group's power. Indeed, a number of observers have credited perceived targeting of racial and ethnic minorities, college students, and urban residents as actually fueling turnout among these groups in 2012. Thus, the unique power of cohesive, highly partisan groups may include the temptation they present to adversaries to overreach and provoke backlash. In 2010 a conservative PAC attempted to deflate the Latino vote in Nevada rather than win it over, running a series of Spanish-language TV ads encouraging Latinos "not to vote," ostensibly because neither party had earned their vote due to insufficient efforts to reform immigration policy. Indeed this group was weighing the likelihood that Democrat Harry Reid could win the state without a strong showing from Latino voters. In the end, the controversial ads seemed to counter-mobilize Latinos, with interest groups reminding Latino voters that "they don't want you to vote; let's prove them wrong," and Latino turnout higher in Nevada in 2010 than in any other state. Putting it bluntly, *Time* magazine proclaimed: "Latino voters saved Harry Reid."

Less visible than influence manifested through negative attention is influence that is realized through *lack of action.* For example, during the 2012 Republican primaries, Texas governor Rick Perry was notably less harsh in his criticism of undocumented immigrants than most of his opponents. His insistence, during one debate, that it would be heartless not to allow undocumented immigrants, brought to the country as youngsters, to attend college at in-state tuition rates was widely viewed as a risky move in light of the power of grassroots conservatives during the primaries. While Perry is by no means a liberal, even on immigration issues, it is safe to assume that political realities in Texas place limits on how extreme he could afford to appear in rhetoric and policy in this area. It is easy to identify the many Latino voters in Texas as a major factor here, but perhaps equally important are the over two million eligible Latino voters who do not yet participate. While, by most measures, the nonparticipation of so many potential voters represents a devastating missed opportunity for influence in Texas, it would be shortsighted to think that these nonvoters have no political influence at all. One lesson that recent elections in California, Arizona, and Nevada have taught us is that campaigns appearing excessively mean-spirited, racist, or explicitly anti-Latino can galvanize Hispanic participation like perhaps no other motivation (Barreto and Ramírez 2013). Thus, while no one would suggest that a group should intentionally refrain from registering or voting, it is true that the *threat of participation* may act as a restraint on extremism, yielding to hidden—but not yet mobilized—power. In fact, since we view uncertainty with regard to group voting preference and/or turnout as an essential component of any definition of voting influence, the fact that Latinos can be found in large numbers at various different levels of formal civic engagement (from unengaged to highly engaged) may be a singular strength. Given sufficient threat, Latinos at each different level are apt to move in the direction of greater engagement, with unauthorized immigrants participating in demonstrations (and petitioning for regularized status), permanent legal residents applying for citizenship, citizens choosing to register, and registered infrequent voters choosing to vote. The lack of clarity on just how large the set of Latino potential voters is at any time may well draw the attention of risk-averse candidates. The fact that the restrictive Proposition 187 was passed in California in 1994, amidst a wave of hostile anti-immigrant activity associated with the Republican Party, is widely credited as driving a major uptick in political participation among Latinos in the state, leading to a long-term dominance for Democrats, especially in elections for national office. It is far too easy to forget how crucial these 53 electoral votes from the "safe state" of California are in allowing Democratic presidential candidates to concentrate time and money elsewhere.

One final obstacle to effectively assessing group (and specifically Latino) voting influence involves confusion over the difference between the probability that voters are pivotal, given that they are group members, and the probability that voters are group members, given that they are pivotal. This was evidenced in 2012 every time a commentator suggested that the high number of Latinos in less competitive states, such as California, Illinois, Texas, New Jersey, and New York, implied lack of influence for Latinos overall. As the *New York Times* blogger Nate Silver (2012) put it, "Almost 40 percent of the Hispanic vote was in one of just two states—California and Texas—that don't look to be at all competitive this year." Carrying this logic to its natural extreme, we might say that non-Hispanic whites have little influence in the nomination process, because 98 percent of this group reside in states other than Iowa and New Hampshire. The relevant issue is not what percentage of all Latinos are in competitive states, but rather what percentage of voters in competitive states are Latino, and whether the margin of victory is likely to make this group crucial to the outcome. To the extent that there are some important shared concerns among many Latinos across the nation, the fact that Latinos represent a growing share of all voters in Nevada, Colorado, Florida, and "new destination" states such as North Carolina, Virginia, Ohio, and Iowa—and therefore have the potential for significant electoral influence—suggests that Latinos do matter, even if Latinos in California, New York, or Illinois did not at all contribute to this influence.

Ramírez (2013) draws attention to three apparent shortcomings of the pivotal voter approach, considering heterogeneity as a challenge to the notion of a Latino voting bloc, the awkwardness of comparing actual outcomes to a hypothetical scenario in which no Latinos voted while assuming candidates would not also change (i.e., the impossibility of 'holding all else constant' in this context), and what one might call a myopic fixation on the current election. Ramírez 's point on the last of these is that demographic trajectories need also be considered, but we would take this point further and assert that it is myopic to give excessive attention to the particular Electoral College configuration and intra-state vote tallies, even in assessing influence in a single election.

DeSipio and de la Garza (2005) identify four closely related forms of Latino voter influence of the type Ramírez critiques. The counterfactual approach they take, asking how electoral outcomes would differ under alternate scenarios, is intuitive and motivates our own definition. However, we replace their somewhat narrow and deterministic notions of influence (according to which each state either is or is not

a "Latino influence state" in a given presidential election) with probabilistic assessments by state and for an election as a whole. Rather than simply asking whether a
state's choice for president would have been different in the absence of Latino voters,
or whether a notable shift in partisan support or turnout actually took place in a given
year, or whether the popular vote in a state wound up being close enough that many
different voter blocs could claim influence over the result (as in DeSipio and de la
Garza 2005), we instead ask: Given our uncertainty about turnout and vote choice
of Latinos and non-Latinos in each state, and the distribution of possible outcomes
across states, how likely is it that a set of states all have votes close enough that they
fall into a range of plausible Latino influence, and that the winner of the election
hinges in turn upon these states?

To capture the range of plausible influence, we consider two realistic scenarios
that are the best for each candidate, respectively. That is, within each state, what is
a plausible level of Latino turnout and percentage of Latino votes cast for Romney
that would be optimal from Romney's point of view, and what combination would
be optimal for Obama, given the constraints of voting history and polling? Then,
given the uncertainty over non-Latino vote percentage for each candidate, we ask
what the probability is of an outcome that falls somewhere between these two
plausible extremes.

Once the election is over, the analysis remains essentially the same, except
that instead of asking how likely it is that the election will be decided by a set of
states that are all themselves decided by a margin within the range of plausible
influence, we ask what was the probability of such an outcome, in retrospect and
given what we know now. If a group is very predictable in its turnout (high or low)
and its partisan voting, the range of plausible influence for that group shrinks; it
is only when a group's turnout and/or partisanship is perceived as less predictable
that it is likely to draw special attention from campaigns, especially if the group
has clear shared interests and can be reached out to efficiently (e.g., through a
shared medium or through policy choices or signals likely to be noticed by a high
percentage of group members).

Paradoxically, it matters less what *did* happen—inasmuch as the precise outcome
involves not just systematic variation but also a random draw from a distribution of
likely outcomes—than what *easily could have* happened, given what is now known.
Uncertainty emerges not only from sampling error in polls, but also from the inher-
ent randomness of voting on Election Day. A clear assessment of which scenarios
are more or less likely is what drives campaign strategy, and a lucid post-election
reassessment must similarly deal with probabilistic considerations. Thus, while some
speculate on how history might have been different had the 2000 Gore campaign
expended a little effort on training the elderly Jewish voters of Palm Beach County

in how to read the now infamous "butterfly ballot," few would think of this small group as singularly influential; we recognize the situation as unique, arising from the confluence of an enormous number of systematic and random factors. Using our best information available (economic models a year before, polls a few months before, and election results during the days after), the question of group influence becomes: What is/was the probability that the Electoral College vote and the vote margins within the states will/would unfold in such a manner that the group of interest may be deemed a decisive factor? This is the question we shall try to answer in the context of the 2012 presidential election, comparing the relative influence of Latinos and African Americans, as well as the combined influence of both groups.

To illustrate the dynamic of Latino influence in the presidential election of 2012, we created an interactive web applet allowing users to visualize what Latino influence looks like.[2] Taking real-time weekly polling data from every state for both Latinos and non-Latinos, coupled with the estimated share of all voters who will be Latino, users of the web app can see what happens if Latino turnout is somewhat lower or higher than expected, if the candidates get more or less of vote support than expected, or both, if Latino turnout is somewhat low in Colorado, or Latino voters break more heavily for Romney in Florida. Users can manipulate two sliders—for Latino vote choice and Latino turnout rate—from low to high and watch various states change from red to blue or vice versa. States that never change colors are those with limited Latino influence. States that flip back and forth with just a slight adjustment of the sliders indicate high Latino influence. And ultimately, one can see whether the magic number of 270 is reached by one candidate or another. Figure 1 approximates the information conveyed by a particular setting of the applet, specifically our best guess a month before the election. Note that the electoral votes under this particular scenario precisely match the eventual outcome. One may also check a box to count those states deemed too close to call as "virtual ties" under a given scenario. As shown, even a slight edge for one candidate is counted as "leaning" in his direction. We encourage the reader to visit the Latino Vote Map web applet online and examine different scenarios from the 2012 election, as this visual demonstration provides some intuition for the theoretical and empirical approach we outline below.

Probability of Swinging an Election: The Special Case of the Electoral College

A key feature of the U.S. presidential election makes the question of group electoral influence especially interesting. The Electoral College system allows for voting power to be distributed unevenly throughout the electorate, so that certain groups may,

Figure 1. Latino Vote Map

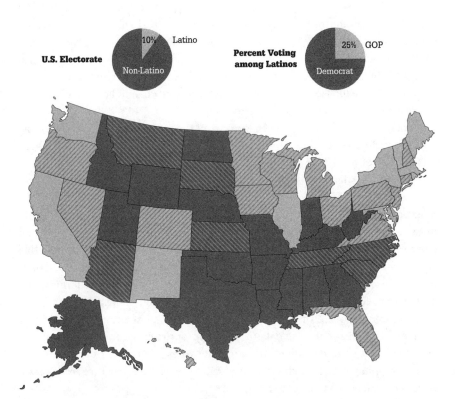

ELECTORAL VOTES

Strongly Obama:	177	Strongly Romney:	148
Obama Leaning:	155	Romney Leaning:	58
	332		**206**

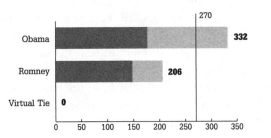

Source: Latino Decisions and American's Voice Education Fund, 2012.

Note: The Latino Vote Map incorporated current polling and measures of uncertainty during the weeks prior to Election Day to allow visitors to the site to discover the implications of different plausible scenarios of Latino turnout and vote choice.

by luck, have greater potential to influence the outcome. This is, of course, a key concern of campaign strategy, and leads to the notion of swing states in the first place. If it weren't for the two-stage approach (where virtually all of a state's electoral votes are awarded to the candidate earning a plurality of popular votes),[3] presidential candidates would likely spend more time in large states with high partisan support, such as California and Texas, in an effort to efficiently mobilize loyal supporters. Instead, eyes are focused each election season on just a handful of states that hold the keys to victory in any close contest.

Political scientists have long been aware of the potential for differential voting power in two-stage elections. Most work in this area examines discrepancies between individuals voting in different subunits. In the United States context, this has taken the form of investigating whether someone in a small state with few electoral votes has more "influence" than someone in a large state with many electoral votes. The most prominent classic analyses, historically, deal with "a priori voting power," found in game theory (social choice theory [Penrose 1946; Banzhaf 1964, 1966, 1968] and cooperative game theory [Shapley and Shubik 1954], plus see a review by Felsenthal and Machover [2005]). As Andrew Gelman and his collaborators have pointed out,[4] however, most of this literature vastly oversimplifies matters by assuming equal probabilities for each possible configuration among subunits (e.g., states). These subunits are thus treated as if voting by independent flips of a coin. An empirically grounded approach must use data to more appropriately account for the relative likelihood that certain configurations of state votes will actually occur, and this means grappling with a potentially complicated correlation structure among state votes (Gelman et al. 1998, 2002, 2004).

Some phenomena will affect votes throughout the nation on any given Election Day, while others will operate on a local level. One straightforward way to model this is via hierarchical random effects, as suggested by Gelman et al. (2002, 2004). Beyond what may be captured by polls (however precise) or predicted from other information, one may model the remaining random variation in terms of a nationwide term, regional terms, state terms, and even district terms. For simplicity, we assume only nation-level and state-level errors in the models specified here. The distribution of these random effects may be estimated by examining several elections, as in Gelman et al. 2002, but while these authors were interested in what may be possible over a long period of time, we are focused on uncertainty surrounding a single election; there will be less unpredictable variation in a specific election with a particular pair of candidates than over several decades with changing candidates and demographics. To better capture the short-term dynamics, we estimate the variance of random effects from weekly poll averages provided by Real Clear Politics (RCP),[5] starting a few months prior to the election.

Table 1. Probability of Latino and Black Influence across States

	Prob(Latino influence)	Prob(black influence)	Prob(black-Latino influence)
Colorado	0.664	0.064	0.835
Florida	0.605	0.778	0.986
Iowa	0.041	0.057	0.112
Michigan	0.013	0.066	0.122
Nevada	0.370	0.095	0.918
New Hampshire	0.040	0.025	0.076
North Carolina	0.237	0.966	0.993
Ohio	0.083	0.486	0.675
Pennsylvania	0.076	0.245	0.403
Virginia	0.125	0.575	0.782
Wisconsin	0.044	0.073	0.183

Note: In 10,000 simulations, centered on the actual outcome of the 2012 election, assuming nation- and state-level variability given by standard deviations (σ_{nation} = 0.02, σ_{state} = 0.01), this table shows the proportion of simulations in which each state's voting puts it in the interval of voting power for Latinos, blacks, and Latinos+blacks, respectively. Nevada exemplified the potential synergy between Latinos and blacks better than any other state, with the probability of combined influence over 90 percent, well more than the sum of the individual probabilities of influence.

Table 2. Probability of Group Relevance in the Electoral College 2012

	σ_{nation} = 0.02 σ_{state} = 0.01 (Short-term estimates, based on polls)	σ_{nation} = 0.03 σ_{state} = 0.015 (Greater uncertainty)	σ_{nation} = 0.06 σ_{state} = 0.04 (Gelman estimates over a few decades)	σ_{nation} = 0.01 σ_{state} = 0.03 (High uncertainty for states, not overall)
Latinos	16.7%	23.2%	18.9%	13.8%
Blacks	26.3%	33.4%	27.3%	28.6%
Blacks and Latinos	65.7%	60.5%	48.7%	69.0%

Note: In what proportion of simulations was a given group "relevant"?—meaning that there was some set of states together determining the outcome of the simulated election, each of which with results that could have plausibly been different depending on group turnout and vote choice. The first column estimates uncertainty at the national and state level, where uncertainty over national and state-specific effects is estimated from movement in average polls provided by Real Clear Politics over the three months prior to the general election. This most naturally captures the short-term variability and a sense of what might have been possible, given the actual final votes within the states. The second column assumes an additional 50% standard deviation in both sets of random effects; this may be considered an allowance for additional uncertainty beyond variation in recent polls. Simulation results in the third column were generated using long-term estimates of variance in state and nation effects, and the final column is based on a hypothetical situation in which the overall nationwide figures are precisely measured, but we are less sure how individual states will vary.

In order to see how robust the results are to the variability of random effects, we analyze voting power both with short-term estimates from RCP and impreMedia/Latino Decisions[6] and America's Voice/Latino Decisions[7] polls (σ_{nation} = 0.02, σ_{state} = 0.01), and the long-term estimates from Gelman et al. (2002) (σ_{nation} = 0.06, σ_{state} = 0.04), as well as two other hypothetical pairs of standard deviations for national and statewide disturbances, in order to check the sensitivity of results to our level of uncertainty pre- and post-election. We center our simulations on the estimates for actual Election Day results by state for non-Latinos, nonblacks, and potential voters who are neither black nor Latino. Parallel analyses may be done throughout the pre-election season, using estimates taken either purely from previous elections, from current polls, or from favorite model-based estimates.

Evaluating Latino Voting Influence on the 2012 Presidential Election

After the election is over and the votes counted, the natural instinct is to ask whether the group with supposed influence did in fact "affect" the outcome. When considering the implications for future elections, the question should not be whether the last one happened to fall on one side or the other of a dividing line, but rather whether the pre-election estimates and assessment of uncertainty (about turnout and vote choice in each state) were realistic. To appreciate this point, it is important to understand that the probability that a given group may be pivotal in a given election is bound to be quite low in absolute terms. However, while neither of two given groups may be likely to swing a particular election, one that has a 5 or 10 percent chance to do so should be more likely to attract attention from campaign strategists and media than one that has a one in a million chance. More precisely, a group whose voting and turnout may make a difference in a state or states that would be pivotal under certain realistic scenarios in the Electoral College will be addressed as part of a comprehensive strategy. Yet, come Election Day, neither group will be expected to actually be a necessary component to the outcome. Suppose a candidate and campaign staff analyze the various "pathways to 270" electoral votes necessary for victory—as Jim Messina, campaign manager for Obama 2012, in fact did publicly (Heilemann 2012)—in order to decide where to allocate attention, money, and political capital (e.g., evolve on gay marriage, implement DACA, visit Ohio and Florida a certain number of times). Some decisions will be aimed at shoring up states and constituencies deemed necessary to a win (e.g., Pennsylvania for Democrats, Florida for Republicans; African American turnout for Democrats, white rural voters for Republicans). Others may be made, resources permitting, as insurance against unexpected scenarios (e.g., a small state unlikely to make a difference, or a state that the candidate feels is safe, but that is deemed necessary to a winning pathway). Whether a particular group such as Latinos will be a key element of a careful strategy should be in part related to an assessment of how efficiently they may be addressed and mobilized, and the degree to which realistic electoral pathways may hinge on the voting behavior of the group in question. This is precisely what we have sought to capture with our simulations.

Based on actual Election Day results, used in our simulation, Florida and Colorado were essential elements of Latino Electoral College voting power. In nearly every one of the simulation runs in which the outcome hinged on a set of states that were each decided within the margin of plausible Latino influence, these two states (worth 38 electoral votes) were in the deciding set. Given how closely contested Florida was, the high percentage of registered Latino voters in the state, the large number of electoral votes (29) at stake, and the relative heterogeneity in partisanship, it is hardly a surprise that this state is currently the linchpin of Latino power. Nevada was close behind the other two states, appearing in over 90 percent of the simulation runs where the outcome hinged on Latino influence.

The probability of black influence was about 10 points higher than the same figure for Latinos in 2012, according to our measure, with several states appearing in the pivotal set (Ohio, Virginia, North Carolina, and Florida) in at least 90 percent of the simulation runs decided within the margin of plausible variability for black turnout and vote choice. Together with Pennsylvania (88 percent), these states account for nearly 100 votes in the Electoral College. Other than Florida, there was no overlap among the top Latino-influence states and the top black-influence states in 2012. And yet, taken together, the opportunity for a possible minority coalition to swing the election outcome is greatly strengthened, with far more states potentially pivotal and at the same time likely to have outcomes driven by Latino and black turnout and vote choice. In states where the power of black or Latino voters will only be manifest in the event of a very close contest, it is much more likely that the *combined* numbers (and uncertainty over those numbers) will be instrumental in a victory.

A fascinating consequence of the complementary demographic strengths of blacks and Latinos is that their voting power, taken together, is stronger—potentially quite a bit stronger—than the sum of their individual contributions. In Wisconsin, the probability of Latinos swinging the state outcome is around 4 percent, while the same probability for blacks is around 7 percent; but the probability of black/Latino combined influence is 18.3 percent. In Nevada, the phenomenon is even more dramatic. While Latinos are estimated to be pivotal with probability 0.37, and blacks with probability 0.10, the two groups taken together are far more formidable; the estimated probability that Nevada will be decided by a margin smaller than the combined plausible variability of blacks and Latinos is over 90 percent! Although Latino and black voters, taken separately, each have between 16 percent and 34 percent chance of being instrumental to the outcome of the presidential election, they together reach over a 60 percent chance of influence measured in this manner.

Looking Ahead to 2016

One of the important contributions of this chapter is that we have outlined an approach to measure Latino influence that is flexible, fluid, and updatable. States such as New Mexico were critical Latino-influence states in 2000 and 2004. By 2012, New Mexico appeared to be a safe Democratic state in the presidential election. Our approach allows scholars and pundits to update and assess Latino influence each year with new data but a consistent model. To this end, we turn our attention forward to the 2016 presidential election. Without question, data from the Census Bureau indicate that the Latino citizen adult population continues to grow across every state. Accompanying these demographic changes are political changes as well, as states begin to appear more competitive and attract the interest of campaign strategists as they map out a plan to gain 270 Electoral College votes. The 3-point margin of defeat for Democratic U.S. Senate candidate Richard Carmona in Arizona in 2012 suggests that Arizona is moving from a leans-Republican to a toss-up state as 2016 approaches. As that happens, the Latino voters who account for roughly 20 percent of the electorate will become incredibly relevant. If Latino turnout is high, Democrats may benefit. If the GOP changes course in Arizona and courts the Latino vote in earnest, it may be able to keep Arizona as a leans-Republican state. Whatever the outcome, Arizona is a state to watch in 2016, and it could be the newest addition to the list of battleground states with sizable Latino electorates.

In addition to Arizona, a state that has drawn a lot of recent attention for its Latino electorate is Texas. A state that has seen twenty-four consecutive years of leadership from Republican governors is now reemerging as a "pre-battleground" state. While it is less likely to be competitive in 2016 than Arizona, the demographic changes are hard to discount. Civic groups that focus on voter registration and voter turnout are flooding the Lone Star State to register the two million Hispanics who are eligible but not yet registered to vote. If these groups make even a dent in the Latino voter registration shortfall, Texas could then very quickly become fertile ground for Latino influence. Should Texas come close to the zone of plausible Latino influence, we should see an enormous spike in outreach to the state's Latino voters and eligible voters. In addition to the untapped potential of the Latino electorate, much has been made about the potential mobilizing power that Julian and Joaquin Castro have as potential statewide candidates for governor, attorney general, or U.S. senator in future Texas elections. With voter-registration drives and a Castro on the ticket, surely Texas will be competitive by 2018 or 2020, and the reason will be Latino voters.

Beyond Arizona and Texas, which have quite significant Latino populations, our data and models suggest that states such as Virginia, North Carolina, Iowa, Ohio, and Georgia have the potential to be strong Latino-influence states in the future. These states are now witnessing very close elections year after year, and all have a Latino citizen adult population that is growing dramatically. The potential for black-Latino synergistic power in new destination states in the South such as North Carolina, Virginia, and Georgia—as well as the Midwest and Mid-Atlantic, such as Ohio, Iowa, and Pennsylvania—may have radical implications for the long-term future of presidential politics in the United States.

NOTES

1. See Erikson (2010) for a thoughtful treatment of the issues involved. In particular, in analyzing appropriate counterfactuals, he gives serious consideration to possible consequences of appeals to Latino voters in terms of the voting behavior of non-Latinos.

2. Latino Decisions/America's Voice Education Fund Latino Vote Map: www.latinovotemap. org.

3. The exceptions are Nebraska and Maine, which allow electoral votes to be shared among candidates.

4. When Gelman and his coauthors discuss "voting power," they are studying the relative power of individual voters, not groups, although they raise the possibility of extending this idea to group voting power. Given our claim that voting influence should not overemphasize the actual election outcome in all its detail, it is interesting to note that even in the absence of any recorded example of a nationwide election decided by a single vote, these authors find value in comparing the relative voting power of individual voters in terms of the tiny, but not identical, probabilities that their votes will be decisive. Gelman, King, and Boscardin (1998) even title their article "Estimating the Probability of Events That Have Never Occurred: When Is Your Vote Decisive?"

5. 2012 RCP polling data is archived here: http://www.realclearpolitics.com/epolls/2012/president/2012_elections_electoral_college_map.html.

6. For example, impreMedia/Latino Decisions weekly national tracking poll: http://www.latinodecisions.com/files/5913/5204/1319/Tracker_-_toplines_week_11.pdf.

7. America's Voice/Latino Decisions final battleground poll: http://www.latinodecisions.com/files/2413/5173/0145/AV_6-state-survey-TOPLINES_-_FINAL.pdf.

REFERENCES

Alvarez, R. Michael, and Lisa Garcia Bedolla. 2003. "The Foundations of Latino Voter Partisanship: Evidence from the 2000 Election." *Journal of Politics* 65, no. 1: 31–49.

Banzhaf III, J. F. 1964. "Weighted Voting Doesn't Work: A Mathematical Analysis." *Rutgers Law Review* 19: 317.

———. 1966. "Multi-Member Electoral Districts: Do They Violate the 'One Man, One Vote' Principle." *Yale Law Journal* 75, no. 8: 1309–38.

———. 1968. "One Man, 3.312 Votes: A Mathematical Analysis of the Electoral College."

Villanova Law Review 13: 304.

Barreto, M. A., L. Collingwood, S. Manzano. 2010. "A New Measure of Group Influence in Presidential Elections: Assessing Latino Influence in 2008." *Political Research Quarterly* 63, no. 4: 908–21.

Barreto, Matt A., and Ricardo Ramírez. 2013. "Anti-Immigrant Politics and Lessons for the GOP from California." *Latino Decisions Research Report*, September 20. Available at latinodecisions.com.

Barreto, Matt, Rodolfo de la Garza, Jongho Lee, Jaesung Ryu, and Harry Pachon. 2002. "Latino Voter Mobilization in 2000: A Glimpse into Latino Policy and Voting Preferences." Claremont, CA: Tomas Rivera Policy Institute.

Barreto, Matt, Luis Fraga, Sylvia Manzano, Valerie Martinez-Ebers, and Gary Segura. 2008. "Should They Dance with the One Who Brung 'Em? Latinos and the 2008 Presidential Election." *PS: Political Science & Politics* 41 (October): 753–60.

Barreto, Matt, Fernando Guerra, Mara Marks, Stephen Nuño, and Nathan Woods. 2006. "Controversies in Exit Polling: Implementing a Racially Stratified Homogenous Precinct Approach." *PS: Political Science & Politics* 39: 477–83.

Beltrán, Cristina. 2010. *The Trouble with Unity: Latino Politics and the Creation of Identity.* New York: Oxford University Press.

Bowler, Shaun, and Gary Segura. 2012. "The Future is Ours:" Minority Politics, Political Behavior, and the Multiracial Era of American Politics. Thousand Oaks, CA: CQ Press.

Cain, Bruce E., D. Roderick Kiewiet, and Carole J. Uhlaner. 1991. "The Acquisition of Partisanship by Latinos and Asian Americans." *American Journal of Political Science* 35, no. 2: 390–422.

Dawson, Michael. 1995. *Behind the Mule.* Princeton, NJ: Princeton University Press.

de la Garza, Rodolfo O. and Louis DeSipio, eds. 1992. *From Rhetoric to Reality: Latino Politics in the 1988 Elections.* Boulder, CO: Westview Press.

———. 1996. *Ethnic Ironies: Latino Politics in the 1992 Elections.* Boulder, CO: Westview Press.

———. 1999. *Awash in the Mainstream: Latino Politics in the 1996 Elections.* Boulder, CO: Westview Press.

———. 2005. *Muted Voices: Latinos and the 2000 Elections.* Lanham, MD: Rowman and Littlefield.

de la Garza, Rodolfo O., Louis DeSipio, and David Leal, eds. 2010. *Beyond the Barrio: Latinos in the 2004 Elections.* Notre Dame, IN: University of Notre Dame Press.

DeSipio, Louis. 1996. *Counting on the Latino Vote: Latinos as a New Electorate.* Charlottesville: University of Virginia Press.

DeSipio, Louis, and Rodolfo de la Garza. 2005. "Between Symbolism and Influence: Latinos and the 2000 Election." In *Muted Voices: Latinos and the 2000 Elections*, ed. R. de la Garza and L. DeSipio. Lanham, MD: Rowman & Littlefield.

Erikson, Robert S. 2010. "Hispanic Voting in the American States." In *Beyond the Barrio: Latinos in the 2004 Elections*, ed. Rodolfo O. de la Garza, Louis DeSipio, and David L. Leal, 73–95. Notre Dame, IN: University of Notre Dame Press.

Felsenthal, Dan S., and Moshé Machover. 2005. "Voting Power Measurement: A Story of Misreinvention." *Social Choice and Welfare*, 25, nos. 2–3: 485–506.

Fraga, Luis R., John Garcia, Rodney Hero, Michael Jones-Correa, Valerie Martinez-Ebers, and Gary M. Segura. 2010. *Making It Home: Latino Lives in the United States.* Philadelphia: Temple University Press.

Gelman, A., J. N. Katz, and J. Bafumi. 2004. "Standard Voting Power Indexes Do Not Work: An Empirical Analysis." *British Journal of Political Science* 34, no. 4: 657–74.

Gelman, A., J. N. Katz, and F. Tuerlinckx. 2002. "The Mathematics and Statistics of Voting Power." *Statistical Science* 17, no. 4: 420–35.

Gelman, A., G. King, and W. J. Boscardin. 1998. "Estimating the Probability of Events That Have Never Occurred: When Is Your Vote Decisive?," *Journal of the American Statistical Association* 93, no. 441: 1–9.

Heilemann, John. 2012. "Hope: The Sequel." *New York Magazine*, May 27.

Krosnick, J. A. 1989. "Question Wording and Reports of Survey Results: The Case of Louis Harris and Aetna Life and Casualty." *Public Opinion Quarterly* 53: 107–13.

Krosnick, J. A., and D. F. Alwin. 1987. "An Evaluation of a Cognitive Theory of Response Order Effects in Survey Measurement." *Public Opinion Quarterly* 51: 201–19.

Layman, Geoffrey. 2001. *The Great Divide.* New York: Columbia University Press.

Leal, David, Matt Barreto, Jongho Lee, and Rodolfo de la Garza. 2005. "The Latino Vote in the 2004 Election." *PS: Political Science & Politics* 38 (January): 41–49.

Lizza, Ryan. 2008. "Making It: How Chicago Shaped Obama." *New Yorker*, July 21.

Lopez, Linda, and Adrian D. Pantoja. 2004. "Beyond Black and White: General Support for Race Conscious Policies among African Americans, Latinos, Asian Americans." *Political Research Quarterly* 57, no. 4: 633–42.

McCain, John. 2013. Interview with Wolf Blitzer. *The Situation Room.* CNN, January 28.

McClain, Paula D., Niambi M. Carter, Victoria M. DeFrancesco Soto et al. 2006. "Racial Distancing in a Southern City: Latino Immigrants' Views of Black Americans." *Journal of Politics* 68, no. 3: 571–84.

McClain, Paula D., Monique L. Lyle, Niambi M. Carter et al. 2007. "Black Americans and Latino Immigrants in a Southern City: Friendly Neighbors or Economic Competitors." *Du Bois Review* 4: 97–117.

Nicholson, Stephen P., Adrian Pantoja, and Gary M. Segura. 2006. "Political Knowledge and Issue Voting among the Latino Electorate." *Political Research Quarterly* 59, no. 2: 259–72.

Oboler, Suzanne. 1995. *Ethnic Labels, Latino Lives: Identity and the Politics of (Re)Presentation in the United States.* Minneapolis: University of Minnesota Press.

Pantoja, Adrian. 2005. "More Alike Than Different: Explaining Political Knowledge among African Americans and Latinos." In *Diversity in Democracy: Minority Representation in the United States*, ed. Gary M. Segura and Shaun Bowler. Charlottesville: University of Virginia Press.

Penrose, L. S. 1946. "The Elementary Statistics of Majority Voting." *Journal of the Royal Statistical Society* 109, no. 1: 53–57.

Ramírez, Ricardo. 2013. *Mobilizing Opportunities: The Evolving Latino Electorate and the Future of American Politics.* Charlottesville: University of Virginia.

Sanchez, Gabriel R. 2006a. "The Role of Group Consciousness in Latino Public Opinion." *Political Research Quarterly* 59, no. 3: 435–46.

———. 2006b. "The Role of Group Consciousness in Political Participation among Latinos in the U.S." *American Politics Research* 34, no. 44: 427–50.

Segura, Gary M. 2009. "Identity Research in Latino Politics." Paper presented at the Annual Meeting of the American Political Science Association, Toronto, Ontario, September 2–6.

Shapley, L. S., and M. Shubik. 1954. "A Method for Evaluating the Distribution of Power in a Committee System." *American Political Science Review* 48, no. 3: 787–92.

Silver, Nate. 2012. "Hispanic Voters Less Plentiful in Swing States." *New York Times–FiveThirtyEight*, June 19. Available at fivethirtyeight.blogs.nytimes.com.

RICARDO RAMÍREZ, EVAN BACALAO, EDELMIRA P. GARCIA,

RANI NARULA-WOODS, and CLAYTON ROSA

Proactive, Reactive, and Tactical

Mobilizing the Latino Vote in 2012

THERE WAS A NOTICEABLE SHIFT IN THE PERCEIVED RELEVANCE OF THE LATINO electorate during the course of the 2012 presidential campaign. In February 2012, *Time* magazine predicted that Latino voters would determine the outcome of the presidential race (Scherer 2012). Within a few months the optimism faded, and there were more skeptics than believers in the growing presence and influence of the Latino electorate. For example, the Pew Hispanic Center anticipated strong Latino support for Barack Obama over Mitt Romney, but cautioned that Latino voters were less certain about voting than other segments of the electorate (Lopez and Gonzalez-Barrera 2012). Others feared that President Obama's failure to deliver on a promise of comprehensive immigration reform during his first term and Mitt Romney's opposition to any pathway to citizenship for undocumented immigrants would leave Latino voters with little incentive to participate in the election (Pino 2012).

In essence, prior to November 6, there was more uncertainty about the overall Latino voter turnout than interest in specific Latino voter preferences. The day after the election, exit polls concluded that Latinos overwhelmingly supported the reelection of President Barack Obama; however, many election analysts and pundits were caught by surprise by the "unexpectedly" strong Latino voter turnout (Rodriguez 2012). Although there were mixed forecasts from journalists, pundits, and think tanks alike of the impact Latinos would make on Election Day, the high Latino turnout challenged many predictions. Similar to 2008, pundits reflexively credited the partisan campaigns (the president's in particular) for increased electoral participation among young voters, African Americans, and Latinos. However, we argue that attributing higher than expected turnout exclusively to partisan, campaign-driven, get-out-the-vote (GOTV) efforts overlooks the combined impact of multiple forms of mobilization within the Latino electorate.

In this chapter, we offer a more nuanced understanding of the role of mobilization in the 2012 general election and seek to provide a framework that delineates why mobilization matters in presidential elections generally, and more specifically in 2012. In the first section, we present three primary forms of voter mobilization (tactical, reactive, and proactive) and describe how these three differing forms of mobilization are interrelated and how they are distinct. The second section focuses on deconstructing the misconception that tactical mobilization of Latino voters by partisan campaigns accounts for variation in turnout rates. The third section explores the role that context plays in the decision of Latinos to vote (reactive mobilization) that is not directly attributable to tactical mobilization. The fourth section demonstrates the efforts and programming by nonpartisan civic institutions to build the electorate in 2012 (proactive mobilization) and their long-term goals of increasing Latino civic participation in the United States. The final section concludes with a consideration of the role of Latino mobilization and the particular significance of proactive mobilization strategies in 2014 and beyond. Overall, this chapter redefines the nature of Latino mobilization by presenting an additional layer that accounts for political context, while challenging voter-turnout assumptions.

Latinos, Mobilization, and American Politics

With the growing attention on Latinos across the United States, it is necessary to explore their impact on the local, state, and national political landscape. Scholars and observers have noted that Latinos played a significant role in key elections across the country in 2012, including the reelection of President Barack Obama (Lopez and Taylor 2012; Foley 2012). According to the U.S. Census Bureau, an estimated 11.2 million Latino voters participated in the 2012 general election (U.S. Census Bureau 2013b). This record turnout was not driven solely by candidate appeal or demographic growth, but by a confluence of historically grounded and multifaceted factors that have stimulated Latino voter participation. As evident in figure 1, the growth is

Figure 1. Latino Citizen Voting-Age Population, Voter Registration, and Turnout, 1988–2012

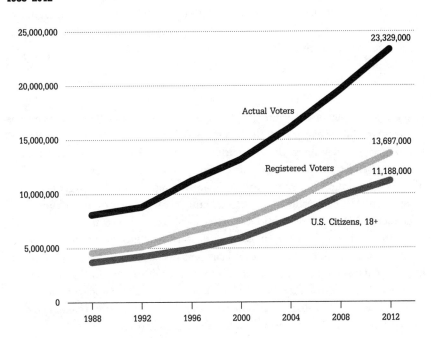

Source: U.S. Census Bureau, Voting and Registration in the November Elections: 1988–2012.

particularly remarkable when considering that fewer than 5 million Latinos voted in 1988 (U.S. Census 2013b).

According to the political participation literature, voter turnout is not only driven by demographic characteristics, such as education, income, and age, but also by recruitment into politics (Rosenstone and Hansen 1993). As such, mobilization is key to understanding why and how Latinos continue to surprise pundits and dispel participation myths. Parsimony may work with respect to identifying general patterns of participation in the overall population, but these patterns require more attention when considering Latinos, precisely because they have been largely neglected by political parties and because of the speed at which the Latino electorate is growing (Wong 2008; Ramírez 2013). Leighley (2001) distinguishes between institutional mobilization and particularized mobilization. The former reflects the extent to which the workplace, church, and voluntary associations are politicized, whereas the latter "reflects the strategic efforts of political institutions such as parties, political candidates, and groups to expand conflict in their favor by mobilizing their supporters" (103–4). While it is important to distinguish between these two forms of mobilization, the analysis does not differentiate between the strategic decisions of partisan versus nonpartisan political elites. We offer a different conceptualization of the recruitment into politics—or mobilization—that identifies three differing forms: tactical, reactive, and proactive.

While it is indeed important that the Latino electorate is now part of the broad strategic decisions of partisan and nonpartisan groups, the consequences for individual Latino voters can be quite distinct. To the extent that presidential campaigns have conscientiously retained Latino outreach directors, these voters may be incorporated into the overall strategic calculus, but this does not speak to the tactics that will be used to mobilize their supporters. The outreach could consist of campaign platforms being translated into Spanish, ensuring that there are key campaign rallies in Latino communities, advertising on Spanish-language media, targeting Latino voters through GOTV campaigns, slating Latina/o candidates, or a combination of these tactics. Tactical mobilization is defined as those voter-engagement efforts that are almost exclusively short-term and focused on a specific outcome in the election (namely, partisan and candidate campaigns) as opposed to those with long-term impact goals, such as Latino electoral presence and growth. In this chapter we explore the role tactical mobilization has played historically in engaging the Latino electorate, and we look to the partisan campaigns of 2012 to better understand their strategic objectives in registering and turning out Latino voters.

Reactive mobilization, defined as political activity in response to a perceived or actual political threat (e.g., legislation or political rhetoric), can have significant impact on the political landscape, and also sets the context for Latino civic participation (Ramírez 2013). This form of mobilization is well-documented, with reactionary politics historically being a major motivating factor for Latino political engagement (Pantoja et al. 2001; Barreto et al. 2005; Barreto et al. 2009). Based on the extant literature, Ramírez (2013) traces the relevance of threat for political activation into protest politics, the decision to naturalize, and electoral politics. While reactive mobilization may last or have consequences beyond one election cycle, it nonetheless begins to dissipate in the absence of imminent political threat. Reactive mobilization can (and often does) take place concurrently with tactical and proactive mobilization.

Finally, proactive mobilization is the coordinated effort of nonpartisan civic institutions—and in some cases with support from philanthropic organizations—to reduce the barriers to engagement and encourage long-term, sustained political participation (Ramírez 2013). Some of these efforts may share similarities in appearance to partisan campaigns, yet the freedom from needing electoral "wins" distinguishes the motivation and goals of these efforts from tactical mobilization. Most significantly, proactive mobilization can contribute to the long-term vision of

Table 1. Overview of Mobilization Types

Type	Tactical	Reactive	Proactive
Definition	Partisan	Real or perceived imminent political threat	Civic infrastructure
Temporal Effects	Short-term	Mid-term	Long-term

expanding the Latino electorate by targeting "low-propensity"[1] Latino voters who are either newly registered or demonstrate irregular voting patterns, both of whom are unlikely to be targeted by partisan campaigns. Later in this chapter we explore examples of proactive mobilization by nonprofit organizations and Spanish-language media, such as the NALEO Educational Fund, Mi Familia Vota, and the ya es hora campaign.

As summarized in table 1, tactical efforts target short-term election-specific participation, reactive mobilization informs intermediary participation, and proactive mobilization influences long-term engagement. Before elaborating on the immediate and long-term consequences of proactive and reactive mobilization, we discuss contemporary instances of tactical mobilization.

Tactical Mobilization: Investing to Win

In the past two decades, presidential campaigns have demonstrated varying degrees of interest in the Latino electorate. The ebb and flow of interest in this community can partially be connected to the disparity between the size of the Latino population and unrealized turnout potential (Durand et al. 2006). However, outreach efforts by the campaigns of President George W. Bush in the 2000 and 2004 elections were lauded for the appeals made to deepen and strengthen relations he had established with Latinos since his time as Texas governor (Armas 2004). More specifically, Bush's campaigns appealed to Latinos on religious and moral grounds connected to issues such as abortion, stem-cell research, and marriage (Johnson 2004). From 2000 to 2004, the Protestant Latino vote for Bush rose from 44 percent to 56 percent (Fry, Passel, and Suro 2005). President Bush won in 2000 and again in 2004 with high support from Latino voters, estimated to be 35 percent and 43 percent respectively (Cillizza 2013).

In 2008, as part of Senator Hillary Clinton's bid for the presidency, Latinos were prioritized as a key voting bloc. At the time, it was believed that on February's "Super Tuesday," Latino voters could be key to unlocking states with large delegations in the Democratic primaries.[2] As Sergio Bendixen, Clinton's head of Latino outreach, pointed out, "The Latino vote in California is the most important part of the firewall . . . if she can win California, no matter what happens the race is on" (Carlton 2008).

Spanish-language ads were developed and disseminated by both campaigns during the 2012 election cycle. The Obama campaign placed a focus on the shared experiences of the candidate as a son of an immigrant, while prominent Spanish-speaking politicians narrated commercials and radio ads as well. Another tactical approach was seen when Obama took on the historical chant "¡Si se puede!" ("Yes we can!") as part of a rally speech, which first began in a Los Angeles appearance and gained immediate popularity. While these approaches may have engaged some Latinos, other Latinos criticized Obama's use of a chant popularized by César Chávez and Dolores Huerta—civil rights leaders and cofounders of the United Farm Workers of America. Dolores Huerta stated that the Obama campaign attempted to establish a relationship with the community using shortcuts, unlike the Clinton campaign (Block 2008). Nonetheless, in the general election, Latinos were touted as a vital force in electing President Obama in Florida, New Mexico, Colorado, Indiana, and North Carolina (Barreto et al. 2010).

For example, in the "swing state" of Colorado, approximately 259,000 Latinos voted in the presidential election, accounting for 10.4 percent of all voters (U.S. Census Bureau 2013b). According to the impreMedia/Latino Decisions 2012 Latino Election Eve Poll, 59 percent of Latinos in Colorado were contacted compared to only 31 percent for the national average. However, in addition to an increased partisan campaign outreach, nonpartisan campaigns also sought out Latino voters. Weeks before the election, Grace Lopez Ramirez, Colorado State director for Mi Familia Vota, explained: "It is important for all of us as a community to engage in these issues, to educate our communities and to get out the vote" (Ryan 2012). Mi Familia Vota's mobilization and outreach efforts, like those of other nonpartisan and partisan local and national organizations, also contributed to higher than average contact rates and increased Latino turnout.[3]

PARTISAN ENGAGEMENT IN THE 2012 PRESIDENTIAL ELECTION

Both President Obama and Governor Romney attended the 2012 NALEO Annual Conference—one of only two organizational conferences both candidates attended on the campaign trail (the other was the annual convention of the Veterans of Foreign Wars). As a nonpartisan and nonprofit organization, the NALEO Educational Fund's conference provides a forum for policymakers from all levels of office and all parties to gather and discuss matters of importance to the Latino community. As such, the conference served as a unique opportunity for partisan campaigns to convey their commitment to the Latino electorate and to Latino leadership in preparation for the general election. Shortly before the conference, Governor Romney launched "Juntos con Romney," while President Obama tapped into his 2008 campaign infrastructure of Obama for America to relaunch "Latinos for Obama." Notably, in the week leading up to the conference, President Obama also announced Deferred Action for Childhood Arrivals (DACA),[4] which was considered a strategic decision for reengagement with the Latino electorate.

As Election Day neared, much of the Latino outreach from both campaigns focused on media buys. The Obama campaign invested more than $2 million on Spanish-language television and radio ads between April and June of 2012, and unions and super PACs committed $4 million for Spanish-language television and radio through the summer in Colorado, Nevada, and Florida (Bravender 2012). These buys were focused on historically competitive "swing" states. PBS NewsHour noted that "President Obama and Mitt Romney have spent eight times more money this year on Spanish-language ads than in 2008." Joseph (2012b), a reporter for *The Hill*, wrote:

> [The Romney campaign] debuted two new Spanish-language ads, one running in all swing states that attacks Obama on jobs and the national debt, with the other featuring Puerto Rico Gov. Luis Fortuño (R), targeted at the fast-growing Puerto Rican population in central Florida, stretching from Tampa to Orlando. Last month he also ran a Spanish-language ad with Sen. Marco Rubio (R-Fla.) addressing Social Security and Medicare (1).

Janelle Ross, from the *Huffington Post*, noted, "Beyond building the base the old-fashioned way, the Obama campaign [was] also running distinctive Spanish- and English-language TV ads targeting Latino voters" (2012). Ross further explained the diversity of the ads depending on the regional landscape—featuring Cubans, South Americans, and Puerto Ricans in areas like Florida versus Mexican American voters in the South and Southwest regions. Young (2012) identified tactics that set the Obama campaign apart from the Romney campaign, such as early registration and early voting, specifically in swing states, and directly targeting eighteen- to twenty-four-year-olds, African Americans, Latinos, and single women. Young continues, "Voter turnout for these four key demographics was about 70% thereby giving him the numbers he needed to push him over the edge."

The Republican National Committee (RNC) launched a Latino outreach campaign targeting Latino voters nationwide and with an eye to local and state races in Colorado, Florida, Nevada, New Mexico, North Carolina, and Virginia for local, state, and national races. With immigration at the forefront, RNC chairman Reince Priebus noted, "We all know it's the fastest growing demographic in America, and Latinos play a vital role in all of our communities" (Republican National Committee

2012b). Bettina Inclan was recruited by the Hispanic Outreach director to lead the campaign, which consisted of increased staff capacity in targeted states, social media promotion, and the "Unéte" mobile-text campaign (Republican National Committee 2012a). From Spanish interviews to blogs and YouTube videos, the campaign messaging highlighted the pitfalls of President Obama's term while focusing on the economy and employment as reasons to support Republican candidates (Harrison 2012; Republican National Committee 2012a).

The Obama campaign's mobilization efforts were lauded by many, but we argue that commentators erroneously conflated enhanced micro-targeting capacity (i.e., use of large quantities of data to identify and reach out to narrow segments of the electorate) with the intention to grow the Latino electorate. A question remains—how did the low voter turnout in 2010 and the projected low turnout of Latino voters in 2012 shift significantly to produce more than 11 million Latino voters? We do not suggest that the Obama campaign would claim credit for directly mobilizing all Latino voters nationally: to wit, during the Obama Campaign Legacy Conference, the Obama campaign released a report suggesting that their strategy was first and foremost geared at winning electoral votes—and doing so through innovative tactics in voter registration, persuasion, turnout, and organization-building in battleground states and border states.[5] Ten battleground states[6] "received a larger share of campaign resources, including organizers, offices, and principal and surrogate trips." According to the report, border states "built organizational strength and capacity to help President Obama win a nearby battleground state. For example, volunteers in California helped [the campaign] win Nevada and Colorado and volunteers in Alabama helped [the campaign] win Florida" (Obama Campaign 2013). At the national level, there was a National Latino Vote director and key personnel focused on communications and the translation of materials to Spanish. In addition, some battleground states[7] also had Latino Vote directors overseeing the operation to mobilize Latino voters locally. Nonetheless, the innovations in voter mobilization in the Obama campaign, while important, cannot account for all Latino turnout nationwide.

In order to determine the likely impact of the Obama campaign's tactical mobilization efforts on overall Latino turnout, it is important to analyze the share of the electorate in the battleground states where Latinos were deemed important.[8] Table 2 reflects the share of the Latino electorate in relation to the overall state electorate in the ten battleground states. Given the importance of electoral votes in these states, there was a strong emphasis placed on mobilization and voter turnout. Moreover, the margin of victory for states such as Colorado, Florida, and Nevada demonstrates the vital role Latino turnout played in securing electoral votes for the Obama campaign (Washington Post 2012).

Table 2. Latino Electorate Share in Battleground States (2012)

State	National share of Latino voters	Latino share of state registered voters	Latino share of total voters	Margin of victory
Colorado	2.31%	10.80%	10.40%	4.70%
Florida	12.50%	17.80%	17.30%	0.90%
Iowa	0.27%	1.80%	1.90%	5.60%
Nevada	1.40%	15.40%	15.00%	6.60%
New Hampshire	0.13%	2.00%	2.20%	5.70%
North Carolina	0.05%	2.20%	2.00%	2.20%
Ohio	0.88%	1.90%	1.80%	1.90%
Pennsylvania	1.64%	3.30%	3.20%	5.20%
Virginia	0.92%	2.70%	2.70%	3.00%
Wisconsin	0.63%	2.30%	2.70%	6.70%

Source: U.S. Census Bureau 2013a.

Given Florida's number of electoral votes, it is a key state for voter mobilization, especially of the Latino electorate. In 2012, nearly 1.4 million Latinos voted on Election Day, accounting for 17.3 percent of all voters (8.1 million) (U.S. Census Bureau 2012). As noted by Casey Klofstad in his chapter titled "Florida's Latino Electorate in the 2012 Election" in this volume, campaign outreach towards Latinos was higher in the state of Florida (37 percent) when compared to other states (31 percent).

According to the Current Population Survey's estimates of registration and voting in 2012, there were 11.2 million Latinos who voted on Election Day; of those, 20.73 percent resided in battleground states.[9] The turnout rate of Latino registered voters in battleground states was noticeably higher than the turnout of those in non-battleground states—87 percent and 80.4 percent respectively. Considering that nearly 80 percent of all Latino voters in the United States live in non-battleground states, tactical mobilization of Latinos in battleground states alone cannot explain the overall turnout of Latino voters nationwide.

It is nonetheless important to consider whether tactical mobilization sheds light on the higher turnout rates in battleground states—for instance, the effect of the Obama campaign's considerable investment in outreach to Latino voters through tailored content and messaging. Unlike Latino outreach in other states, given the larger share of non-immigrant Latinos in New Mexico, the Obama campaign strategically disseminated more English-language content than Spanish. As the Obama campaign confidently expected to win the state, they soon redistributed their resources in Colorado instead, thus exemplifying the essence of tactical mobilization (Obama

Table 3. 2012 Self-Reported Mobilization of Latino Registered Voters by Selected Characteristics

	State Characteristic		Nativity		Preferred Language	
	Non-Battleground	Battleground	Naturalized	Native-Born	Spanish*	English
Contacted	28.32%	43.13%	24.64%	36.61%	23.53%	36.49%
Not Contacted	71.68%	56.87%	75.36%	63.39%	76.46%	63.51%

Source: impreMedia/Latino Decisions Election Eve Poll. Analyses presented are weighted.

Note: Response to survey question: "Over the past few months, did anyone from a campaign, political party, or community organization ask you to vote, or register to vote?

*Totals under "Spanish" do not equate to 100 percent due to rounding.

Campaign 2013). Yet various policy debates in New Mexico arguably contributed to an increase in Latino voter turnout. For instance, the issue of granting state driver's licenses to undocumented immigrants was an important factor for 70 percent of Latino voters. The visibility of this issue, coupled with partisan outreach, mobilized Latino voters to make it count on Election Day.[10]

According to the impreMedia/Latino Decisions 2012 Latino Election Eve Poll results, 71 percent of Latino voters in Ohio felt President Barack Obama truly cared about Latinos, with only 13 percent believing the same about Governor Mitt Romney. This sentiment translated into an overwhelming 82 percent of Latinos in Ohio casting their votes for President Obama. However, the contention in Ohio went beyond presidential candidates, where the economy and job growth (issues ranking as high priority for Latino voters) took center stage in the Ohio U.S. Senate race. Republican state treasurer Josh Mandel and Democratic incumbent Sherrod Brown differed in their stances on economic development, and Senator Brown's position and ongoing political mobilization help him win reelection and secure another term in the Senate. As with all voters, Latino voters in Ohio were also tactically mobilized by connecting with them on key issues like the economy and jobs.[11]

Likewise, in the race for Nevada's 3rd Congressional District seat, incumbent congressman Joe Heck (R) and his Democratic opponent, John Oceguera, led campaigns with Latino voters in mind, investing nearly $200,000 combined on Spanish-language ads (Damon 2012). In an attempt to connect with Latino voters, John Oceguera launched a Spanish-language ad campaign featuring his family and education values, and highlighting the fact that he was raised by a single mother and that he worked his way through college. Additionally, Oceguera made several appearances at local events and met with key Latino leaders. On the other hand, as a means to appeal to Latino voters on a wide political spectrum, Congressman Joe Heck was a keynote speaker at the Hispanic Leadership Network business conference

Table 4. 2012 Partisan Mobilization Type by Selected Characteristics among Latino Registered Voters Contacted

	State Characteristic		Nativity		Preferred Language	
	Non-Battleground	Battleground	Naturalized	Native-Born	Spanish	English
Partisan	54.96%	60.08%	50.78%	58.84%	47.86%	60.32%
Non-Partisan	35.08%	29.38%	42.16%	29.26%	46.19%	27.54%
Both	9.96%	10.54%	7.05%	11.90%	5.95%	12.15%

Source: impreMedia/Latino Decisions Election Eve Poll. Analyses presented are weighted.

Note: Response to survey question: "Were you contacted by the Democrats, Republicans, both parties, or by representatives of community organizations?" (only asked of those who responded yes to having been contacted).

and also attended a Hispanics in Politics event to discuss his platform (Hispanic Leadership Network 2012). Despite his opposition to the DREAM Act, right-of-birth U.S. citizenship, and immigration reform, Congressman Joe Heck won the election by nearly 8 percentage points (Nevada Secretary of State 2012).

Some of this difference in turnout can be attributed to increased rates of tactical mobilization in battleground states. Table 3 illustrates that the rate of self-reported contact for Latino registered voters living in battleground states was about 15 percent higher than for those Latinos registered as living elsewhere (43 percent vs. 28 percent). The tactical mobilization, however, was not solely based on geography but also on key demographic characteristics. Naturalized Latinos and those who opted to respond to the 2012 Latino Election Eve Poll in Spanish were less likely to report being contacted to register or to vote (12 percent and 13 percent respectively). The difference in reported contact highlights that Latino turnout nationally was not solely driven by presidential campaigns' tactical mobilization. In both battleground and non-battleground states, there are partisan campaigns for legislative districts and statewide offices that may have reached out to Latino voters. Even in the battleground states, the mobilization of Latino registered voters should not be interpreted as only representing the efforts of partisan campaigns, because nonpartisan Latino organizations were also active.

To further explore these emerging patterns, table 4 demonstrates additional characteristics of the type of Latino voters contacted by state and campaign type.

The focus and type of campaign outreach aimed at Latinos in 2012 varied considerably. Partisan campaigns constituted the largest share of reported contact among Latino registered voters—65 percent of Latino voters in non-battleground states and 71 percent in battleground states report being contacted by partisan campaigns. There were also marked differences among demographic subgroups. For example, English-dominant Latino voters were more likely to receive encouragement to register or vote from partisan sources, and 60 percent of native-born Latinos reported contact from partisan campaigns.

The relevance of nonpartisan groups in mobilizing the oft-ignored segments of the Latino electorate (i.e., naturalized, Spanish speakers, and those in non-battleground states) is evident in the rates of reported contact. While a large share of all registered Latino voters in both battleground and non-battleground states reported contact from nonpartisan sources (45 percent and 41 percent respectively), nonpartisan outreach efforts appear to have placed greater emphasis on engaging immigrant and Spanish-dominant Latinos than partisan outreach efforts. For example, 42 percent of naturalized Latino voters contacted by a campaign indicated that they were contacted only by nonpartisan organizations, versus 29 percent of native-born Latino voters. Similarly, among Spanish speakers, they were about equally as likely to be contacted by partisan as nonpartisan campaigns. These characteristics in voting demographics and preferences are important to keep in mind as campaigns develop micro-targeted methods of outreach. As we discuss in the next section, this illustrates the proactive mobilization strategy of Latino nonpartisan civic institutions with an eye to long-term electoral presence of Latino voters.

The language-specific effects of tactical mobilization are not only evident with respect to GOTV efforts, but also by the amount of resources spent on reaching out to the Spanish-speaking community by partisan campaigns.[12] While the amount spent in 2012 on Spanish-language media was more than in 2008, this is not commensurate with the size of the Latino electorate. Based on comprehensive data on local television advertising from Kantar Media's CMAG, an October 2012 report by the Hispanic Chamber of Commerce (USHCC) found that between April 10th and September 25th of 2012, Spanish-language advertising constituted less than 5 percent of the $358,898,420 total spending on political advertising. With a reported 38.3 million (13 percent) U.S. Spanish-speaking population (U.S. Census Bureau 2014a) and 23.5 million eligible Latino voters (U.S. Census Bureau 2013b), there is a stark difference in investment. Javier Palomarez, president and CEO of the USHCC, reacted to the notable disparity, pointing out that "While political advertising spending records are being shattered, neither political party is investing a comparable percentage of their advertising dollars to reach these voters. The difference between rhetoric and action is striking and, frankly, troubling" (Hartfield 2012). Striking as it may be for Latino elites, this is consistent with expectations of tactical mobilization of expending only enough resources to get to 270 Electoral College votes.

Reactive Mobilization: Unexpected Mobilization, Unexpected Turnout?

Two major policy issues, immigration and voting rights, shaped the political land-scape in the run-up to the 2012 general election, particularly in regard to the Latino community. As it has in the past, immigration became a contentious issue with strong resonance among Latino voters, while new election-administration policy changes emerged as a potential threat to the participation of this historically marginalized segment of the electorate. Although discussed in different public dialogues and to different degrees (immigration being a much wider part of public discourse), both issues shaped the mobilization of Latino voters.

THE IMMIGRATION DEBATE

The 2012 election was not the first to see immigration being used as a wedge issue, nor the first in which it served as a catalyst for mobilization. The civic unrest of the 1990s occurred within a weaker civic infrastructure, while more recent protests showcased the impact of increased coordination and strengthening civic infrastructure, allowing for proactive mobilization to respond more effectively to perceived political threats. Such was the case early in 2012, when Governor Romney's statements regarding "self-deportation" during a Republican primary debate drew outrage nationally from immigration and Latino advocates alike. After securing his party's nomination, however, Romney's views and stances on immigration evolved, resulting in a softening of his position in an effort to appeal to and court Latino voters (Joseph 2012b).

The Obama campaign also faced challenges in regard to its position on im-migration. Besides the Obama administration failing to fulfill the promise of comprehensive immigration reform during the president's first term, there have been record deportation numbers reaching almost 2 million removals from 2008 to 2012 (Department of Homeland Security 2012). According to the Pew Hispanic Center, polls (comprising primarily Latinos) report high disapproval ratings of 59 percent for the Obama administration in respect to deportations (Lopez, Gonzalez-Barrera, and Motel 2011a). However, with the announcement of "Deferred Action for Childhood Arrivals (DACA), presidential approval ratings reached 75 percent among Latino voters by the end of 2012 (Pew Hispanic Research Center 2013).

Even though the intent and timing of this announcement was hotly debated among partisan strategists and columnists, the impact of this decision on mobi-lization cannot be understated. With an overwhelming majority of adult Latinos (89 percent) and Latino registered voters (86 percent) approving of the Obama administration's DACA policy (see Lopez, Gonzalez-Barrera, and Motel 2011b), this new policy had an instrumental impact on the political landscape and the mobilization efforts that followed. For example, a poll by America's Voice found that DACA was a mobilizing factor for many Latinos, with 38 percent of Latinos naming the policy as "the single most important issue" or a "very important issue" in determining their vote. The impreMedia/Latino Decisions 2012 Latino Election Eve Poll further confirmed the mobilizing factor of DACA and the candidates' stances on immigration, with the poll reporting that 58 percent of Latinos were more enthusiastic about voting for President Obama following the announcement of DACA, while 57 percent were less enthusiastic about Governor Romney and his stance on immigration.

While DACA may have been a strategic political move for President Obama, ongoing immigration-reform advocacy efforts continued to elevate the importance of immigration among Latino communities throughout 2012. Local and statewide groups mobilized the Latino community in Arizona around immigration. United We Dream, for instance (founded in Phoenix in 2008), expanded nationwide with fifty-two affiliates and stands as an example of how nonpartisan organizations can educate and mobilize voters in response to an imminent threat or to prevent one. In 2012, United We Dream launched the "Right to Dream Campaign," seeking to raise awareness of immigration policy debates and identify elected officials as opponents and supporters of immigration (United We Dream 2012). As a result, organizers were able to connect directly with community members with resources and recruit them to participate in other issue-based campaigns. Also in Phoenix, Somos America (We are America) organized community events to address questions about immigration and encourage eligible voters to stand against anti-immigration laws by voting (Cornish 2012). Daniel Rodriguez, a "Dreamer" and president of Somos America, spoke to participants at the event: "Raise your hand . . . if you know someone who's not here but needs this information. Raise your hand if you know someone who's been deported. Raise your hand if you know someone who has the power to vote." Rodriguez and others persuasively connected with the networks and experiences of undocumented voters while also prompting eligible voters to take action. This proved essential in mobilizing Latino voters to vote.

VOTING RIGHTS AND THE STATE HOUSE

Despite numerous levels of federal, state, and local legal protection, voters faced an unprecedented number of challenges to casting their ballots and making their voices heard in the 2012 general election. With cuts to early voting, limitations to same-day and third-party voter registration, and new identification requirements (among many other policies), the 2012 election was particularly challenging for Latino participation. At the polls, a lack of personnel and ill-preparedness were also factors in increased waiting and long lines across the country (up to eight hours in Florida), while some organizations allegedly misinformed volunteers and poll workers (Charles 2012).

In October 2012, the NALEO Educational Fund released an assessment of restrictive voting and registration measures across the country, uncovering the systemic harm that such legislation would impose on Latino voters and other underrepresented segments of the potential electorate (NALEO Educational Fund 2012). These measures were shown to disproportionately have a negative impact on access to voting among certain segments of the population (e.g., Latinos, blacks, immigrants, youth, etc.).

For instance, a new regulation in Pennsylvania (enacted in March 2013) required all voters to present photo identification in order to cast a ballot, generating voter anxiety and confusion and a perceived threat to the electoral process. Rather than expending their energies on fighting the legislation in the courts, many community-based organizations focused on mobilizing and preparing the Latino electorate of Pennsylvania to vote with identification. For example, the Pennsylvania Voter ID Coalition (an advocacy group of organizations from numerous sectors) coordinated efforts to ensure that every voter in Pennsylvania attained the identification required to cast a ballot (Loeb 2012). Ultimately, just weeks prior to the election, a federal judge ruled that the requirement would be placed on hold until after the 2012 election cycle due to the limited turnaround time for implementation, a ruling applauded by the Coalition and others fighting restrictions to the voting process (Gregg 2012). However, this translated into organizations mobilizing in order to provide additional voter education, legal advocacy, and outreach to ensure that voters, poll workers, and other community members knew that there would be no identification requirements on Election Day after all (Johnson and Terkel 2012).

Many community-based organizations focused on traditional "in-field" voter registration, and some of these mobilization efforts faced challenges as a result of new legislation and electoral regulations ahead of the 2012 general election. In Florida, restrictions on third-party registration activities "contributed to the decision of organizations including the National Council of La Raza's Democracia program and the League of Women Voters to temporarily suspend their work in the state while litigation over the law ensued" (United States District Court 2011; NALEO 2012). These regulations included the requirement that all canvassers register with county registrar offices and submit all voter-registration applications within forty-eight hours, lest the individual assisting in the registration (rather than the organization behind the effort) be assessed fines (NALEO 2012).

For underrepresented voters, the impact of these regulations was projected to be devastating; according to the Brennan Center for Justice, "African-American and Latino citizens register through drives [registration] at twice the rate as whites" (Kasdan and Weiser 2012). Professor Daniel Smith, from the University of Florida, conducted a post-election analysis demonstrating that in comparison to voter registration in the 2008 presidential election cycle (prior to the new regulations taking effect) there was a decrease in approximately 80,000 registrations (Allen 2012). Nonetheless, the League of Women Voters and National Council of La Raza ultimately fought against the new regulations in the courts, and adapted in-field registration efforts to the new regulations.

Florida governor Rick Scott initiated a purge of alleged noncitizens from the state's voter rolls ahead of the 2012 general election ("Florida Voter Purge" 2012). Many nonpartisan civic institutions joined together and challenged these efforts on grounds that the voter-list purge "mostly [targeted] the wrong people" and "some voters who [became] citizens a few years before [were] now receiving letters saying they [had] to prove their citizenship" (Lilley 2012). NALEO Educational Fund partners like the Florida Latino Immigrant Coalition helped ensure that eligible voters were not removed from the voter rolls by coordinating with media to make certain that voters were fully educated about the process and their rights as voters and what steps to take should they be incorrectly purged from the voter rolls. Despite the potential to disenfranchise Latino voters, those efforts ultimately generated modest reactive mobilization and galvanized organizational and voter efforts.[13]

Proactive Mobilization: Nonpartisan Campaigns and Latino Mobilization

The nonprofit sector has not always played such an active role in Latino voter engagement. In 2000, the Tomás Rivera Policy Institute's (TRPI) evaluation of Latino voter mobilization efforts found minimal to nonexistent infrastructure of nonprofit services and programs promoting political participation. The study pointed to the most common mobilization strategy as voter registration (de la Garza et al. 2002). TRPI noted that

> Overall, there is little to be said about Latino GOTV efforts. In California, which we consider to have the most effectively organized Latino communities in the nation, those few Latino mobilization campaigns identified were episodic, under-funded and dependent on volunteers (7).

Thirteen years later, nonpartisan civic institutions play a distinct and vital role in the mobilization of the Latino electorate. Partisan campaigns inherently operate with the goal of "winning" electoral outcomes—typically defined as their candidate winning 50 percent or more of all votes cast in a race. Resources are therefore strategically allocated to ensure high turnout of supporters, persuade "undecided" but regular voters, and focus on geographies that are most critical in the campaign's political calculus. Nonpartisan campaigns, however, cannot have electoral goals. Laws governing 501(c)(3) organizations mandate that any political-engagement work be educational in nature and strictly nonpartisan. With the exception of some activity around ballot measures, this allows nonprofit programming to focus on outreach that would likely be overlooked by partisan campaigns and activities that are essential for building long-term participation and a vibrant democracy—from unbiased voter education to engagement of infrequent voters.

The engagement of infrequent or low-propensity voters has proven to be a successful tactic for integrating Latinos into the civic process. Until recently, partisan and nonpartisan campaigns alike were inclined to focus engagement efforts on "most-likely" or "higher propensity" voters, consequently disregarding other voters (Ramírez 2005). In 2002, the NALEO Educational Fund carried out a GOTV campaign, Voces del Pueblo, designed to specifically target low-propensity voters with the goal of converting nonvoters to voters, and most importantly, reach segments of the population overlooked by traditional campaigns' methods. Results demonstrated that with a combination of live calls, "robo" calls, and mailers, Latino voter participation increased. More specifically, the live calls played the greatest role in determining voting behavior, with every twenty-two live calls translating into one voter (Ramírez 2005). With campaign experiments dating back to 2000, NALEO Educational Fund has continued to design programs and outreach activities utilizing empirically tested and proven strategies for engaging Latino voters, including a special focus on low-propensity and "unengaged" voters. Moreover, with the growing literature pointing to the intricacies and nuances of the Latino electorate and the importance of nonpartisan mobilization efforts, other nonpartisan campaigns have also adjusted their outreach strategies.

According to national polling from November 2012, partisan campaigns contacted the largest share of Latino registered voters in all states. With the depth of resources raised and expended in federal campaigns, this is to be expected. Estimates suggest nearly $2 billion spent (Ashkenas et al. 2013). Yet, the long-term vision of community-based organizations is evident when comparing non-battleground states to battleground states. As noted in table 4, in non-battleground states, a greater share of registered Latino voters report that the outreach they received was nonpartisan in nature. This reflects the relatively high investment of nonpartisan efforts in engaging those voters and geographies overlooked by partisan campaigns, with the intent to build a more participatory Latino electorate for the long term.

Of particular note are the mobilizing factors of key propositions throughout California. Education and public safety, issues ranking in importance among Latino voters, were central for several ballot measures in 2012. Specifically, Proposition 30, or the "Temporary Taxes to Fund Education, Guaranteed Local Public Safety Funding Initiative," drew overwhelming support from Latino voters. This speaks to the saliency of key issues and the value of coupling proactive mobilization with localized messaging.[14]

Overall, across all states where polls were conducted, 33 percent of voters were contacted by a community organization. Table 5 further reflects the role of community organizations in voter mobilization in relation to partisan candidate campaigns. The highest contact rates were found in California, New Mexico, Colorado, Texas, Massachusetts, and Arizona, demonstrating how the national Latino turnout in battleground states was not solely driven by presidential campaigns' tactical mobilization.

BUILDING PARTNERSHIPS TO MOBILIZE LATINOS

In a concerted effort to maximize reach and minimize redundancy in the nonpartisan outreach to Latino voters, the nation's leading Latino nonprofit advocacy and civil rights organizations joined together in 2011 to form the National Latino Civic Engagement Table (NLCET).[15] The historic collaboration of the NLCET led to the registration of more than a quarter of a million Latino voters and calls to nearly 3.5 million registered Latino voters in key states such as Arizona, California, Colorado, Florida, Maryland, Nevada, New Mexico, North Carolina, Texas, and Virginia (table 6). Moreover, the NLCET provided a forum for dissemination of voter-education and voter-rights information, sharing of best practices, strategic planning, and other essential elements for large-scale outreach and engagement.

Specifically, the focus of NLCET efforts on ten states with significant, influential, and growing Latino populations contributed to an increase in Latino mobilization and Latino turnout. In Arizona, in-person canvassers walked various communities to promote voter registration and voting (Drummond and Sinclair 2013). Further east, campaigns in Texas and Florida included large-scale voter registration, while outreach efforts in North Carolina and Virginia sought to engage relatively new and emerging Latino communities. For example, Latino population growth in North Carolina is translating into stronger political clout, with registered Latino voters increasing from 10,000 in 2004 to more than 113,000 in 2012. Overall, the NLCET

Table 5. Latino Voters Contacted by Type of 2012 Campaign

	Democrats	Republicans	Community organization
National	59%	39%	33%
Arizona	54%	33%	30%
California	55%	31%	46%
Colorado	75%	40%	33%
Florida	53%	51%	29%
Massachusetts	61%	37%	32%
North Carolina	58%	34%	29%
New Mexico	66%	44%	22%
Nevada	67%	44%	22%
Ohio	74%	54%	27%
Texas	54%	43%	32%
Virginia	76%	67%	23%

Source: impreMedia/Latino Decisions 2012 Latino Election Eve Poll.
Note: Response to survey question: "Were you contacted by Democrats, Republicans, both parties, or by a representative of an organization?"

Table 6. NLCET Phone Canvassing Efforts

State	Voters canvassed	State	Voters canvassed
Arizona	242,523	New Mexico	350,035
California	359,238	North Carolina	7,573
Colorado	761,272	Texas	522,937
Florida	459,685	Virginia	242,605
Maryland	97,256	Total	3,461,554
Nevada	418,430		

proved to be an effective method of developing and implementing a shared national drive in coordination with local, state, and regional programming.

"National Voter Registration Day" (NVRD), which was described as "a national day of action and push people to register to vote before it's too late for the November election," also offered an opportunity for civic institutions to collaborate (Froomkin 2012). One of NVRD's objectives was to challenge common confusion and dispel misinformation about the voter-registration process. Head Count, a nonpartisan voter-registration group, found that 52 percent of eligible first-time youth voters from the 2008 election did not know whether they were still registered to vote at their current address for the 2012 election (A. Bernstein 2012). Hundreds of grassroots organizations and volunteers collaborated to organize voter-registration drives across the nation, using both online technology and traditional methods. The outcome was that hundreds of thousands registered to vote as a result of the coordinated NVRD efforts in 2012, and the momentum continued into 2013.[16]

In addition to national partnerships, local coalitions have also garnered the resources and capacity to serve the Latino community, with the short-term goal of voter registration and education leading to a long-term change of the political landscape and electorate. For instance, in North Carolina, El Pueblo (another NALEO Educational Fund partner) collaborated with local groups at a credit union to conduct in-field voter registration and voter-rights education for the Latino community. El Pueblo also designed a voter-registration campaign targeting multigenerational families, encouraging different generations to provide education to one another and assistance with registering and voting. As outlined by Betina Wilkinson in the chapter titled "North Carolina Latinos: An Emerging, Influential Electorate in the South" in this volume, the greatest potential in the Latino electorate of North Carolina may reside with young voters, who represent the largest and youngest electorate among all ethnic groups in the state. This presents an opportunity to build continuous and long-term Latino voter participation.

Similarly, increased Latino growth in Virginia is fueling coalition-building at the local and state level. In 2012, Latinos made up 8 percent of the state population, but by 2020 they are expected to be well over 11 percent. The Virginia Coalition of Latino Organizations (VACOLAO) has coordinated mobilization and advocacy efforts with faith-based and civil-rights groups, in addition to legal and civic organizations in the area, to raise awareness around voter-protection and voting-regulation issues with legislators, election administrators, and the Latino community. In addition to voter outreach, VACOLAO conducts workshops and advocacy on immigration, which is a fundamental mobilization issue for the Latino community in Virginia. As D. Xavier Medina Vidal points out in the chapter titled "The New *Virginiano* Electorate and the Politics of Immigration in Virginia" in this volume, immigration was a unifying force in bringing together Latinos from diverse economic, educational, and ethnic backgrounds in the state and motivating them to become citizens and registered voters. Based on the role Virginia plays in presidential elections, the growing Virginia Latino community positions the state as a ground for demonstrating the importance of Latino mobilization and turnout.

ROLE OF SPANISH-LANGUAGE MEDIA IN MOBILIZATION

Unlike most of their English-language media counterparts, Spanish-language media has historically been very involved in informing their viewers and involving them in civic engagement opportunities (Ramírez 2013). Building on collaboration across several election cycles, NALEO Educational Fund along with hundreds of local partners and national coordinating partners (including Entravision Communications, impreMedia, Mi Familia Vota Education Fund, National Council of La Raza, and Univision Communications) relaunched the historic ya es hora campaign in 2012. After the election, Lizette Alvarez of the *New York Times* noted the impact of the ya es hora campaign and the unique multilayered approach it took to connect with Latino voters, gain their trust, provide them with information, and mobilize them to participate:

> In countless households, Latinos tuned their television sets to Univision and heard Jorge Ramos, the host of *"Al Punto,"* the Spanish version of "Meet the Press," discuss the candidates' positions on issues critical to them. They switched on Spanish-language radio and heard myriad reasons their vote could spur change. . . . And if voters in some battleground areas needed a ride to the polls, television and radio stations owned by Entravision Communications, Univision's largest affiliate, offered those, too. (Alvarez 2012).

The synergistic partnership between Spanish-language media and Latino nonpartisan efforts such as the ya es hora campaign helped expand the potential electorate. The *New York Times* noted that with ya es hora campaign, "how Latinos got [the] message—the relentless call to register, to vote, to participate—was as important as the message itself: Hispanic television and grass-roots groups working together generated a civic campaign they called ya es hora—Now Is the Time" (Alvarez 2012).

Mobilization in 2014 and Beyond

Latino mobilization efforts reached new heights during the 2012 election cycle, with a unique combination of tactical, reactive, and proactive mobilization contributing to the community's historic impact. Partisan campaigns actively targeted and reached out to Latino voters at unprecedented levels as part of the tactical mobilization of the Latino electorate. Perceived political threats and the short-term and long-term effects of restrictive voting measures, coupled with the debate on immigration, primed the political landscape for increased participation and led to heightened awareness and reactive mobilization.

Tactical forms of mobilization in 2014 and beyond will need to incorporate concerted efforts to connect with Latino voters. Partisan campaigns specifically may need to modify outreach in regions with large Latino populations and also augment infrastructural investment in areas with emerging Latino communities. With considerable regional differences, utilizing the same surface-level tactics across all geographies may no longer be a viable method to genuinely connect with Latino voters. In order for tactical mobilization to remain relevant and effective, partisan campaigns will have to shift from a homogeneous method of outreach to a multipronged approach that better suits the tremendous diversity within the Latino electorate.

Coordination among nonpartisan civic institutions to conduct voter registration, GOTV, and other programs to proactively mobilize the Latino electorate ensured Latino voter engagement in states without competitive presidential contests in the 2012 election cycle. Most importantly, these efforts contributed to an infrastructure vital to the long-term political mobilization of the Latino community. These successes were not devoid of challenges, with new administrative changes proving to be taxing for Latino voters and organizations. For example, operators on the NALEO Educational Fund's 888-VE-Y-VOTA hotline assisted hundreds of potential voters who lacked information and resources (39 percent), were denied provisional ballots (16 percent), needed language-specific materials and assistance (13 percent), or unfairly faced impositions to prove their identity or registration status (4 percent) during the election cycle. Nonetheless, these examples serve as opportunities to continue to build and promote effective engagement of the Latino electorate.

A potential game-changer in regards to Latino voter mobilization could come in the form of changes to the Voting Rights Act (VRA). On June 25, 2013, the Supreme Court of the United States released their decision in the case of *Shelby County, Ala. v. Holder*, which ruled as unconstitutional the formula (Section IV of the VRA) used to determine which jurisdictions are required to receive preclearance from the United States Department of Justice prior to implementing any change to their election policies (Section V of the VRA), due to a history of deliberate voter disenfranchisement. The State of Texas (a Section V jurisdiction) has already implemented its new voter-identification requirement, which was deemed discriminatory (particularly against Latinos) by the Department of Justice during a preclearance review in August 2012. In order to prevent discriminatory practices and threats to voting rights through election-administration changes, advocacy groups are working with Congress to develop and pass legislation with a new coverage formula.[17] Before and after a new formula is implemented, we will likely see an increase in both reactive and proactive mobilization in the Latino community, both in response to the debate and as additional voter education around election policy changes is needed.

The uncertainty surrounding comprehensive immigration reform (CIR) will also bring additional opportunities for multiple forms of mobilization. Despite setbacks in Congress, national nonpartisan civic institutions continue to build cross-sectional and multi-jurisdictional advocacy efforts to champion reform in 2014 and beyond. The struggle for CIR will likely be central to strategic voter-mobilization efforts by nonpartisan organizations in 2014—both as a catalyst for action (in essence, leveraging reactive mobilization), and to build bridges between the advocacy and voter-engagement worlds. Organizations will also have the capacity to tap into the networks built over years of proactive mobilization to enhance and encourage reactive mobilization. Moreover, parties and candidates will also likely utilize CIR as a tool for tactical mobilization of those for and against CIR, in addition to using it as a wedge issue for reactive mobilization. However, the extent to which the dialogue and political struggles around CIR and the reforming of the VRA will contribute to the growth and engagement of the Latino community remains to be seen.

The U.S. Census Bureau projects that the Latino population will more than double from an estimated 53.3 million in 2012 to a projected 128.8 million in 2060 (R. Bernstein 2012). With an increasingly large majority of Latinos being born in the United States and therefore citizens eligible to vote upon turning eighteen, it is vital that mobilization efforts increasingly prioritize Latino voters. This is particularly relevant for partisan campaigns, whose deep resources and prominence can reach millions, and whose future is dependent upon successful and long-term engagement of Latino voters. It is also critical that nonpartisan efforts are sufficiently resourced to continue their essential role in building the electorate over the long term. Combined with the strategic leveraging of reactive mobilization, these strategies are vital to ensuring that the Latino community fully participates in the political process.

NOTES

1. A discussion of low-propensity voters is provided later in this chapter.

2. "Super Tuesday" took place on February 5, 2008, when twenty-three states held the Democratic Party primary.

3. For a detailed discussion on Colorado, see the chapter by Robert Preuhs titled "The 2012 Latino Vote in Colorado," in this volume.

4. DACA, announced on June 15, 2012, would allow for certain people who came to the United States as children to apply for deferred "action" (deportation) for a period of two years, subject to renewal, and would then be eligible for work authorization.

5. The report defined "border states" as those expected to be decided by a wide margin, such as California, and that were geographically located close to a battleground state.

6. The ten battleground states included Wisconsin, Nevada, Iowa, New Hampshire, Pennsylvania, Colorado, Virginia, Ohio, Florida, and North Carolina.

7. These included Colorado, Iowa, Nevada, New Hampshire, Ohio, Virginia, and Wisconsin. In Florida, there were two Latino Vote directors.

8. The sample-size population for the registration and turnout information in New Hampshire, Ohio, and Iowa is relatively small and may have a higher margin of error;

however, they are included in a table given their political significance as battleground states.

9. 2.7 million of the 13.7 million Latino registered voters live in the selected ten states.

10. For more information on New Mexico, see the chapter titled "The 2012 Latino Vote in New Mexico: Immigration Emerges in Unexpected Ways," in this volume.

11. For more information on Ohio, see the chapter titled "Brown Ballots in the Buckeye State," in this volume.

12. The Obama campaign invested more than $2 million on Spanish-language television and radio ads between April and June of 2012, while union supporters and super PACs committed $4 million on Spanish-language television and radio through the summer in Colorado, Nevada, and Florida.

13. Nearly two years later, the U.S. Court of Appeals for the 11th Circuit ruled in April 2014 that Florida's voter purge violated federal law. In a 2–1 decision, the Court concluded that the voter purge violated the National Voter Registration Act (NVRA), due to systemic removal programs being unconstitutional within 90 days of a federal election (Alvarez 2014).

14. NALEO Educational Fund carried these best practices into proactive mobilization efforts in local races in 2013, confirming the importance of increased investments across all levels of campaigning.

15. Partners include Center for Community Change (CCC), the Hispanic Federation, the Labor Council for Latin American Advancement (LCLAA), the League of United Latin American Citizens (LULAC), Mi Familia Vota Education Fund, NALEO Educational Fund, National Council of La Raza, Presente, and Voto Latino.

16. National Voter Registration Day 2012, http://nationalvoterregistrationday.org.

17. The Voting Rights Amendment Act of 2014 was introduced in the U.S. House of Representatives (and a companion bill in the U.S. Senate) on January 16, 2014. As of writing, neither bill has yet to be heard in committee.

REFERENCES

Allen, Greg. 2012. "In Florida Registering Voters a Whole New Game." *NPR*, May 14. Available at npr.org.

Alvarez, Lizette. 2012. "For Latino Groups, Grass-Roots Efforts Paid Off in Higher Number of Voters." *New York Times*, November 27.

——. 2014. "In Florida, Bid to Cut Voter Rolls Is Set Back." *New York Times*, April 2.

Armas, Genaro C. 2004. "Hispanic Outreach Pays Off for Bush." *New York Sun*, November 5.

Ashkenas, Jeremy, Matthew Ericson, Alicia Parlapiano, and Derek Willis. 2013. "The 2012 Money Race: Compare the Candidates." *New York Times*, November 26.

Barreto, Matt A. 2005. "Latino Immigrants at the Polls: Foreign-Born Voter Turnout in the 2002 Election." *Political Research Quarterly* 58(1): 79–86.

Barreto, Matt A., Sylvia Manzano, Ricardo Ramírez, and Kathy Rim. 2009. "Mobilization, Participation, and *Solidaridad*: Latino Participation in the 2006 Immigration Protest Rallies." *Urban Affairs Review* 44(5): 736–764.

Barreto, Matt A., Loren Collingwood, and Sylvia Manzano. 2010. "A New Measure of Group Influence in Presidential Elections: Assessing Latino Influence in 2008." *Political Research*

Quarterly 63(4): 908–921.

Bernstein, Andy. 2012. "Millions of Young Voters Unsure of Voter Registration Status after Moving." *Headcount*, September 18. Available at headcount.org.

Bernstein, Robert. 2012. "U.S. Census Bureau Projections Show a Slower Growing, Older, More Diverse Nation a Half Century from Now." *U. S. Census Bureau*, December 12. Available at census.gov.

Block, Melissa. 2008. "Clinton, Obama Target Latino Voters in California." *NPR*, February 1. Available at npr.org.

Bravender, Robin. 2012. "Obama Spanish Language Ad Blitz Aims to Wrap Up Latino Vote." July 1.

Calvo, Dana. 2000. "Bush Hopes Spanish Ads Will Garner Votes." *Los Angeles Times*, February 7.

Carlton, Jim. 2008. "Clinton Courts Hispanics for Crucial Super Tuesday." *Wall Street Journal*. January 11.

Charles, Deborah. 2012. "As Election Nears, Efforts Intensify to Misinform, Pressure Voters." *Reuters*, October 24. Available at reuters.com.

Cillizza, Chris. 2013. "Why George W. Bush Was Right." *Washington Post*, January 31.

Cornish, Audie. 2012. "Arizona Immigration Activists Mobilize Latino Vote." *NPR*, July 11. Available at npr.org.

Damon, Anjeanette. 2012. "The Damon Political Report: Oceguera Set to Launch Spanish-Language Ad Campaign." *Las Vegas Sun*, October 2.

de la Garza, Rodolfo O., Carolyn Dunlap, Jongho Lee, and Jaesung Ryu. 2002. "Latino Voter Mobilization in 2000: Campaign Characteristics and Effectiveness." *Tomás Rivera Policy Institute*.

Department of Homeland Security. 2012. "ICE Total Removals." *U.S. Immigration and Customs Enforcement*, August 25. Available at ice.gov.

Durand, Jorge, Edward Telles, and Jennifer Flashman. 2006. "The Demographic Foundations of the Latino Population." In *Hispanics and the Future of America*, ed. National Research Council. Washington, DC: The National Academies Press.

Drummond, Amy, and Christina Sinclair. 2013. "A Brief Look at Voter Registration and Non-Partisan Voter Contact." *NLCET 2012 Report*, September.

File, Thom. 2013. "The Diversifying Electorate—Voting Rates by Race and Hispanic Origin in 2012 (and Other Recent Elections)." *U.S. Census Bureau*. Available at census.gov.

"Florida Early Voting Lawsuit." 2012. *Huffington Post*, November 4. Available at huffingtonpost. com.

"Florida Voter Purge: Judge Allows State to Remove Potentially Ineligible Voters from State Rolls." 2012. *Huffington Post*, October 4. Available at huffingtonpost.com.

Foley, Elise. 2012. "Latino Voters in Election 2012 Help Sweep Obama to Reelection." *Huffington Post*. November 7. Available at huffingtonpost.com.

Froomkin, Dan. 2012. "National Voter Registration Day: The Time to Register Is Now." *Huffington Post*, September 25. Available at huffingtonpost.com.

Fry, Richard, Jeffrey Passel, Roberto Suro. 2005. "Hispanics and the 2004 Election: Population, Electorate and Voters." *Pew Research Hispanic Center*, June 27. Available at pewhispanic. org.

Gonzalez-Barrera, Ana, and Mark Hugo Lopez. 2012. "Latino Voters Support Obama by 3–1

Ratio, but Are Less Certain Than Others about Voting." *Pew Research Hispanic Center*, October 11. Available at pewhispanic.org.

Green, Donald, and Alan Gerber. 2005. "Recent Advances in the Science of Voter Mobilization." *Annals of the American Academy of Political and Social Science* 601: 6–9.

———. 2008. *Get Out the Vote: How to Increase Voter Turnout*. Washington, DC: Brookings Institute.

Gregg, Cherri. 2012. "Judge Rules Photo ID Won't Be Required." *CBS Philly*, October 2. Available at philadelphia.cbslocal.com.

Harrison, Carlos. 2012. "Bettina Inclan, Hispanic Outreach Director, May Have Toughest Job in GOP Circus." *Huffington Post*, February 10. Available at huffingtonpost.com.

Hartfield, Elizabeth. 2012. "Spanish Language Campaign Ad Spending Lags." *ABC News*, October 1. Available at abcnews.go.com.

Hispanic Leadership Network. 2012. "Hispanic Leadership Network Announces Agenda, Speakers of Small Business Invitational in Las Vegas." *Hispanic Leadership Network*, March 27. Available at hispanicleadershipnetwork.org.

impreMedia/Latino Decisions. 2012. "2012 Latino Election Eve Poll." *Latino Decisions*, November 7. Available at latinodecisions.com.

Johnson, Kirk. 2004. "Hispanic Voters Declared Their Independence." *New York Times*, November 9.

Johnson, Luke, and Amanda Terkel. 2012. "Pennsylvania Election Day Plagued by Confusion over Blocked Voter ID Law." *Huffington Post*, November 6. Available at huffingtonpost.com.

Joseph, Cameron. 2012a. "Romney Increases Efforts to Win Over Hispanic Voters." *The Hill*, October 3. Available at thehill.com.

———. 2012b. "Romney Tells Hispanics 'You Deserve Better' in New Ad." *The Hill*, October 9. Available at thehill.com.

Kasdan, Diana, and Wendy Weiser. 2012. "Voting Law Changes: Election Update." *Brennan Center for Justice at New York University School of Law*, October 28.

Leighley, Jan E. 2001. *Strength in Numbers?: The Political Mobilization of Racial and Ethnic Minorities*. Princeton, NJ: Princeton University Press.

Lilley, Sandra. 2012. "Florida Voter Purge Should Be Stopped, Say Latino Civic Leaders." *NBC Latino*, June 20. Available at nbclatino.com.

Loeb, Pat. 2012. "Even after Judge's Ruling, Pa. Voter ID Opponents Not Slowing Down." *CBS Philly*, October 2. Available at philadelphia.cbslocal.com.

Lopez, Mark Hugo, and Anna Gozalez-Barrera. 2012. "Latino Voters Support Obama by 3–1 Ratio but Are Less Certain Than Others about Voting." *Pew Hispanic Research Center*, December 28. Available at pewhispanic.org.

Lopez, Mark Hugo, Ana Gonzalez-Barrera, and Seth Motel. 2011a. "As Deportations Rise to Record Levels Latinos Oppose Obama's Policy." *Pew Hispanic Research Center*, December 28. Available at pewhispanic.org.

Lopez, Mark Hugo, and Paul Taylor. 2012. "Latino Voters in the 2012 Election." *Pew Hispanic Research Center*, November 7. Available at pewhispanic.org.

Montopoli, Brian. 2012. "Group Seeks to Define Obama as 'Worse Than Joe Arpaio' on Immigration." *CBS News*, May 25. Available at cbsnews.com.

NALEO Educational Fund. 2012. "Latino Voters at Risk." *NALEO Educational Fund*, October 23.

Available at naleo.org.

National Voter Registration Day. 2013. Available at nationalvoterregistrationday.org.

Nevada Secretary of State. 2012. "Silver State Election Night Results 2012." *Nevada Secretary of State: Board of Elections*, November 27.

Obama Campaign. 2013. "Legacy Report." Report presented at the National Obama Campaign Legacy Conference, January 20.

Pantoja, Adrian D., Ricardo Ramírez, and Gary M. Segura. 2001. "Citizens by Choice, Voters by Necessity: Patterns in Political Mobilization by Naturalized Latinos." *Political Research Quarterly* 54(4): 729–750.

Pew Hispanic Research Center. 2013. "If No Deal Is Struck, Four in Ten Say Let the Sequester Happen." *Pew Hispanic Research Center*, February 21. Available at pewtrusts.org.

Pino, Camilo. 2012. "First NBC News/WSJ/Telemundo National Poll: Obama Leads Romney by 34 Percentage Points among Latinos." *NBC Universal*, May 23. Available at nbcuniversal. com.

Ramírez, Ricardo. 2005. "Giving Voice to Latino Voters: A Field Experiment on the Effectiveness of a National Non-Partisan Mobilization Effort." *Annals of the American Academy of Political and Social Science* 601: 66–84.

———. 2013. *Mobilizing Opportunities: The Evolving Latino Electorate and the Future of American Politics*. Charlottesville: University of Virginia.

Republican National Committee. 2012a. "GOP Expands National Latino Effort." *GOP.com Communications*, January 11. Available at gop.com.

———. 2012b. "Highlights from Conf. Call w/ Chairman Preibus Announcing Expanded National Latino Outreach Effort." *GOP.com Communications*, January. Available at gop.com.

Rodriguez, Cindy. 2012. "Latino Vote Key to Obama's Re-election." *CNN*, November 9. Available at cnn.com.

Rosenstone, Steven J., and John Mark Hansen. 1993. *Mobilization, Participation, and Democracy in America*. New York: Macmillan.

Ross, Janell. 2012. "Latino Voter Outreach Breaks New Ground, Putting Obama Ahead." *Huffington Post*, September 17. Available at huffingtonpost.com.

Ryan, Kathleen. 2012. "Colorado Latino Voters: Enthusiastic, Immigration Matters." *Public News Service*, October 11. Available at publicnewsservice.org.

Scherer, Michael. 2012. "Why Latino Voters Will Swing the 2012 Election." *Time*, March 5.

Smith, Donna. 2007. "Senate Kills Bush Immigration Reform Bill." *Reuters*, June 29. Available at reuters.com.

Supreme Court of the United States. 2013. *Shelby County, Alabama v. Holder, Attorney General, et al.* June 25.

Suro, Roberto, Richard Fry, and Jeffrey Passel. 2005. "Hispanics and the 2004 Election: Population, Electorate and Voters." *Pew Hispanic Research Center*, June 27. Available at pewhispanic.org.

United States District Court for the District of Columbia. 2011. "Memorandum in Support of Motion to Intervene as Defendants" (Docket No. 16-3, Sept. 9, 2011) 5–7, *Florida v. United States* (D.D.C. 2011)(No. 1:11-cv-1428-CKK-MG-ESH)." September 9.

United We Dream. 2012. "Immigrant Youth Launch National Right to Dream Campaign Calling on Obama to Provide Relief for all Dreamers." *United We Dream*, May 17. Available at unitedwedream.org.

U.S. Census Bureau. 2013a. "Current Population Survey. Table A-6. Reported Voting and Registration for Total and Citizen Voting-Age Population by Race and Hispanic Origin: Presidential Elections 1980 to 2012." *Voting and Registration*, November 2012. Available at census.gov.

————. 2013b. "Current Population Survey: The Diversifying Electorate—Voting Rates by Race and Hispanic Origin in 2012 (and Other Recent Elections)." *Voting and Registration*. Available at census.gov.

————. 2014a. American Community Survey 1-Year Estimates 2012, File B16008. *American Community Survey*. Available at census.gov.

————. 2014b. American Community Survey 1-Year Estimates 2012, File B05003I. *American Community Survey*. Available at census.gov.

Washington Post. 2012. "2012 Presidential Election Results." *Washington Post: Campaign 2012*, November 19. Available at washingtonpost.com.

Wong, Janelle. 2008. *Democracy's Promise: Immigrants and American Civic Institutions*. Ann Arbor: University of Michigan Press.

Young, Antony. 2012. "How Data and Micro-Targeting Won the 2012 Election for Obama." *Mindshare North America*, November 20. Available at mediabizbloggers.com.

Immigration
Defining Candidates, Deciding Elections

IN ORDER TO DISCUSS THE INFLUENCE THE ISSUE OF IMMIGRATION HAD ON THE 2012 elections, we need to go back to 2008—and to the developments that have unfolded around immigration in the intervening four years. In 2008, in the middle of a brutal Democratic primary against fellow senator Hillary Clinton, young Illinois senator Barack Obama promised the unthinkable: he would pass comprehensive immigration reform in the first year of his presidency. The declaration (made in an interview with Univisión anchor Jorge Ramos) has been immortalized as the famous Promesa, and it has continued to dog the president to this day.[1] The promise of immigration reform helped Obama succeed in taking on Clinton, despite her greater familiarity among Hispanics and her association with Bill Clinton (a president much beloved by Latinos, despite his role in passing an "immigration reform" bill in 1996 that proved disastrous for legal immigrants). The Promesa was also just what Obama needed to appeal to Latinos in his general-election fight against the Republican nominee, Senator John McCain of Arizona.

McCain, for his part, represents the starting point for the trend in declining Latino support for Republican presidential nominees. More to the point, he was the candidate whose political strategy caused that support to begin to unravel. In the summer of 2007, just one year before the general-election campaign started, McCain had suffered a legislative defeat on immigration (the second such defeat in two years). The senator from Arizona had tried to pass comprehensive immigration reform in a bipartisan fashion; this plan had two flaws that proved fatal. First of all, his Democratic counterpart was not just any Democrat, but Senator Ted Kennedy of Massachusetts—the Liberal Lion of the Senate himself—and for the extreme right of the Republican Party, alliance with Kennedy constituted a mortal sin. Second of all, that same extreme right bore deep antipathy toward McCain himself for his stance on immigration and his previous willingness to work with Democrats on other bills. The defeat of immigration reform fed the anti-immigrant flames around the country. When McCain decided to seek the Republican presidential nomination, taking all this into account, he chose a costly strategy that has since become standard among Republican candidates: appealing to the anti-immigrant base of the Republican Party by rejecting immigration reform and, in McCain's case, saying that he would vote against his own comprehensive immigration reform bill.[2] Flouting pundit predictions, McCain won the Republican nomination in 2008 and went on to face Obama.

McCain might have been competitive with Obama among Latinos if he hadn't distanced himself from his long history of championing immigration reform. In any event, elections are cyclical, and there's no doubt that McCain chose a poor moment to run. The country, beset by wars in Iraq and Afghanistan, the war on terror, a housing crisis, and a collapsing economy, was more than ready to turn the page on eight years of Republican ownership of the White House. Voters gave a chance to a young, relatively inexperienced Democrat who offered some new ideas, but mostly Hope and Change.

Merely being a Republican had become a liability for McCain, but being a Republican who turned his back on the immigration reform he'd once proposed certainly played a role in alienating Latino voters and in McCain's defeat by Obama. At the beginning of the 2008 primary campaign, McCain was in a position to compete with Obama for Latino votes. After all, of the two of them, McCain was the one who had introduced bipartisan comprehensive immigration reform bills and fought his own party on behalf of reform; McCain was the one with a track record of compromise. But he threw his own legacy under the bus, and the price was high. When the votes were counted in November, Obama had won the presidency with 67 percent of the Latino vote. The young senator who had promised Latinos immigration reform had won their support; the older senator had abandoned a Latino vote motivated by immigration to appeal to a base that didn't support him anyway. With this, McCain and the Republicans alienated the fastest-growing demographic group and electoral bloc in the country, and one that has continued to leave its mark in successive elections.

At the end of the day, McCain won only 31 percent of the Latino vote—compared to the 44 percent George W. Bush had won in the 2004 presidential election.

The effect of the Latino vote was such that, while McCain won his home state of Arizona by 9 percentage points (54 to 45 percent), Obama won the Latino vote in Arizona 56 to 41 percent. Furthermore (and more significantly), in 2008 Obama won four of the states Bush had won in 2004 and where the Latino vote is key: Nevada, New Mexico, Colorado, and Florida. The story line—the connection between the Latino vote, immigration, and Republicans' inability to win a presidential election—began to come into focus, but few predicted what would happen in the next four years on the immigration front. Certainly not immigrant families, for whom the developments proved horrific, and neither political party, both of whom proved they had lessons yet to learn. Those lessons particularly applied to Republicans, who ignored the signs from 2008 and continued to accelerate their march over the demographic (and therefore electoral) cliff.

2008–2012: Lessons Still Unlearned

The hope and change Obama promised in 2008 rapidly evaporated in a harsh political climate as the new president's plans collided with the reality of a divided Congress. Obama faced a Republican Party with the sole mission of guaranteeing he would be a one-term president, and a Democratic Party divided over which of the president's promised reforms (health care, financial regulation, or immigration) should become legislative priorities. After the first one hundred days of the Obama administration, there was still no sign of any immigration reform bill. In fact, at no point during the president's entire first term was a bill brought to light. The administration's attention was consumed with trying to prevent a budget crisis, an unemployment level that is still recovering, and an acrimonious debate over health-care reform that stretched over nearly two years—taking up all the oxygen that could have been used for other legislation, including immigration reform.

And incredibly enough, the Obama administration decided to apply the same political logic as Republican administrations had done on immigration: double down on immigration enforcement in the hopes of shutting up critics and winning over supporters for eventual broad reform. With this in mind, they proceeded to fund every increase in border security specified in the 2007 bill—a bill that had initially provided for broad reform, but now was being enacted only as enforcement (Khan 2013). Furthermore, the Department of Homeland Security, which hosts the government's various immigration agencies, decided to expand its programs of local-federal collaboration on immigration enforcement, including 287(g) and Secure

Communities (Fox News 2010). Attacks on these programs from immigrant-rights and civil-rights groups, alleging that the programs lent themselves to racial profiling and discrimination against Hispanics and other minorities simply because of the color of their skin, fell on deaf ears, and the two programs became the principal points of intake for a massive deportation pipeline. This is how the president who promised immigration reform in his first term became the president who (at a rate of 400,000 per year) deported more immigrants than any of his predecessors, including George W. Bush (Lopez and Gonzalez-Barrera 2013).

At the same time, Republicans (ignoring the effect of their anti-immigrant rhetoric and policies alienating the Latino vote and perpetuating their political irrelevance in the last presidential election) began to push anti-immigrant laws at the state level. Their justification: in the absence of immigration reform at the federal level—reform Republicans themselves had blocked whenever it was considered for the past several years—Republican-led states were obligated to take things into their own hands. Dozens of Republican-majority state legislatures began to pass harsh anti-immigrant laws, provoking a (justified) panic that spread throughout immigrant communities across the country. The effects of the state laws weren't just felt by the undocumented immigrants who were their ostensible targets, but among Hispanics who were naturalized citizens, many of them voters and legal residents. Some began to experience direct discrimination, while others simply resented the treatment to which state legislatures and their anti-immigrant laws were subjecting their relatives, friends, and Hispanic brethren. This is supported by a robust 76 percent of respondents to the June 2011 impreMedia/Latino Decisions Tracking Poll that believed "that an anti-immigrant or anti-Hispanic environment" exists today (Sanchez 2012).

Arizona's and Alabama's laws are probably the best known: Arizona's SB 1070 was passed in 2010 at the height of campaign season for the midterm elections, and Alabama's HB 56 was enacted in 2011, a year before the presidential election. Arizona, governed by Republican Jan Brewer, has long been the home of the most feared sheriff in the West, Joe Arpaio, who was already negatively impacting the immigrant community of Maricopa County with the cooperation of the federal government under 287(g). It's also the home of Senator McCain (who rather than denouncing SB 1070, gave it his seal of approval) and former senator Jon Kyl (who was still in office when SB 1070 was passed), one of the Republicans who killed the immigration reform bills of 2006 and 2007 (Smith 2007).

Ultimately, a federal judge blocked the worst sections of SB 1070 from going into effect, but the atmosphere of fear persisted among undocumented immigrants, legal residents, and citizens alike. Ultimately, it gave rise to efforts to respond to the attacks in the only language politicians would understand: the vote. As the midterm elections of 2010 approached, groups intensified their voter registration and mobilization campaigns, and immigration was certainly a prime motivator. Interviewing Hispanics at an early voting site in Phoenix in 2010, America's Voice found immigration to be the number-one issue driving them to the polls. Hector Hernández voted for the first time in 2010 because of the immigration laws that were being passed: "While it doesn't affect me on a personal level, I know a lot of people who are suffering, and I feel it's my job as a citizen to vote so that this changes" (quoted in America's Voice 2010). Brewer and McCain both won reelection in 2010, but since then their historically conservative and Republican state has begun to show signs that it might eventually turn purple. To be sure, the influence of the Latino vote is a large factor in this equation.

Rudy Espino, an associate professor of political science at Arizona State University (ASU), told *America's Voice* that it is probable that Arizona will become more competitive with each election.

> In each electoral cycle, the growth of the Latino population, combined with the fact that the Republican Party in Arizona continues to push Latinos away more and more, makes it possible that Arizona could be placed in the category of "swing states" we hear about like Florida, New Mexico and Nevada. I don't know whether it will be quite as competitive as New Mexico or Nevada, but it is certainly moving in that direction (quoted in Hastings 2012b).

In 2010, Latino voters in other states—places that weren't ground zero in the immigration battle—still felt the impact of the lack of reform. Take, for example, Nevada. Immigration was the central issue in the 2010 race between Senate majority leader and Democrat Harry Reid and Republican tea party favorite Sharron Angle. Angle's negative campaign featured openly racist ads and false information, exploiting anti-immigrant fears. While Reid supports broad immigration reform, Angle (an opponent of reform) declared her support for Arizona's SB 1070. Sheriff Joe Arpaio campaigned for her. Her ads presented dark and menacing images of Hispanics and claimed that "illegals" were receiving public benefits and tax credits. After voting early, one Las Vegas Latina told *America's Voice*: "To Sharron, we're all illegals. She comes off as very racist to me. It's like bringing Sheriff Arpaio up here." Another added: "We can't let the Republican Party win because we'd have serious problems, worse than what we have now" (quoted in America's Voice 2010). All six Spanish-language weekly newspapers in the state published editorials supporting Reid's reelection. Ultimately, Reid won with 90 percent of the Latino vote, a vote that had been mobilized by immigration. But Republicans also found victory in several 2010 races, including in Nevada itself, where Hispanic Republican Brian Sandoval won the governorship. Another Hispanic Republican, Susana Martinez, won the gubernatorial race in New Mexico. Both opposed immigration reform, and both won without the support of the Latino vote. The House of Representatives passed into Republican hands. Obama described the election as a "shellacking" (Branigin 2010).

Immediately, the Republican Party forgot the electoral lesson of the McCain defeat in 2008: assuming anti-immigrant positions alienates the Latino vote, and Republicans need the Latino vote to win the White House. Emboldened by their 2010 victory, Republicans felt secure in the notion that they did not need Latinos for their survival, and that anti-immigrant rhetoric or policies would not cause them lasting political damage. Thus in December 2010 they voted as a bloc in the Senate to filibuster the DREAM Act (which would legalize some undocumented youth) after it was passed by the Democratic-majority House of Representatives. But two years later it was the Republicans who were on the receiving end of the "shellacking."

Election 2012: The Year of the Latino Vote

By the beginning of 2012, various factors had combined to create a perfect storm that threatened to drive down Latino voter participation in the election. The year 2011 had been one of intense battling to stop the implementation of anti-immigrant state laws. At the beginning of 2012, the unemployment rate among Latinos was higher than the national average (Hooda 2012). Millions had lost their homes as victims of foreclosure (Taylor et al. 2012), and the lack of immigration reform, and the separation of families caused by deportation, made its impact felt not only on undocumented immigrants, but on Hispanics in general: those affected were relatives, friends, neighbors, and coworkers. And even if that hadn't been the case, basic empathy would have led Latino voters to resent the anti-immigrant atmosphere. It topped the list of complaints they already had about other issues. And beyond even that, anti-immigrant laws and panics imposed economic costs, not just on immigrants but on their communities and the businesses they patronized.

As preparations for the 2012 Republican presidential primary proceeded, strategists began to survey the political landscape. Polls showed that President Obama continued to command the support of Latino voters at the national level, and particularly in Latino-heavy swing states. But the question was clear: Would Latinos turn out to vote in the same numbers as they had in 2008? Or would they send Obama the bill for the hits they'd taken to their wallets and call in the creditors for his unfulfilled promise of immigration reform and his record of over a million deportations? Matt Barreto of Latino Decisions, a professor of political science at the University of Washington, formulated the question this way at the beginning of 2012:

"The question is what the level of participation will be: how many Latinos will vote. This is where the president and Democrats need to focus their efforts: on explaining to the community how they will fix the areas where they've failed, and what they've done to improve the lives of Latinos. If they can make those connections, that will help them." Obama and Democrats, Barreto continued, had to overcome "the lack of enthusiasm and motivation among voters" (quoted in Hastings 2012a). But when the 2012 Republican primary began in earnest, and candidates launched their own unofficial competition to see who could be the most anti-immigrant, Democrats tended to assume that the spectacle the other party was making of itself had solved all their problems. Whichever candidate emerged from the fracas could never win Latino support after so much venom had already been spilled.

They weren't wrong, but the reality was more complicated. Not voting for the Republican challenger didn't necessarily mean Latinos would vote for President Obama. In a worst-case scenario, they wouldn't turn out to vote at all, an outcome that, from the Democratic perspective, would be tantamount to them voting Republican. As it turned out, the leading Republican candidate, Mitt Romney, appeared to hand Obama the Latino vote on a silver platter. Romney (who had once supported George W. Bush's comprehensive immigration reform bill) won the contest for horrible immigration proposals (and subsequent alienation of Latino voters) in a single move: taking on as an immigration advisor the architect of Arizona's SB 1070 and Alabama's HB 56, Kansas secretary of state Kris Kobach. Furthermore, Romney claimed that the solution to the current limbo in which 11 million undocumented Americans remain stuck was "self-deportation." He also promised to veto the DREAM Act if he were elected president and Congress passed the bill, and he claimed that Arizona's immigration laws served as a "model" for the country (Madison 2012). In May 2012, Romney accumulated enough Republican delegates to secure the party's nomination. While the anti-immigrant tone of his rhetoric and positions provoked condemnation from pro-immigrant organizations around the country, it was hardly the case that Obama didn't still have work to do as the general-election campaign began.

Many of these same national immigrants' rights organizations and Hispanic groups had long warned of the need for Obama to show a degree of leadership on the issue of immigration and send Latino voters a signal that he was willing to spend political capital on the immigration reform he'd failed to accomplish in his first term. In particular, since the defeat of the DREAM Act in 2010, the DREAM movement (composed of undocumented youths) had called on the administration to provide DREAMers with deferred action, a form of temporary relief from deportation that would also allow recipients to receive work permits. The Obama administration had long maintained that the president lacked the authority to do this. But DREAMers didn't abandon the case. They put intense pressure on the administration and sent a clear message: relief for DREAMers—even if it would only temporarily protect them from deportation—was a winner, morally and politically. Not only was it unfair to treat young people who had come to the country through no fault of their own (brought instead by parents or relatives) so harshly, but from an economic point of view, deporting DREAMers represented a significant "brain drain" of future professional and military leaders who could aid the economy. Furthermore, politically speaking, relief offered Obama the chance to demonstrate to Latino voters that he was exercising leadership on immigration, a down payment on finally fulfilling his promise of immigration reform in his second term.

The warnings from the immigrants'-rights groups and DREAMers were hardly unfounded. America's Voice went to Florida (a state Obama won in 2008, but that in mid-2012 appeared to be leaning Romney) to speak with voters and the organizations working to mobilize them, such as Mi Familia Vota. The voter apathy was palpable, and the significance of immigration in influencing the Latino vote was equally evident. Take this selection from an *America's Voice* article:

> In gas stations, supermarkets, restaurants and churches, the common denominator Hispanic voters share is lack of motivation. "I'm going to vote because it's an obligation. But honestly, I'm not enthusiastic, because the presidential candidates don't motivate me. There's nothing in this campaign making us say, 'This is the person we need to bring change for everyone, not just one group,'" says Deborah Soto, a Republican who considers herself an undecided voter. Soto, born in the U.S. to Puerto Rican parents, says that she's concerned about two issues: the absence of a program to assist people who are emptying their savings and retirement plans to pay their mortgages, and immigration. "The breaking up of families is very sad to me," she says.
>
> Soto also supports the efforts of undocumented young people—the "DREAMers"—to win relief. Like others we interviewed—Democrats, Republicans, and independents alike—she agreed that if Obama, in the absence of immigration reform, issued an executive order to stop these young people from being deported, it would inspire her to vote for him. "That would make me enthusiastic. If he says 'I'm going to do this, and here's how,' he'd definitely have my vote," she says. Another undecided voter—an independent—agrees. "I'd definitely be motivated to vote for him." The possibility that Obama might sign an executive order to help the DREAMers resonates even among Republicans, who find Romney's hard line on immigration off-putting. Wilmer Enoch González, a Republican born in Puerto Rico and raised in the U.S., says that the economy will determine who he votes for—but immigration is also an important issue to him. That's especially true because immigration relief would help talented young people "who can contribute to what I'm most concerned for, which is the economy." He's undecided, though

he's leaning toward Romney. "But if the president signs an executive order [giving relief to DREAMers], I'd be one foot in, one foot out again," he says, using an idiom to indicate an even split between the candidates. "But right now I'm not so inclined to support Mr. Obama." (Hastings 2012d).

On June 15, 2012, Obama announced temporary relief for DREAMers (DACA). This was "the Harry Reid theory" of tackling immigration head-on to carry Latino voters to the polls, and with them, Obama to reelection. But before the election, and after both parties held their presidential conventions (in August and September of 2012), Latino Decisions, together with America's Voice, conducted a series of polls in key states that were important swing states in the fight for the White House, and where the Latino vote has continued to grow in size and importance: Florida, Nevada, Colorado, New Mexico, and Arizona. They aimed to capture the effect Obama's decision to grant relief to DREAMers and Romney's anti-immigrant proposals and rhetoric had been having on Latino voters. The results illustrated the enormous influence immigration had on Latinos' perception of the candidates and their decisions about whether, and for whom, to vote.

An *America's Voice* article on the results of the polls in Florida and Nevada illustrated the enormous effect Obama's decision to grant DREAMer relief had on Latino voter enthusiasm and how Romney's anti-immigrant positions had hurt him with Latino voters. It also showed that for Latino voters, immigration is hardly a cold and impersonal matter of public policy, but a personal and mobilizing issue:

On June 15th, Obama introduced the Deferred Action program, which provides temporary relief from deportation to undocumented youth (DREAMers)—a reversible, administrative measure taken in the face of the impossibility that Congress will pass the DREAM Act. The announcement appears to have inspired pro-Obama enthusiasm among Latino voters: 63% of Latino voters in Nevada and 53% of Latino voters in Florida told pollsters that the announcement had increased their enthusiasm for voting for the president's reelection. Romney's positions, on the other hand—his support for "self-deportation" and his opinion that Arizona, with its anti-immigrant state law SB 1070, should be a "model for the country"—have had the opposite effect among Florida's and Nevada's Latino voters, according to the poll. 67% of Latino voters in Nevada, and 57% in Florida, said that Romney's immigration positions had made them less enthusiastic about him. The Florida and Nevada polls demonstrate that immigration is a defining issue that touches all Latinos. 69% of Latino voters in Nevada and 49% in Florida say they have a friend or relative who is undocumented. Obama, who told a Univision town hall that his biggest failure in his first term had been his failure to pass immigration reform, seems to have the numbers on his side when it comes to the Latino vote—but his challenge continues to be ensuring that Latinos turn out to vote, and to turn their theoretical support into reality. That said, Latino enthusiasm appears to be on the rise. We see that in an October poll from 2012 68% and 70% of Latino voters in Nevada and Florida, respectively, said they are more enthusiastic about participating in the election than they were in 2008, while in a poll conducted earlier in the 2012 season 64% of Latino voters in Nevada and 57% in Florida said they are more enthusiastic about voting in 2012 than they were in 2008.[3]

In the other states that were polled, the results were similar, but the case of Florida carries special importance. The state hosts a conservative Cuban and Cuban American bloc in the south of the state and a Puerto Rican swing vote in Central Florida. Furthermore, it's the home state of Republican senator Marco Rubio. Rubio was not as centrally involved in the immigration debate in 2012 as he is in 2013; instead, like other Republican Hispanic politicians, he attempted to limit the damage Romney's strategy was doing to his campaign among Latinos while stopping short of confronting it openly (and revealing divisions in the party).

America's Voice covered both conventions. At the Republican Convention in Tampa, Florida, we saw abundant evidence of the Republican campaign's "Hispanic problem." In the column "The GOP and Hispanics: It's Complicated," we laid out the difficulties facing Hispanic Republicans: they could neither defend Romney's statements on immigration nor admit that he was destroying any chance his party had of competing effectively for the Latino vote:

> Romney's spokespeople and surrogates, wherever they go, keep getting dogged with questions about how anti-immigrant rhetoric has buried the Republican Party's chances of being seen as a viable alternative for Hispanic voters. But their preferred strategy continues to be to evade the topic entirely, attempting to steer the conversation toward the economy. On the first of the campaign's daily press calls with the Spanish-language press, Republican Rep. Quico Canseco of Texas got the question, and his answer was "we have a nearly bankrupt economy." Seventy days before the election, Romney's level of support among Hispanics is abysmal. Polls don't show him reaching 30 percent in vote share. The message that Romney will offer a solution for the economy and fix unemployment isn't working with Hispanics—and this is a voter bloc with one of the highest unemployment rates across all demographics. And if it's not working now, it doesn't take a genius to conclude that the anti-immigrant—and, really, anti-Hispanic—rhetoric coming from the GOP has made a profound impression on Latino voters. That impression has been reinforced by their presidential candidate—a man who has embraced "self-deportation," promised to veto the DREAM Act in its current form and sworn to pull the plug on the Department of Justice's lawsuits against states like Arizona and Alabama for their anti-immigrant laws (S-1070 and H-56, respectively). As far as deferred action for DREAMers

goes: All Romney's surrogates say he wants a "permanent solution," not a two-year reprieve. But Republicans voted en masse against that same permanent solution—the DREAM Act itself. And while deferred action is similar to Florida senator Marco Rubio's long-gestating "DREAM Act light," in that neither would grant a path to citizenship for DREAMers, Rubio has yet to produce a bill. Former United States Treasurer Rosario Marín called deferred action an "insult to the Latino community because [Obama] did it at the last possible moment." Marín is among those who think that Romney's economic message will strike a chord with Latinos. For the past four years, she said, the community has been afflicted by unemployment, and another four years of President Obama would bring more of the same. "If that's what you want, vote for him," she said. "Here [at the convention] we see Latinos who are very enthusiastic about the possibility of having Mitt Romney and Paul Ryan as president and vice president. Ask any of them. We're excited because we know that they're going to take care of the most important issue first: the economy," she continued.

When told that while this might be true in the convention hall, it's not true of Latino voters in the rest of the country—as shown in poll after poll—Marín responded: "We're all voters here." Head, meet sand. (Hastings 2012c)

On November 6, 2012, Barack Obama was reelected to a second term as president of the United States. He won more than 71 percent of the Latino vote, surpassing his 2008 performance. Romney won 27 percent of the Latino vote, less than the 31 percent won by John McCain in 2008. Not twenty-four hours after the election, leading conservatives and Republicans, including Speaker of the House John Boehner and commentator Sean Hannity, were saying the Republican Party needed to address immigration reform in order to take it off the table with Latino voters as an electoral issue. The Latino vote and immigration had a starring role in the 2012 election. The message was unequivocal: immigration mobilizes voters and defines their preferences and their decisions in the polling booth.

In a country where it's always campaign season, politicians took note. Obama wants immigration reform, not just deportation records, to be part of his legacy, and immigration reform would help to solidify Latino support for Democrats. But Latino Decisions polling has shown that Republicans can be competitive if they demonstrate effective leadership on reform and don't use the issue to attack Hispanics and the immigrant community.

The immigration debate continues in full force, and it will serve as a test case: have both parties—especially Republicans—learned the lessons of the last five years on immigration? Apparently not. The Senate passed a comprehensive immigration reform bill on June 27, 2013, but the Republican-controlled House of Representatives refused to debate the measure, opting instead for more of the same failed strategies and the pre–2012 election mentality. Faced with Republican inaction and with the prospect of ending his presidency with nothing to show on immigration except deportation records, president Obama announced that he will use his executive authority to stem deportations.

What happens next?

The story of immigration and the Latino vote is still being written . . .

NOTES

1. See the direct quote from the president here: http://www.thedailybeast.com/articles/2010/06/28/univisions-jorge-ramos-obamas-immigration-promise.html.

2. Republican presidential hopeful Marco Rubio has used a strategy similar to McCain's as referenced here: http://www.dailykos.com/story/2013/06/06/1214212/-Rubio-like-McCain-pledges-to-vote-against-his-own-immigration-bill#.

3. This data comes from numbers taken from http://www.latinodecisions.com/files/2413/5173/0145/AV_6-state-survey-TOPLINES_-_FINAL.pdf and http://www.latinodecisions.com/files/4013/4083/4006/LD_AV_Battleground_Webinar.pdf.

REFERENCES

America's Voice. 2010. "America's Voice Research on Immigration Reform: Report 'March to the Polls' 2010." *America's Voice*, October 27. Available at act.americasvoiceonline.org.

Branigin, William. 2010. "Obama Reflects on 'Shellacking' in Mid-term Elections." *Washington Post*, November 3.

Fox News. 2010. "Homeland Security Expands Local Law Enforcement Pilot Plan to Arrest Criminal Aliens." *Fox News*, April 9. Available at foxnews.com.

Hastings, Maribel. 2012a. "After Nevada: Placing Bets on the Latino Vote in November." *America's Voice*, February 6. Available at americasvoice.org.

———. 2012b. "America's Voice: Obama's Push among Latinos to Paint Arizona Blue." *Sun Sentinel*, February 29. Available at sun-sentinel.com.

———. 2012c. "The GOP and Hispanics: It's Complicated." *North Jersey.com*, September 4. Available at northjersey.com.

———. 2012d. "The Latino Swing Vote: On the I-4 Corridor, Voters Are Hearing All Comers." *America's Voice*, June 13. Available at americasvoice.org.

Hooda, Samreen. 2012. "Unemployment Rates Highest amongst Blacks and Latinos." *Huffington Post*, September 10. Available at huffingtonpost.com.

Khan, Mahwish. 2013. "Suzy Khimm: Nearly All Border Security Targets from 2007 Immigration Bill Have Been Hit." *America's Voice*, January 30. Available at americasvoice.org.

Lopez, Mark Hugo, and Ana Gonzalez-Barrera. 2013. "High Rate of Deportations Continue under Obama Despite Latino Disapproval." *Pew Research Center*, September 19. Available at pewresearch.org.

Madison, Lucy. 2012. "Romney on Immigration: I'm for 'self-deportation.'" *CBS News*, January 24. Available at cbsnews.com.

Sanchez, Gabriel R. 2012. "Taking a Closer Look at Latino Pan-ethnic Identity." *Latino Decisions*, April 18. Available at latinodecisions.com.

Smith, Donna. 2007. "Senate Kills Bush Immigration Reform Bill." *Reuters*, June 29. Available at reuters.com.

Taylor, Paul, Mark Hugo Lopez, Gabriel Velasco, and Seth Motel. 2012. "Hispanics Say They Have the Worst of a Bad Economy." *Pew Hispanic Trends Project*, January 26. Available at pewhispanic.org.

ROBERT R. PREUHS

The 2012 Latino Vote in Colorado

IN THE 2012 GENERAL ELECTION, COLORADO ONCE AGAIN LIVED UP TO ITS swing-state status. Democrat Barack Obama won the presidential election with 51.45 percent of the popular vote, while 46.09 percent of Colorado's voters preferred Republican Mitt Romney. The 5.5 point margin for Obama contracted from the 9 point spread in 2008, when Obama garnered 53.66 percent versus Republican John McCain's 44.71 percent of the vote. Nevertheless, both Obama victories highlight a shifting political tide in Colorado, a state that, prior to 2008, produced victories for Democratic presidential candidates only twice since 1948 (Clinton in 1992 and Johnson in 1964).

The growing Latino population in Colorado, and Latinos' subsequent influence in electoral politics over the last several decades form an important backdrop for the "purpling" of Colorado, moving from a safe Republican state for presidential candidates to one, given the wins in 2008 and 2012, with a definite "bluish" hue. Latinos accounted for 20.9 percent of the population in Colorado in 2012, increasing from 17.1 percent in 2000, and 12.9 percent in 1990 (Guzman 2001; U.S. Census 2013). The growth in the Latino population accounts for just over 40 percent of Colorado's population increase over the last decade. Latinos in Colorado are primarily of

Mexican origin (about 75 percent), and a significant proportion of the growth in the Latino population is due to immigration (particularly from Mexico) and a growing under-eighteen population. Nevertheless, the Pew Hispanic Center estimates that about 46 percent of Latinos in Colorado are eligible to vote, slightly higher than the 42 percent of the Latino population nationally (Motel and Patten 2012).

Colorado's large and growing Latino population has resulted in the group's unprecedented levels of electoral influence. In 2012, higher estimates placed Latinos at about 13.7 percent of Colorado's electorate (Motel and Patten 2012), up from an estimated 12.6 percent in 2010, and approximately 12.2 percent in 2008 and 2006 (Pew Hispanic Center 2006, 2008, 2010). The following discussion explores the impact of the growing Latino population, its share of the electorate in the 2012 presidential election, and the influence of Latino policy preferences on Colorado politics using a unique set of survey data compiled by Latino Decisions that closely followed the Latino electorate in Colorado leading up to the 2012 election.[1] Colorado Latinos decisively voted Democratic in 2012, and this overwhelming support is responsible, to a large extent, for the changing dynamics of Colorado politics and its role in presidential elections.

Latino Vote Choice, Influence, and the 2012 Presidential Election

Latinos in Colorado generally affiliate with the Democratic Party and prefer Democratic presidential candidates, and the combination of these preferences with Latino growth in the electorate proved to be a pivotal factor in the Obama win in 2012. The influence of Latinos was also apparent in the two general elections leading up to 2012, and exit polls conducted during these elections underscore the Democratic leanings of Latinos. In 2008, Latinos supported Barack Obama by a 70–18 percent split, while statewide elections for governor and U.S. senator in 2010 suggest a split closer to 80–20 in favor of the Democratic candidates—and these splits can account for winning margins for both the Obama campaign in 2008 and the U.S. Senate campaign of Democrat Michael Bennet in 2010 (Latino Decisions 2010; NALEO 2008). In other words, while 2012 is the topic of the present discussion, Latino preferences for Democratic candidates were firmly established leading up to the 2012 general election. The Democratic orientation of Latinos in Colorado likely reflects both the general orientation of Latinos across the nation and a state-specific context of recent public policy debates and candidate effects that are discussed in more detail below.

The Latino electorate's 2012 presidential and congressional preferences are presented in figure 1 for the series of three Latino Decisions tracking polls taken in June, September, and just days before the November general election (the 2012

Figure 1. Colorado Latinos' Presidential and Congressional Preferences, 2012 General Election

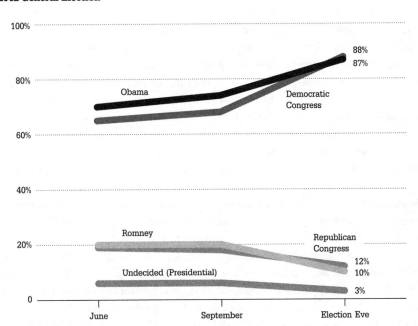

Latino Election Eve Poll). Figure 1 reveals two important aspects of Latino electoral preferences. First, reflecting previous elections, Latinos signified a strong preference for Democratic candidates (both presidential and congressional) in the summer and fall of 2012. Support for Obama and congressional Democratic candidates remained strong throughout the pre-election period, with Latinos certain or leaning toward a vote for Obama averaging 78 percent of respondents over the three polls, and those certain or leaning toward their Democratic congressional candidate averaging just over 73 percent of respondents during the same period. As a point of contrast, exit polls from the *New York Times* estimated that 54 percent of white non-Latino Colorado voters supported Romney ("New York Times Exit Polls" 2012). A second point to note from figure 1 is the consistent trend favoring Democrats throughout the general election campaign. While random sampling error may account for some of the shift, support for Democratic candidates grew substantially over the months leading up to the election. Clearly, not only was baseline support for Obama and Democratic candidates initially high, but the campaign period was marked by the movement of Latino voters in Colorado toward Democratic candidates and away from Republican candidates.

The magnitude of Latino support for Obama in 2012 helped tip the election in Colorado. With estimates of the Latino proportion of the electorate in 2012 ranging from 13.1 to 13.7 percent at the high end, the considerable level of support for Obama translated to substantial margins attributable to the Latino vote. To account for some error in estimates of both the levels of support and proportion of the electorate, prudence calls for a calculation of a range of marginal effects of the Latino vote on the Obama win in Colorado. For instance, a very low estimate of the Latino proportion of the electorate comes in at 12.4 percent and then ranges to 13.7 percent (with the midpoint of the two at 13.05 percent). Similarly, support for Obama was estimated over the span of the Latino Decisions polls to range from 70 to 87 percent (with the three-poll average of 78 percent—similar to results of the *New York Times* [2012] and the Pew Hispanic Center [Lopez and Taylor 2012] estimates of 75 percent). Calculating the range of election impact from the low and high estimates (and generously assuming that all non-Obama voters chose Romney), the Latino vote accounted for Obama margins of between 5.0 percent (at 12.4 percent of the electorate and 70 percent support) to 10.1 percent (at 13.7 percent of the electorate and 87 percent support). At the midpoints of support and the proportion of the electorate, the estimated Latino vote impact lies at 7.3 percent—more than enough to account for Obama's 5 point margin. In other words, given the most likely scenarios of support and turnout, remove the Latino vote, or neutralize the Obama lead among Latinos, and Romney could have won Colorado. Latinos in Colorado were critical to Obama's win.

Immigration Policy, General Policy Alignment, and the Latino Vote in Colorado

Why did Latinos so overwhelmingly support Obama and the Democrats in Colorado and subsequently become a pivotal voting block? One answer is that in Colorado, as in much of the nation, the narrative of a conflicted Latino electorate where cross-cutting social and economic interests leave room for Republican support seems more myth than reality. The 2012 Latino Election Eve Poll conducted by Latino Decisions reveals a relatively consistent liberal orientation among Latino voters across a variety of general policy positions. When asked about a favored approach to the $1.4 trillion U.S. budget deficit, 41 percent of Latinos in Colorado favored "raising taxes on the wealthy," and an additional 39 percent preferred "some combination of tax increases and spending cuts." Only 14 percent of respondents cited "only spending cuts" (a position parallel to GOP preferences) as the best approach.[2] About 72 percent of Latinos preferred to let the Affordable Care Act (popularly known as Obamacare) stand rather than having it repealed, and 70 percent felt the government should play a role in ensuring that all people have access to health care (20 percent said people should get their own).[3] In terms of these two major issues related to the role of government in the economy, Colorado's Latinos more closely align with Democratic positions than with Republican positions.

While Latinos displayed liberal economic-policy preferences, gay rights represents an issue space that further undermines the myth of a conflicted Latino electorate due to preferences for more conservative social policies. Following a contentious 2012 state assembly session where legislation allowing civil unions was defeated on procedural grounds in a special session (after a similar defeat during the regular session), gay rights became a highly salient issue in Colorado's political landscape. The following June, a Progress New America/Keating poll of Colorado voters was conducted to gauge support for gay-rights legislation in the upcoming 2013 session.[4] The results revealed a generally high level of support for legal recognition of gay and lesbian couples across all Coloradoans. Among Latinos, 55 percent supported full legal rights to marriage, while an additional 18 percent supported full legal rights that would not be called "marriage." Combined, about 73 percent of Colorado Latinos supported some sort of legal recognition. Only 12 percent opposed any legal recognition of gay and lesbian couples. This level of support was lower than Democrats as a group, but closer to Democrats than Republicans.

Support for full marriage rights among Latinos was also higher than among whites, of whom 41 percent supported such a policy and 22 percent opposed any legal recognition. Moreover, in national polling conducted by Latino Decisions in early 2012, Latinos across the country indicated that moral issues were low-salience issues to them, with "just 14% say[ing] that politics is more about moral issues such as abortion, family values, and same-sex marriage" (Barreto 2012). In short, baseline support for Obama and Democratic candidates can be attributed in part to the rather straightforward explanation that, across a broad set of policy issues, Latino preferences simply aligned with the Democratic Party to a greater degree than with the Republican Party. And, even if alignment with moral issues was less than complete, Latinos may not have been voting based on those issues. In the case of Latinos in Colorado, rational voters pursued their policy priorities and preferences.

While ideological and partisan alignment was present, an equally important factor in Obama's (and the Democrats') success with Latino voters in Colorado lies in the issue of immigration. Immigration consistently placed near the top of important issues to Latino voters throughout the election cycle in 2012. As shown in table 1, immigration came second only to issues of jobs and the economy when respondents in the Latino Decisions polls were asked to identify the most important issues facing the Hispanic/Latino community that politicians should address. From June through

Table 1. Four Most Important Issues Facing the Community That Politicians Should Address, June 2012 through Election Eve Polls

	June	September	Election Eve
Jobs/Economy	50%	45%	50%
Immigration Reform/DREAM Act	39%	44%	34%
Education Reform/Schools	12%	19%	17%
Health Care	17%	14%	16%

Note: Cells report percentage of respondents indicating the category as one of the top issues. Top four responses reported. All other issues during the period garnered less than 5 percent of responses.

November, 33 to 44 percent of Latinos indicated that immigration was one of the most important issues and clearly on the minds of Colorado's Latino voters.

Part of immigration's importance to Latinos is a recent history with immigration policy and politics in Colorado marked by both anti-immigrant sentiment and small victories for Latinos. Perhaps the most notable of these events was the election of Tom Tancredo in 1998 and his subsequent rise as the congressional leader of the movement to seek strict and conservative approaches to undocumented immigrants. His high-profile role in the Republican Party in Colorado likely helped to solidify Latino Democratic leanings during his tenure in Congress, which ended in 2009. Tancredo briefly revived his presence during a losing gubernatorial campaign in 2010 as a candidate for the American Constitution Party. Also significant, in 2006 the state passed into law a measure that restricted social services to only those who could prove legal residency. While passed by a Democratic-controlled legislature, it was a result of a compromise to avoid the appearance on a statewide ballot of a stricter measure associated with the Republican governor Bill Owens and anti-immigrant groups. The year 2006 also witnessed the passage of a ballot initiative requiring the attorney general to sue the federal government to enforce immigration laws and the passage of SB 90, which required police to contact Immigration and Customs Enforcement officials if individuals are suspected of being undocumented immigrants at the time of arrest. In 2011, a Republican-controlled statehouse committee defeated the ASSET Bill, which would have allowed children of undocumented immigrants who graduated from Colorado high schools to attend state colleges and universities with a modified resident tuition rate substantially lower than the nonresident rate required at the time. It was the fifth straight year that such legislation was defeated. While early opponents in that committee seemed to be wavering during the 2012 legislative session, Republican leadership in the House signaled opposition and assigned the bill to a committee where a "no" vote was assured. The ASSET Bill was defeated once again in 2012. In terms of victories, voters in 2002 defeated a ballot initiative requiring schools to instruct students solely in English, and 2004, while generally lacking an explicit immigration component, marked the election of two Latinos to Congress: Ken Salazar to the Senate and John Salazar to the U.S. House—with strong Latino support. In 2011, the state Senate defeated Arizona/Alabama-style immigration legislation.

Overall, the past policy positions of the Republican Party (as well as GOP lawmakers' continued efforts to pass Arizona/Alabama-style legislation) have worked to the advantage of Democrats. In 2012, Republicans were still vying for primary votes in contested state legislative races based on conservative credentials, which included jousts over whose position most closely reflected Tom Tancredo's stance on immigration. It is clear that in terms of party activists and party leadership, Republican support of anti-immigration policy continued leading up to the 2012 election, and national candidates seemed to reflect this position as well—a strategy that continued to undermine support from the growing Latino voter pool in Colorado.

Polling data regarding the impact of state-specific policy issue preferences and immigration policy debates at the national level, and particularly positions by the two major parties' nominees, suggest that immigration issues solidified Latino support for the campaigns of Democratic candidates and Barack Obama. On the state front, the September 2012 Latino Decisions Poll indicated that 76 percent of Colorado Latinos either strongly or somewhat supported the ASSET Bill. And, as figure 2 illustrates, support was not isolated to Latino Democrats. While 80 percent of Latino Democrats supported the legislation, 59 percent of Latino Republicans in

Figure 2. Support for ASSET Bill among Colorado Latinos by Partisanship

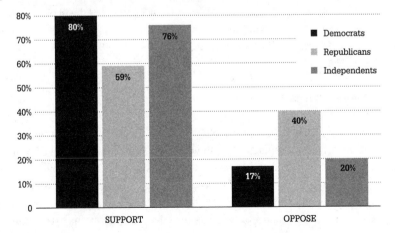

Colorado supported the bill as well. Republican opposition to the ASSET Bill seemed to counter even the preferences of their co-partisans within the Latino community.

Nationally, the difference between the two presidential candidates' positions on undocumented immigration policies overwhelmingly led Latinos in Colorado to favor Obama over Romney. Romney's campaign comments supporting self-deportation of undocumented immigrants and a pledge to not provide work permits for undocumented youth resulted in 68 percent of Latinos polled in Colorado reporting themselves to be less enthusiastic about the Romney campaign (5 percent were more enthusiastic). In comparison, 62 percent were *more* enthusiastic for Obama after hearing about "the Department of Homeland Security policy (established in June of 2012) to stop the deportation of any undocumented immigrant youth who attends college or serves in the military and to provide them with a legal work permit that is renewable" (only 4 percent were less enthusiastic about Obama due to this policy). The difference in the impact of the two presidential candidates' immigration positions on Latino voter enthusiasm was striking and consistent across the months leading up to the election (June 2012 polling demonstrated similar results).

The role of immigration in the election of 2012 in Colorado was indeed significant. How exactly the Latino community came to view immigration policy, and particularly policy aimed at dealing with undocumented immigration, is complicated by both state and national forces. However, one factor that likely played a role is the personal side of undocumented immigration policy for Latino voters in Colorado. Almost two-thirds (63 percent) of respondents in the November 2012 Latino Decisions poll indicated that they knew someone who was an undocumented immigrant. This personal connection to the issue may have led Colorado's Latino community to react negatively to Republican positions within the state (as well as to Mitt Romney's campaign) just as much as it fostered enthusiasm for Democratic candidates at both levels. What is clear (regardless of the specific candidate effects or underlying causes) is that Latinos in Colorado saw immigration as a major policy issue where preferences decisively favored Democratic positions.

Obama's Win or Romney's Loss?

The presidential race in Colorado showed traces of campaign effects that significantly benefited the Obama campaign's Latino vote share. As discussed above, immigration policy differences clearly led to greater enthusiasm for Obama over Romney. Campaign effects, however, reached beyond this single policy. Over the course of the campaign, Democrats engaged in more outreach activity to the Latino community and crafted a campaign that resulted in a sense that Barack Obama cares about the community, while the Romney campaign's efforts simultaneously failed to instill a similar sense of empathy. Combined, outreach and message aligned for Obama in Colorado, much like immigration policy. Colorado Latinos' disposition to vote for Democratic candidates likely led to strategic voter mobilization and campaign contact efforts for both parties. With an estimated two-thirds of Latinos in Colorado identifying with the Democratic Party, GOP efforts to contact and mobilize the community would undoubtedly lag behind the Democrats'. Yet, in what was expected to be another close race in this swing state, the Democrats led by far in terms of contact and mobilization efforts. Overall, 59 percent of Colorado Latinos were contacted in 2012 according to the 2012 Latino Election Eve Poll. The level of contact exceeded the national average of 31 percent of Latino respondents and even outpaced other swing states such as Nevada, where 51 percent of Latinos polled were contacted, and Ohio, with 52 percent contacted. In fact, of the eleven battleground states sampled by Latino Decisions prior to the election, Colorado's Latino community was contacted at the highest rate. Given its swing-state status and statewide polls just weeks before the election confirming an extremely close race, heightened get-out-the-vote activities were expected and evidently materialized.

The margin between those contacted by Democrats and Republicans in Colorado was the striking aspect of the mobilization and contact story. Nationally, 59 percent of those contacted were contacted by Democrats, compared to 39 percent who were contacted by Republicans—a 20 point margin. In Colorado, the margin was 35 points, with 75 percent of Latinos who were contacted by a campaign in Colorado contacted by Democrats and 40 percent contacted by Republicans. Beyond New Mexico's 31 point margin, Colorado's was the highest among the eleven states polled by Latino Decisions. The Democratic Party's contact efforts (and presumably the Obama campaign's as well) clearly dominated the GOP's.

The contact and campaign-policy position effects across parties accompanied, and perhaps led to, an indicator of a more serious problem for the Republican Party—Latinos' sense that the GOP did not care about their community. Figure 3 presents the summary responses for questions regarding the degree to which each of the presidential candidates "cares" about the Latino community. Specifically, respondents were asked, "Thinking about the 2012 campaign for President, would you say that [Barack Obama/Mitt Romney] is someone who truly cares about the (Hispanic/Latino) community, that he didn't care too much about (Hispanic/Latino)s, or that [Obama/Romney] was hostile towards (Hispanics/Latino)s?" As figure 3 reveals, substantial differences emerged in terms of Latinos' perceptions of the degree to which the candidates cared about the community. By the 2012 election (data are from the 2012 Latino Election Eve Poll), 80 percent of Colorado Latinos felt that Obama "truly cares" about the Latino/Hispanic community. Only

Figure 3. Perceptions of Obama's and Romney's Degree of Caring for the Latino Community in Colorado

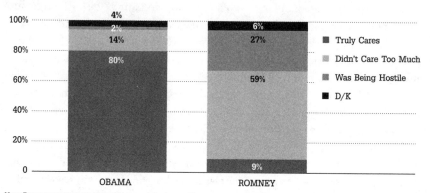

Note: Percentages may not add to 100 percent due to rounding.

2 percent responded that Obama was hostile toward the community. This placed Colorado at the top of states surveyed by Latino Decisions on the eve of the election. Conversely, only 9 percent of respondents indicated that Mitt Romney "truly cares" about the Latino/Hispanic community, while 27 percent indicated that Romney was "hostile towards" the community. The modal response for Romney, at 59 percent, was that he "didn't care too much" about the community. These data reveal that the Obama campaign benefited from perceptions of empathy, while at the same time Romney, while not universally viewed as hostile, certainly lagged behind Obama. Between the perceived empathy gap and the party contact gap discussed above, two plausible explanations emerge: either the Democrats and Obama were very effective in pulling Latinos toward their candidates, or Republicans and Romney managed to push Colorado Latinos away from their candidates. Regardless of the mechanism, the candidate and party preference gaps that emerged were certainly linked to campaign effects, whether in terms of mobilization, policy positions, or the degree of perceived empathy.

While Obama and the Democrats held the policy, empathy, and mobilization advantage, part of the backstory of the Latino electorate during the summer and much of the fall in 2012 was the expectation of a lack of enthusiasm among Latinos that presumably would mitigate preference gaps when Latinos failed to show up at the polls. With the 12.4 to 13.7 percent estimated range of Latinos' percentage of the electorate, a significant drop in turnout might lead to margins allowing for a Republican victory. That drop in turnout never materialized, of course, and the margins provided by Latinos in Colorado ultimately helped to account for much (if not all) of the Obama win.

While the narrative of low Latino enthusiasm seemed plausible given the lack of movement on immigration policy and a slow economic recovery that left Latinos worse off in most economic indicators, polling during the summer and fall revealed that enthusiasm was not as low as popular accounts suggested. The Latino Decisions polls in June and September in Colorado actually describe fairly healthy baseline levels of enthusiasm that increased during the June to October period. Figure 4 presents the results of two questions from the June and September Latino Decisions poll of Colorado Latinos that measured the degree of enthusiasm both in overall terms ("How enthusiastic are you about voting in the upcoming election?") and as relative to the 2008 election, which witnessed unparalleled levels of Latino enthusiasm ("Compared to 2008, are you more/less enthusiastic about the election?"). Between June, when 60 percent of respondents indicated that they were very enthusiastic about voting, and the end of September, when 69 percent reported being very enthusiastic, levels of excitement increased from a reasonably high initial rate (see figure 4). Additional evidence dispelling the narrative of an apathetic Latino electorate in Colorado was the increase in enthusiasm relative to 2008. Recall that 2008 could reasonably be called a high expectations/enthusiasm election for Latinos, and thus a drop in enthusiasm should be expected as presidential promises met institutional constraints in Obama's first term. However, as results of the June and September polls (presented in figure 4) reveal, enthusiasm was remarkably high relative to 2008. In June less than half of the respondents (44 percent) indicated that they were more enthusiastic than in 2008, still a rather solid level of enthusiasm given

Figure 4. Enthusiasm for Voting and the 2012 Election

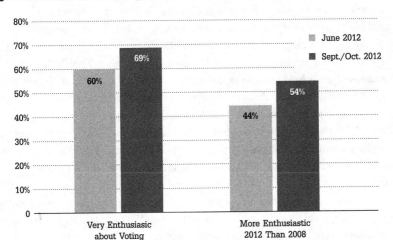

the nature of the 2008 campaigns. Relative enthusiasm also increased over the next several months of the campaigns. By the end of September 2012, some 54 percent of Latinos in Colorado responded that they were more enthusiastic about the election in 2012 than in 2008. These data are likely related to policy differences across the presidential candidates, as indicated by the increase in enthusiasm spurred by the deferred-action order in June. However, they also signify the growing political clout of the Latino community in Colorado. With less variation in turnout (and indeed continued attention to, and enthusiasm for, elections), Latinos demonstrated a commitment to the electoral process as a mechanism for policy change and influence. Ultimately, the popular narrative of low enthusiasm and weak turnout that was so prevalent in media narratives leading up to the election was more myth than reality.

The Impact of the 2012 Election and Latino Influence in Colorado

The outcome of Colorado's 2012 general election and the role of Latino voters in both the presidential and state-level contests in many ways reflected a continuation of the politics of the 2008 presidential and the 2010 midterm elections. Coloradoans sent all of their incumbent U.S. House members back to Washington. Obama won the suburbs, and ultimately the state, by about 5.5 percent of the vote. And while Obama's margin was smaller than in 2008, the general patterns of support were reflected in the 2012 contest.

At the same time, an argument could be made that the election resulted in a substantial shift in Colorado politics. Aside from the high-profile legalization of marijuana, several important changes to Colorado politics resulted, both directly and indirectly, from the election. A few of these shifts are highlighted below, with particular attention paid to the role of, and effects on, Latinos in Colorado.

As the 2013 state legislative session began, Democrats controlled both chambers of the body. The Democrats took control of the lower chamber from the Republicans (who had previously held a one-vote majority) and presently command the legislative agenda that had stalled significant policy proposals for civil unions and the creation of special tuition rates for undocumented immigrants. The Republicans' obstruction of these bills in the 2012 legislative session may have hurt them in the polls, or at least did not help them carry Latino voters, who overwhelmingly supported Democratic candidates as well as the ASSET Bill (the undocumented-immigrant tuition bill). The legislature has since passed the ASSET Bill, and it was signed into law on April 29, 2013. Provisions allowing civil unions were signed into law in March 2013. Among supporters of the ASSET Bill in particular were a handful of Republican state legislators who seemed to be responding to Latino constituencies and their strong desire for tuition reform within the state. In addition, the state repealed SB 90 (the requirement to contact Immigration and Customs Enforcement at the time of arrest of suspected undocumented immigrants) in April 2013 through passage of the Community and Law Enforcement Trust Act, and in May of that year the governor signed into law a process allowing undocumented immigrants to obtain a driver's license.

The influence of Latino voters in the 2012 election has also reached the state's congressional delegation. Democratic Party recognition of Latino preferences was reflected in late 2012 when prominent Democrats in Colorado's U.S. House delegation commended the Metropolitan State University of Denver for its introduction of a new tuition rate for "DREAMers" prior to the passage of the ASSET Bill (Zayed 2012). Moreover, congressional Democrats were not the only ones changing their policy preferences in the wake of the Latino electorate's influence in the 2012 Colorado elections. Republican congressman Mike Coffman of Congressional District 6 (who holds the seat previously held by the outspoken critic of undocumented immigration, Tom Tancredo) narrowly defeated his Democratic opponent in the newly redistricted 6th Congressional District. The 6th CD's Latino population increased from 9 percent to 20 percent after redistricting, and Latino voters likely helped make this a close race for the relatively unknown Democratic challenger. In previous policy statements, Coffman called the DREAM Act a "nightmare," was a proponent of English-only ballots, and supported Arizona's immigration laws in an amicus brief. In February 2013, he shifted his position to one of support for some path to citizenship for undocumented immigrants and their children (Isenstadt 2013). The strong preferences of a large Latino constituency undoubtedly led to the competitiveness of what would otherwise have been a safe seat for the third-term Republican, as well as the shift in policy orientation looking forward to the 2014 campaign. Coffman may well be adopting a strategy suggested by results of the 2012 Latino Election Eve Poll conducted by Latino Decisions in Colorado, which revealed that 24 percent of Colorado Latinos would be more inclined to vote for Republicans if the party took a position on immigration reform that included a pathway to citizenship.

Another important change in Colorado politics is the increased diversity of the legislature. When the Colorado General Assembly convened in January 2013, the makeup of the House and Senate included twelve Latino and five African American legislators—highpoints for both groups. Colorado's diversifying state legislature reflects new gains nationally at the congressional level, particularly in terms of a record thirty-one Latinos expected to serve in Congress in 2013. These gains should translate into more representation of the interests of minority constituents in the future (Juenke and Preuhs 2012; Preuhs and Juenke 2011), and the 2013 legislative session's activity certainly indicates such a movement. Thus, not only has party control shifted towards Latino interests, but the diversity of elite decision-makers has as well. (Colorado also has a record number of openly gay legislators in 2013, and its first openly gay Speaker of the House).

How has this come about? One answer is that Latinos in this election solidified and expanded their political influence in Colorado in 2012. The 2012 Latino Election Eve Poll indicated that almost 87 percent of Colorado Latinos supported Obama and 88 percent supported the Democrat in congressional elections. Those numbers are staggering. Combine this overwhelming support for Democrats with what the Pew Center estimates as just below 14 percent of the electorate (up from 8 percent in 2004) (Lopez and Taylor 2012), and Latinos have become a key constituency for Democratic success in Colorado. Questions of Latino mobilization and enthusiasm all fell by the wayside in November 2012. Going forward, it is hard to imagine Latino preferences regarding policy issues being neglected by state leaders. Moreover, in 2012 Latinos made up about 21 percent of the population and are projected to constitute a third of the population by 2040—the fastest growing demographic group over that period (Colorado Division of Local Government 2012). Combining demographic shifts in Colorado with political preferences, it is foreseeable that Colorado's purple hue will reflect New Mexico's blue tilt and it will fade from swing-state status. In many ways that would represent a sea change—and one that is in great part a result of the political participation of the Latino community in Colorado in the 2012 general election and beyond.

NOTES

1. This chapter relies heavily on three polls of Latino voters in Colorado conducted over the course of the election by impreMedia/Latino Decisions, as described in the appendix. References will be made to the "June," "September," and "2012 Latino Election Eve" polls to distinguish the individual polls and corresponding polling periods.

2. Question: "As you may know, the U.S. budget deficit is currently about 1.4 trillion dollars. There are a number of different solutions being discussed for reducing this deficit. These are cutting existing programs, raising taxes on the wealthy, or some combination of the two. Which approach do you think is best?"

3. Question: "Do you think the Affordable Care Act, sometimes called Obamacare, should be left to stand as law, or do you think it should be repealed?"

4. The question was: "Which ONE of the following statements do you agree with most? Gay and lesbian couples should have the same legal right to marry as do a man and woman. Gay and lesbian couples should be allowed to form a civil union, which gives the same legal rights as marriage, but it should not be called marriage. [Or,] There should be no legal recognition of a relationship between gay and lesbian couples."

REFERENCES

Barreto, Matt. 2012. "Moral Values Not a Defining Issue for Latino Voters." Blog post. *Latino Decisions*, September 16. Available at latinodecisions.com.

Colorado Division of Local Government. 2012. "Table 2. Colorado Ethnic Groups Share of Total Population, 2000–2040." October. Available at colorado.gov.

Guzman, Betsy. U.S. Census Bureau. 2001. "The Hispanic Population: 2000: Census 200 Brief. Report No. C2KBR/01-3." Washington, DC: Department of Commerce.

Isenstadt, Alex. 2013. "Mike Coffman Does a 180 on Immigration." *Politico*, February 26. Available at politico.com.

Juenke, Eric Gonzalez, and Robert R. Preuhs. 2012. "Irreplaceable Legislators? Rethinking Minority Representatives in the New Century." *American Journal of Political Science* 56, no. 3: 705–16.

Latino Decisions. 2010. "Latino Decisions Election Eve Poll—State by State Results." November 2. Available at latinodecisions.com.

Lopez, Mark Hugo, and Paul Taylor. 2012. "Latino Voters in the 2012 Election." *Pew Research Hispanic Center: Washington, D.C.* Available at pewhispanic.org.

Motel, Seth, and Eileen Patten. 2012. "Latinos in the 2012 Election: Colorado." *Pew Research Hispanic Center: Washington, D.C.* Available at pewhispanic.org.

NALEO. 2008. "2008 Latino Vote Survey in Key Battleground States." *NALEO Educational Fund: Los Angeles.* Available at naleo.org.

"New York Times Exit Polls from Battleground States." 2012. *New York Times*, November 8, p. 1.

Pew Hispanic Center. 2006. "Hispanics and the 2006 Election." *Pew Research Center: Washington, D.C.* Available at pewhispanic.org.

———. 2008. "Hispanics and the 2008 Election." *Pew Research Center: Washington, D.C.* Available at pewhispanic.org.

———. 2010. "Latinos in the 2010 Elections: Colorado." *Pew Research Center: Washington, D.C.* Available at pewhispanic.org.

Preuhs, Robert R., and Eric Gonzalez Juenke. 2011. "Latino U.S. State Legislators in the 1990s: Majority-Minority Districts, Minority Incorporation, and Institutional Position." *State Politics and Policy Quarterly* 11, no. 1: 48–75.

U.S. Census Bureau. 2013. "State and County QuickFacts." Data derived from Population Estimates, American Community Survey, Census of Population and Housing, State and County Housing Unit Estimates, County Business Patterns, Nonemployer Statistics, Economic Census, Survey of Business Owners, Building Permits, Consolidated Federal Funds Report. Last Revised: Thursday, 14-Mar-2013 11:17:49 EDT.

Zayed, Michelle. 2012. "Colorado Dems Push for Immigration Reform and DREAM Act." *VivaColorado*, November 12. Available at vivacolorado.com.

GABRIEL R. SANCHEZ and SHANNON SANCHEZ-YOUNGMAN

The 2012 Latino Vote in New Mexico

Immigration Emerges in Unexpected Ways

As the rest of the nation takes note of Latinos' growing political influence, New Mexico provides an opportunity to understand what these shifting demographics may mean for long-term electoral politics.[1] It is the nation's most Hispanic state, with a large proportion of third- and fourth-generation Latinos with an English-language preference. Perhaps more importantly, due to their long historical presence in the founding and development of the state, Latinos have achieved high levels of political power relative to Latinos from other U.S. states. New Mexico has also gained a reputation as both a bellwether and a swing state in recent elections.

For example, in the 2000 presidential election, Democrat Al Gore won the state over George W. Bush by only 366 votes, the closest margin in the country. Four years later, former President Bush won the popular vote over his Democratic rival by 5,988 votes in the state, making New Mexico one of only three states in the nation to switch parties from 2000 to 2004 in its vote for president (Garcia, Sanchez, and Sierra, 2012). This battleground-state status led to numerous visits to New Mexico by presidential candidates and their surrogates in these races and in 2008 as well, when President Obama made six trips to New Mexico during his campaign, outdone by Senator McCain, who made eight visits to the state during the campaign.

Driven largely by Latino support, President Obama won New Mexico by a surprisingly wide margin in 2008, which raised questions regarding the state's battleground status. According to the National Association of Elected and Appointed Officials (NALEO), the Hispanic population was essential to Obama's success in New Mexico. Specifically, the organization's report found that Latinos accounted for 41 percent of the vote (a significant increase from 2004), and 69 percent of these Hispanics voted for Obama, giving Obama a victory margin of 117,897 votes among Hispanics in New Mexico (NALEO 2008). McCain would have won New Mexico if it had not been for Hispanic and other minority voters. National exit polls estimated that non-Hispanic white voters in New Mexico supported McCain, 57 percent to 41 percent for Obama (Garcia, Sanchez, and Sierra, 2012).

As we discuss in this chapter, the 2012 election solidified the fact that 2008 was not an anomaly, with an even larger margin of victory for President Obama than 2008 in New Mexico, once again driven by growth in nonwhite voters in the state and an even greater Democratic advantage among Latino voters. In 2012, Hispanic voters from New Mexico were indeed reflective of Latinos from across the nation. Not only did they select the Democratic candidate, Barack Obama, at historic levels, but the issue of immigration played a significant role in their selection of the 44th President of the United States. The chapter will highlight how the growth of Hispanics in the New Mexico electorate, coupled with their increasing support for Democratic candidates in national elections have removed the state from true battleground status. It will also examine the factors that led immigration to be salient in a state where immigration is generally a nonfactor.

The Latino Electorate in New Mexico

Demographics and history shape the importance of Latinos in New Mexico. Latinos constitute 47.3 percent of the state's population, the largest percentage of any state in the nation. Combined with Native Americans (who constitute 10.4 percent of the population), this makes New Mexico one of the few majority-minority states in the U.S. The state's largest cities comprise even higher proportions of Latinos. For instance, in the Albuquerque metropolitan area, Latinos constitute 46.7 percent of the population. In the other large cities such as Santa Fe and Las Cruces, Latinos make up even greater proportions, at 48.7 percent and 56.8 percent respectively.[2]

In addition to contemporary demographics, Latinos have actively participated in New Mexico state politics for quite some time. Dating back to the 1600s, even before there was an independent nation of Mexico, Latinos in New Mexico created communities with organized governments (Garcia and Sanchez 2008). As a result, Latinos have been an integral part of the political system of their colony, their territory, and their state for approximately four hundred years. Latinos' current demographics and their longstanding participation in state politics translate into their political power and leverage in contemporary politics. For instance, in every presidential election in which Latino voting patterns have been analyzed, New Mexican Latinos have been a significant part of the state's electorate. Over the several past decades, Latinos have constituted between 33 and 40 percent of voters in the state (Garcia and Sapien 1999; Garcia and Sierra 2005; Sierra and Garcia 2010). In 2012, Latinos accounted for 37 percent of the electorate—representing the highest proportion of Latino voters compared to other U.S. states (Hugo-Lopez and Taylor 2012).

Strong Latino electoral participation and historical political prowess have led to high levels of descriptive representation in New Mexico as well. For example, the proportion of Latinos in the state legislature is similar to the proportion of Latinos in the state's population. In addition, Latinos hold several key positions in statewide offices, on county commissions, city councils, school boards, and in other local governments. Susana Martinez became the first Latina governor in U.S. history in 2010, but she is the sixth Latino governor of New Mexico. At the national level, 66 percent of New Mexico's members of Congress are of Latino descent. In short, Latino descriptive representation is deeply rooted across time and multiple levels of office.

Latino Support for Democrats

In terms of raw votes, Democrats won big in New Mexico. The Obama-Biden campaign won handily over Romney-Paul by a vote of 53 to 42 percent. In an open-seat Senate race, Democrat Martin Heinrich defeated his Republican opponent Heather Wilson by a 5-point margin. Democrats also won two out of three contested House seats, and in both the 1st and 3rd Congressional Districts, Latino candidates Michelle Lujan Grisham and Ben Ray Lujan were elected. Michelle Lujan Grisham defeated her Republican opponent, Janice Arnold Jones, in the state's largest congressional district (CD1) 59.1 to 40.9 percent, and Ben Ray Lujan was reelected to the 3rd Congressional District (located in northern New Mexico) with a 26-point margin of victory. These victories produced Hispanic representatives from two of the three congressional districts in the state, by far the highest levels of representation in the nation.

Obama won in seventeen of the state's thirty-three counties, including the largest counties in the state: Bernalillo (Albuquerque), Dona Ana (Las Cruces), and Santa Fe, by large margins, along with the less populous but important counties of the Hispanic north, and Grant and Hidalgo, two border counties along the southwest corner. For example, voters in Bernalillo County gave Obama a substantial winning margin of 16.3 percentage points over Mitt Romney. In Rio Arriba County, the heart of the Hispanic north, President Obama defeated Romney by a whopping 52.6 percent.

While New Mexico was not considered a swing state in the 2012 election, it is indeed a part of what has been termed the "Western Latino firewall." Obama won an overwhelming 75 percent of the Latino vote, while Romney carried 23 percent of Latino voters.[3] Based on these election poll numbers and Obama's overall gains in New Mexico, Latinos added a net contribution of 22.2 percentage points to Obama. As in the western states of Nevada and Colorado, the Latino vote in New Mexico ensured a Democratic vote advantage that prevented Romney from victory. The overwhelming victory for Democrats in 2012 among Latinos is a significant departure from 2004, when former President Bush won 44 percent of the Hispanic vote in New Mexico according to a CNN exit poll.

Although the early indication that New Mexico would not be a tight race down the stretch led the state to move outside of key battleground lists in 2012, this led to positive consequences for Latinos just north in Colorado. Recognizing that victory was in sight, the Obama campaign decided to move their Latino outreach personnel from New Mexico to Colorado, a state where the race was projected to be much tighter and where Latino voters were going to be vital. This shift in resources undoubtedly helped secure the state for Obama and led to increased mobilization of Latino voters in the neighboring state.

Latinos in New Mexico also influenced congressional election outcomes in 2012. For instance, Latinos supported Democrat Martin Heinrich over Republican Heather Wilson by a margin of 79 to 20 percent, helping to ensure Heinrich's victory. More specifically, we calculate that Heinrich's net gain from this wide margin of Latino voters was 21.8 percent, a number much greater than his overall margin of victory. This means that Senator Heinrich joins Senators Bennett and Reid among U.S. senators directly owing their victories to Latino voters in 2012. Michelle Lujan Grisham defeated Janice Arnold Jones by an 80 to 20 percent margin among Latino voters. Considering these election returns along with the overall trend of increases in the Latino share of total voters suggests that Latinos decisively influenced the outcomes of both presidential and congressional elections in New Mexico.

Mobilization in New Mexico

Campaign organization and mobilization were key ingredients in Obama's victory in the state. Building on a very successful ground operation from the previous election, the campaign modified its get-out-the-vote efforts to reflect the 2012 electoral and demographic context of the state. In particular, the 2012 campaign decreased its number of field offices to thirteen, compared to forty in the 2008 election, for two primary reasons. First, during Obama's first run in 2008, New Mexico was a key battleground state, as President Bush won New Mexico's electoral votes in 2004. By 2012, however, New Mexico was the least contested among battleground states, with Obama obtaining a significant lead in early election polls. Consequently, it was less imperative for the campaign to cast a wide net in this geographically diffuse and rural state. Second, and as Masket (2009) suggests, while greater numbers of field offices are associated with better electoral performance, data from the 2008 election suggest that field offices were most effective in states that were not saturated with them. For example, Indiana, which had a minimal field presence, saw the biggest effects on vote, while New Mexico, where most counties had offices, saw smaller ones. Learning from mobilization efforts in the 2008 election, the Obama campaign undertook a more surgical approach in 2012 to garner support from Latino voters in a blue-leaning state.

While the 2012 Obama campaign clearly decreased its overall presence in New Mexico compared to 2008, it still obtained a stronger presence in New Mexico relative to the Romney campaign. In a strategy similar to their ground strategy across all the states, the Romney campaign dismissed the Democrats' ground game, calling it a waste of time (Dickerson 2012). Moreover, the Romney campaign spent most of its efforts targeting voters in large metropolitan areas like Albuquerque, and they failed to implement aggressive outreach to large Hispanic communities in the less urban areas of the state. In contrast, realizing the impact of Latinos in New Mexican politics, the Obama campaign positioned eight out of its thirteen field offices in counties with heavily concentrated Hispanic populations (Santos 2012).

Survey data from the 2012 Latino Election Eve Poll conducted by Latino Decisions demonstrate the disparity in each party's efforts to reach Latinos. Among those contacted, 70.41 percent were contacted by Democrats, compared to just 4.62 percent contacted by Republicans. Indeed, not only were Latinos more likely to be contacted by Democrats, various community organizations outperformed Republican operatives, as 24.97 percent of Latinos said they were contacted by these groups.

Not only did the Obama campaign extend more Latino outreach in New Mexico than Romney, Adrian Saenz, the president's national Latino Vote director, adapted the *content* of the campaign's messaging strategy in New Mexico to more effectively reach Hispanics in a state with "deep political roots, influence and familiarity with the electoral process" (Santos 2012, 2). For instance, the campaign spent less money and time on Spanish-language advertising and Spanish-language news media relative to other states, as New Mexicans are more likely to speak English. Further, given that Hispanics make up 40 percent of the state's electorate, get-out-the-vote efforts were modified from messages like "Votemos Todos" to events that were designed to draw in multiple generations of Latinos and New Mexico's growing population of recent immigrants. Finally, given the state's high levels of Latino descriptive representation, campaign officials relied less on national public Latino figures to mobilize voters, and more on local Latinos to make introductions for campaign events and to make inroads into well-established Latino communities. For instance, in Albuquerque's South Valley, a political stronghold among Latinos, the campaign worked with well-established local Hispano elites to organize events like car shows to build support for the president.

In sum, the Obama campaign undertook vastly different strategies to mobilize voters in New Mexico. Obama's campaign not only used tactics that created personal contacts in the most vital regions of the state, but they adapted their messages to appeal to the dynamics of New Mexican politics. Most importantly, the campaign appealed to New Mexicans by recognizing longstanding Latino electoral participation and by leveraging Latinos' strong presence in state and local political institutions to garner support for the president's second term.

Immigration Policy and Support for Obama

As reflected in this overall volume, the role of immigration policy on Latino voting behavior dominated discussions of the Latino vote during the 2012 election. In particular, Romney took an especially aggressive stance on immigration reform during the primary season—promising to veto the DREAM Act, applauding Arizona's immigration policies, and supporting the radical notion of self-deportation. In contrast, the Obama administration signed an executive order in June 2012 giving temporary legal status to many undocumented immigrants who entered the country as children. Although Romney attempted to soften his stance toward immigration to appeal to Latino voters after Obama signed the executive order in June, opinion data suggest that Romney's aggressive stance alienated Latino voters.

For instance, the 2012 Latino Election Eve Poll conducted by Latino Decisions found that immigration policy was salient to Latinos across key battleground states and central to Latino enthusiasm levels. Specifically, 57 percent of Latinos in New Mexico stated that Romney's position on immigration resulted in less enthusiasm among voters, while 58 percent of Latino voters stated that Obama's deferred-action policies resulted in more enthusiasm for the president. The context that immigration provided to the election was captured well by President Obama, who acknowledged in the final weeks of the campaign that if he were to win reelection, it would largely be due to the GOP alienating the Latino community (Fabian 2012).

This statement by the president reflected the perceptions of the Latino community just prior to the election. For instance, a Latino Decisions pre-election poll demonstrated that while 37 percent of Latino voters believed that the reelection of President Obama would make no difference regarding comprehensive immigration reform being passed, 51 percent believed that the prospects for reform would get worse if Romney were to be elected.

The shift in Latino attitudes toward immigration policy has been rather striking, as many studies of Latino political behavior conducted in the 1990s noted that Latino public opinions toward immigration were rather divided. For example, the Latino National Political Survey (1990) indicated that 75 percent of Mexican Americans, 79 percent of Puerto Ricans, and 70 percent of Cuban Americans agreed with the statement that there are "too many" immigrants coming to the United States. While beyond the scope of this chapter, the 2012 election suggests that Latino voting behavior was driven, at least in part, by a Latino perception that Republicans were hostile toward the nation's most rapidly growing minority population.

The Influence of Immigration Policy on Latino Vote Choice

While immigration was a deciding factor in the 2012 election outcome at the national level, it is less clear whether immigration policy is the most critical issue for many New Mexicans who themselves are far removed from the immigration experience. Indeed, as in the context of Colorado, there are many plausible reasons why immigration would be less likely to influence Latinos in New Mexico compared to other Latinos in states such as California. First, the foreign-born population in New Mexico (approximately 10 percent) is smaller than the national average, which means that Hispanics in New Mexico are less likely to be immigrants than in other southwestern states. With such a small immigrant population and high numbers of Latinos who are third- and fourth-generation U.S. citizens, it seems plausible that New Mexicans may not place immigration high on their list of priorities when selecting a president.

Second, Acuña (1972), Barrera (2008), and Gomez (2007) argue that both U.S. and Spanish colonialism have played a central role in constituting Mexican Americans as a marginalized group in this state. In particular, they suggest that through a constellation of factors including legal institutions, land-grant distributions, labor-market patterns, and residential segregation, Latinos who claim Spanish descent occupy higher social status compared to Mexicans and recent immigrants. For instance, through a historical analysis of the construction of race in the state, Gomez suggests that New Mexicans' continuing claims of Spanish heritage are a tactic that evolved from intense anti-Mexican racism dating back to the 1800s. According to Gomez, current ethnic cleavages continue to reproduce social hierarchies grounded in myths of national-origin status. In sum, national-origin cleavages suggest that Mexicans and Spanish Latinos have defined such different conceptions of ethnic identity that they have historically competed more than they have cooperated as each group struggles to evade the marginalized stigma of an "abject" minority group within constructions of ethnic difference within New Mexico.

Despite these historical cleavages and demographic realities, the narrative of a conflicted Latino electorate is now largely a historical narrative in New Mexico. The 2012 election highlighted a growing movement toward increased commonality and collective identity among the Hispanic population that has been brewing for the last decade. Related to demographics, while not as extreme as other border states, there have been significant increases in the foreign-born population in New Mexico overall. In fact, the percentage of foreign-born New Mexicans in the state's largest city, Albuquerque, has more than doubled since 1990.

These demographic shifts have impacted the interactions of U.S.-born Hispanics and more recently arriving Latino immigrants. In an America's Voice/Latino Decisions survey of Hispanic voters in New Mexico conducted in October 2012, nearly 60 percent of Hispanic voters in New Mexico indicated that they knew someone who was undocumented personally, as a friend, a family member, or a coworker. Although slightly lower than percentages in neighboring Colorado (69 percent) or Arizona (66 percent), the 60 percent in New Mexico was higher than many observers of New Mexican politics anticipated and provided the context for the surprising salience of immigration policy in the Land of Enchantment.

The personal connection Latino voters in New Mexico have to immigrants may have had major implications for how Latino voters viewed both immigration policy and President Obama in 2012. On the one hand, and according to the racial-contact hypothesis, increased interaction among immigrants and third- and fourth-generation Latinos may have led to greater empathy for newcomers among Latino citizens, consequently leading to more liberal views on immigration (Oliver and Wong 2003). On the other hand, and according to the theory of racial group competition, interactions could lead to increased competition and hostility among these Latino subpopulations (Blalock 1967; McClain et al. 2006).

Related to perceived historical cleavages, there is evidence that divisions between native and foreign-born Latinos are largely overblown. New Mexico has seen immigration policy become a major topic of political debate since 2010 with the election of Governor Susana Martinez, who made immigration-related issues the focus of that election (Sanchez 2010). In fact, Martinez made immediate headlines for her aggressive approach to immigration policy, which included an executive order issued on her first day in office that requires state law-enforcement officials to verify the citizenship status of individuals arrested, and several failed efforts to repeal a law allowing undocumented immigrants to acquire driver's licenses in the state.

In 2010, Dianna Duran, the first Republican secretary of state elected in New Mexico since 1928, sent a shock wave through the state when she speculated, after cross-checking voter registration files with the state motor vehicle database, that there were as many as 64,000 noncitizens registered to vote in the state. After intense criticism from the public, Duran later announced that her office had evidence that only 117 undocumented immigrants had obtained driver's licenses and registered to vote in New Mexico, with 37 voting in elections between 2003 and 2010. Following a lawsuit by the ACLU of New Mexico and substantial pressure from other interest groups to produce the results of her office's report, Duran's office clarified that there were only two confirmed cases of foreign nationals being registered to vote, and only one individual who actually voted—albeit unintentionally. Duran and Martinez have also unsuccessfully pushed to pass a voter ID law in New Mexico that would require voters to present photo ID before being allowed to vote in person.

While Martinez continues to have high approval ratings among voters, her controversial immigration policies at the state level may have influenced Latino voters

Figure 1. The Most Important Issues Facing the Latino Community in New Mexico That Politicians Should Address

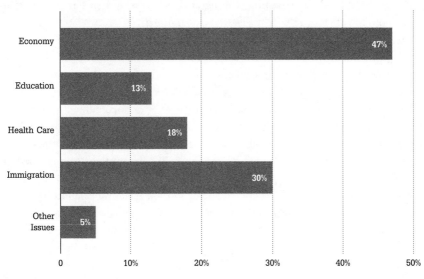

Source: Latino Decisions Poll October 29, 2012; *n* = 400

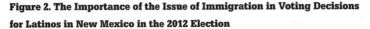

Figure 2. The Importance of the Issue of Immigration in Voting Decisions for Latinos in New Mexico in the 2012 Election

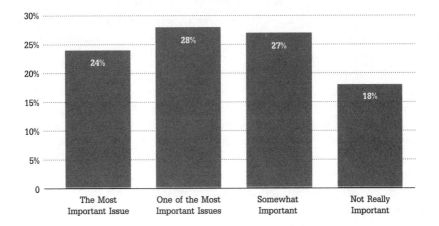

in the 2012 election. In fact, as figure 1 demonstrates, immigration policy was clearly important to Hispanic voters in the state of New Mexico, as immigration trailed only the economy as the "most important issue facing the Hispanic community" according to respondents in the 2012 Latino Election Eve Poll conducted by Latino Decisions. Furthermore, in a Latino Decisions poll conducted two weeks prior to the presidential election, a combined 79 percent of Hispanic voters in New Mexico indicated that debates surrounding immigration influenced their decision to vote and whom to vote for in the 2012 election (see figure 2).

More directly assessing the outcome of increased contact with immigrants among native-born Hispanics, the same poll queried Hispanic voters about the driver's license issue that became a lightning rod in many state legislative races in the 2012 cycle. As reflected in figure 3, an overwhelming 70 percent of Hispanic voters in New Mexico indicated that they prefer that undocumented immigrants be provided the opportunity to apply for a driver's license that has some added restrictions, compared to a much smaller 21 percent who support not allowing undocumented immigrants to apply for a license. The descriptive data provided in this chapter clearly suggest that Latino voters in New Mexico were unified in their belief that immigration would be a key factor in their electoral calculus, and that Latino voters' ideology about immigration had moved from moderate to liberal following the national trends among Hispanic voters. What is very interesting and worthy of future study is how Governor Martinez has remained highly popular among Latino voters in New Mexico despite the right-of-center immigration policy agenda she has pushed during her first term in office.

Figure 3. Hispanic New Mexican Attitudes toward Providing Undocumented Immigrants a Driver's License

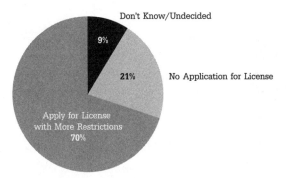

Note: The question states, "When it comes to the driver's license issue, some people have said undocumented immigrants should not be able to apply for a driver's license, other people have said the law should be reformed so that undocumented immigrant drivers are required to be licensed, but should be subjected to stricter identity and residency requirements as well as tougher penalties for fraud. Which approach comes closer to your views on this issue?"

Source: Latino Decisions/America's Voice Six State Latino Voter Survey, October 2012. Available at latinodecisions.com.

Immigration and Latino Vote Choice

Immigration was clearly a priority for New Mexicans in the 2012 election, but did this policy issue impact Latino vote choice? The Latino 2012 Election Eve Poll data suggest that immigration contributed to Latino support for President Obama in the state. For instance, 60 percent of New Mexican Latinos stated that Obama "truly cares about Latinos," compared to only 20 percent who felt the same way about Mitt Romney. Specifically related to immigration reform, Romney's self-deportation immigration policy led 52 percent of Latinos in New Mexico to feel less enthusiastic about the Republican candidate, while a meager 8 percent of Latinos were less enthusiastic about Obama's candidacy as a result of his deferred-action immigration stance. On the flip side, only 9 percent of Latinos in New Mexico expressed more enthusiasm toward Romney as a result of his immigration position, while a whopping 50 percent of Latinos were more enthusiastic about Obama as a direct consequence of his immigration views.

We also provide more direct evidence that the candidates' immigration positions also led to decisive Latino support for Obama. Simple bivariate analysis suggests that immigration impacted New Mexicans' decisions at the ballot box. As shown in figure 4, of those Latinos who cited immigration as the most critical issue facing politicians, 89.29 percent were significantly more likely ($p < 0.01$) to vote for Obama compared to only 10.71 percent who voted for Romney. As political pundits have

Figure 4. Impact of Immigration on New Mexican Vote Choice

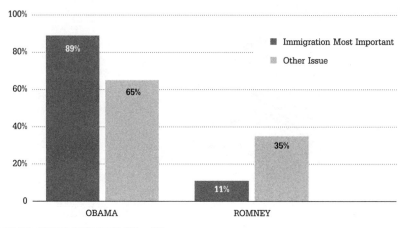

Source: Latino Decisions Poll October 29, 2012; n = 356.

suggested, immigration is a key factor impacting Latino voting behavior nationally, and at least in this instance there is no evidence of the New Mexico exceptionalism that has been such a strong component of the narrative regarding Latino politics in the state.

Conclusion

New Mexico is a microcosm of the future of U.S. electoral politics. With a long-standing presence of Latino residents and a deep history of Latino political power, New Mexico offers an excellent venue to understand what other states' electoral politics may look like in the future. Three main themes emerge from the 2012 election. First, immigration is a key policy issue that impacted how Latinos selected the 2012 president. Even in a state where most Latinos are far removed from the immigrant experience, New Mexicans of Hispanic origin attached great importance to the issue. More importantly, in the context of a polarized political climate at both the national and state level, New Mexicans responded by choosing the candidate who supported comprehensive immigration reform and relatively pro-immigrant policies. This finding suggests that even as Latinos who have lived in the country for generations experience political and social incorporation, immigration remains a pivotal issue for Hispanics.

Second, New Mexico demonstrates the impact of racial stratification on vote choice. In this state, Spanish descendants have maintained a higher position relative to other groups such as Mexicans, and these historical dynamics continue to impact electoral politics. In multivariate analysis not presented in this chapter, we found that Latinos who self-identify as Spanish were less supportive of President Obama than those who are of Mexican origin. The New Mexican experience therefore suggests that while the content of specific stratifications may vary by region, between-group differences may lead to systematic differences between different Latinos. However, we must not overstate the importance of these differences, because the impact of them in our model was relatively small compared to other factors, and Latinos of both groups voted for Obama in wide numbers. Thus, it is clear that substantive policy issues trump cleavages, as the importance of immigration was a more potent factor in selecting Obama among New Mexicans. Indeed, the lesson here is that when Latinos perceive hostility toward immigration, they are likely to behave as a unified group supporting candidates who support their interests.

Finally, New Mexico highlights the importance of campaign factors in electoral outcomes. As in other states, Latinos who were mobilized to vote were more likely to choose the Democrat, Barack Obama. While not directly tested here, the results suggest that Obama's tailored outreach to Latino voters proved successful. Not only did the Obama campaign work harder to reach Latinos, they astutely used messages and events that reflected New Mexicans' relatively high electoral participation levels and their entrenched community engagement throughout the state.

NOTES

1. Latino and Hispanic are used interchangeably throughout the chapter.
2. See the United States Census Bureau's "State and County Quick Facts" sheet for New Mexico at http://quickfacts.census.gov/qfd/states/35000.html.
3. See the "ImpreMedia/Latino Decisions 2012 Election Eve Poll" at http://www.latinovote2012.com/app/.

REFERENCES

Acuña, Rodolfo. 1972. *Occupied America: A History of Chicanos*, 5th ed. New York: Pearson Longman.

Barrera, Mario. 2008. "Are Latinos a Racialized Minority?" *Sociological Perspectives* 51, no. 2: 305–32.

Blalock, Hubert. 1967. *Toward a Theory of Minority Group Relations*. New York: Wiley.

Dickerson, John. 2012. "Why Romney Never Saw it Coming." *Slate*, November 9. Available at http://www.slate.com/articles/news_and_politics/politics/2012/11/why_romney_was_surprised_to_lose_his_campaign_had_the_wrong_numbers_bad.html.

Fabian, Jordan. 2012. "Obama: If I Win, It Will Be Because GOP Alienated Latinos." *ABC News*,

October 14. Available at abcnews.go.com.

Garcia, F. Chris, and Gabriel R. Sanchez. 2008. *Hispanics and the U.S. Political System: Moving into the Mainstream.* Upper Saddle River, NJ: Pearson, Prentice-Hall.

Garcia, F. Chris, and Bianca Sapien. 1999. "Recognizing Reliability: Hispanos and the 1996 Elections in New Mexico." In *Awash in the Mainstream: Latino Politics in the 1996 Election*, ed. Rodolfo O. de la Garza and Louis DeSipio. Boulder, CO: Westview Press, 75–100.

Garcia, F. Chris, and Christine Marie Sierra. 2005. "New Mexico Hispanos in the 2000 General Election." In *Muted Voices: Latinos and the 2000 Elections*, ed. Rodolfo O. de la Garza and Louis DeSipio. Lanham, MD: Rowman & Littlefield Publishers, 101–29.

Garcia, F. Chris, Gabriel R Sanchez, and Christine Marie Sierra. 2012. "Hispanos in the 2008 Elections in New Mexico." Unpublished manuscript.

Gomez, Laura. 2007. *Manifest Destinies: The Making of the Mexican American Race.* New York: New York University Press.

Hugo-Lopez, Mark, and Paul Taylor. 2012. "Latino Voters in the 2012 Election." *Pew Hispanic Center*, November 7. Available at pewhispanic.org.

Masket, Seth. 2009. "Did Obama's Ground Game Matter? The Influence of Local Field Offices during the 2008 Presidential Election." *Public Opinion Quarterly* 73, no. 5: 1023–39.

McClain, Paula D., Niambi M. Carter, Victoria M. DeFrancesco Soto, Monique L. Lyle, Jeffrey D. Grynaviski, Shayla C. Nunnally, Thomas J. Scotto, J. Alan Kendrick, Gerald F. Lackey, and Kendra Davenport Cotton. 2006. "Racial Distancing in a Southern City: Latino Immigrants' Views of Black Americans." *Journal of Politics* 68, no. 3: 571–84.

Oliver, Eric, and Janelle Wong. 2003. "Intergroup Prejudice in Multiethnic Settings." *American Journal of Political Science* 47: 567–82.

Sanchez, Gabriel R. 2010. "Hispanic Vote Will Decide Next Governor of New Mexico." *Latino Decisions: Everything Latino Politics* (blog post), October 19. Available at latinodecisions.com.

Santos, Fernanda. 2012. "New Mexico Offers Look at U.S. Elections of the Future." *New York Times*, September 29.

Sierra, Christine Marie. 2008a. "From Hillary to Barack." Notes from the DNC: An On-the-Spot Blog from the 2008 Democratic National Convention, posted by KNME TV-5 and *New Mexico Independent*, August 28. Available at newmexicoindependent.com.

———. 2008b. "Political Advertisements in the 2008 Election: Immigration Transcriptions." Author's files.

———. 2008c. "Timelines: Candidate and Surrogate Visits in the 2004 and 2008 Elections." Author's files.

Sierra, Christine Marie, and F. Chris Garcia. 2010. "Hispanic Politics in a Battleground State: New Mexico in 2004." In *Beyond the Barrio: Latinos in the 2004 Elections*, ed. Rodolfo O. de la Garza, Louis DeSipio, and David L. Leal. South Bend, IN: University of Notre Dame Press.

JASON L. MORIN and ADRIAN D. PANTOJA

The *Reconquista* of California
Latinos and the 2012 Election

IN 2012, LATINOS IN CALIFORNIA WENT TO THE POLLS IN RECORD NUMBERS and overwhelmingly voted for President Barack Obama over the Republican challenger, Governor Mitt Romney. In this chapter, we focus on the state of California and examine the extent to which Latinos exerted their political influence in the 2012 general election. California provides an excellent opportunity to examine Latinos in the 2012 presidential election. California is home to the largest Latino population in the United States. In 2011, Latinos accounted for well over one-third of California's residential population. Its population is diverse, young, and the number of Latino residents within the state continues to grow every year (Pew 2013). Not surprisingly, the potential to shape political outcomes is tremendous. As the most populated state in the union, California carries a great deal of weight in presidential elections. After the 2012 Census, the state was reallocated fifty-five delegates in the Electoral College, which is the most of any other state by far. In presidential elections, where candidates need to capture 270 votes to win, the ability to carry California can create a significant advantage. The stakes, therefore, are quite high—not only for the candidates themselves, but also for Latinos when the polls open in November.

Despite the size of California's Latino population, there has been much debate about whether Latinos have any influence over California politics and presidential elections. In comparison to other states discussed in this volume, some pundits have suggested that Latinos will be less influential than they are in in other key battleground states. Over the past two decades, California has been a safe state for the Democratic Party and has continuously voted for Democrats at the state and national level of politics. We, however, take issue with this assessment because it neglects the very demographic changes that make California a safe seat—a growing Latino population that also heavily supports the Democratic Party. In this regard, we suggest that having electoral influence moves beyond the ability to impact close or hotly contested elections. It also involves the ability to promote sustained support for a political party and candidates already in power.

In what follows, we provide a brief historical account of California politics in the 1990s and a discussion of the growing Latino population in the Golden State. Using the highly regarded impreMedia/Latino Decisions 2012 Latino Election Eve Poll, we examine patterns of Latino outreach, participation, and voting behavior in the 2012 election. Our results indicate that Latinos overwhelmingly showed their support for Barack Obama in the presidential election. Although California garnered much less attention than other battleground states, Latinos remained enthusiastic about the election. In part, this enthusiasm was driven by the larger national debate over policies, such as immigration, that was reminiscent of prior political battles in California. Consistent with Latinos' attitudes towards the candidates and their stance on the national policy debate, our results also indicate that Latinos were influential in the passage of key propositions on the ballot. While Latinos overwhelmingly preferred Proposition 30 to 38 when it came to funding public education, they did not support measures to limit the electoral influence of unions. We conclude by suggesting that Latinos will continue to play a critical role in determining political outcomes in California. However, Latinos' interests will be better served if both Republicans and Democrats provide greater outreach to Latinos.

California Politics and the Growing Influence of Latinos

During much of the Cold War era, California could be classified as a Republican stronghold given that the GOP won every presidential contest from 1952 to 1988, except LBJ's 1964 landslide over Goldwater (Mataconis 2012). Today, the Republican Party in California is in free fall. Since 1992, no Republican presidential candidate has won the state. Presently, Republicans do not hold any statewide office and have seen their numbers fall below one-third in the Senate and Assembly. In the 2010 midterm elections, when Republicans picked up sixty-three House seats nationally, they failed to pick up a single seat in California. In the 2012 election, the GOP lost seven legislative seats and four congressional seats. The Democratic Party has a two-thirds majority in the state legislature for the first time since the 1880s. The share of Californians registered as Republican has declined from 37 percent in 1992 to less than 30 percent in 2012 (Nagourney 2012). If these trends continue, by the decade's end, there will be more persons registered as Independents than Republicans. Whether the GOP has politically hit rock bottom in California remains to be seen. What is clear is that unless the GOP undertakes a major reorientation, it is likely that things could get grimmer.

Since the 1990s, the Republican Party has clearly lost much of its electoral influence in California. The political decline of the GOP in California is not only the result of the changing composition of the state's electorate, i.e., larger numbers of Latino and Asian American voters. A more significant factor was the decision of Republican candidates and elites to pursue policies and campaigns that alienated immigrants, Latinos, Asian Americans, and other minorities in the state. The beginnings of this march of folly was the 1994 election, when Proposition 187, the so-called "Save Our State" initiative, became the centerpiece policy of Governor Pete Wilson's reelection campaign. The initiative was designed to deny social services, including public education, to undocumented immigrants, as well as require state officials, doctors, and nurses to report suspected undocumented immigrants to the Immigration and Naturalization Service for deportation. The rhetoric and campaign in support of the initiative was racially charged, and essentially blamed Latinos and immigrants for most of the state's economic and social hardships (Nicholson 2005). Latinos felt under threat, and record numbers of them naturalized and voted to counter this and other racially charged initiatives, e.g., Propositions 209 and 227 (Barreto, Ramirez, and Woods 2005; Pantoja, Ramirez, and Segura 2001).

In retrospect, attacking Latinos, immigrants, and other minorities was a shortsighted strategy given that the share of the non-Hispanic white population declined from 69.9 percent in the 1980s to 42.8 percent in 2010, while its share of the electorate declined from 83 percent to 65 percent (Field Research Corporation 2009). During the same period, the share of Latino population grew from 19 percent in 1980 to 38 percent in 2010, while its electorate increased from 8 percent in the 1980s to 26 percent in 2010. Today, one in four Californians is an immigrant. Of the 18 million registered voters in the state, 28.9 percent are "New Americans" ("New Americans in California" 2012). Yet, demographic shifts alone do not explain why California has undergone a radical political transformation in the last three decades. The political transformation is the result of a partisan shift brought about by a growing minority electorate that has moved away from the Republican Party (Segura, Falcon, and Pachon 1997).

Analysis of Latino voting behavior reveals that prior to the 1994 election, the GOP had been making inroads (Bowler, Nicholson, and Segura 2006; Jacobson 2004). Although polling data on Latinos have historically been unreliable, the available data show a steady increase in support for Republican presidential candidates. For example, polling data from a Field Poll show that Ronald Reagan increased his share of the Latino vote from 35 percent in 1980 to 45 percent in 1984 (Barreto et al. 2009). The decision on the part of Governor Pete Wilson and other supporters of Proposition 187 to criminalize immigrants resulted in a dramatic turn away from the GOP by Latinos and other minorities. Research by Bowler, Nicholson, and Segura (2006) also finds that the anti-immigrant campaigns led many non-Hispanic whites to distance themselves from the Republican Party in California. Thus, there was an overall movement in the state by minorities and whites toward the Democratic Party. The political consequences of the GOP's short-sighted strategy have been devastating, and it will take decades and radical change for the GOP to recover its image in the state.

As the GOP's fortunes have been in decline, Latinos have been politically ascendant in the Golden State. First, demography matters, as it provides a base for potential citizens and voters. Figure 1 shows the growth of the Latino population since the 1950s. Latinos have essentially turned California into a majority-minority state. Second, demographic growth has led in an increase in the size of California's Latino electorate (as noted in figure 2). Third, the increase in the size of the Latino electorate has been facilitated by fewer registration restrictions and the availability of online registration in both English and Spanish (García Bedolla and Vélez 2013). Fourth, Latino voting strength has increased the number of Latino elected officials in the state (see figure 3). Fifth, Latinos have made California a solidly blue state, which has led to a decline in the number of Republican officeholders in the state and a denial of 55 electoral votes to Republican presidential candidates. These factors make Latinos a major force behind the Democratic *reconquista* of California.

Latinos in California and the 2012 Election

What impact did Latinos in California have in the 2012 election? As noted before, the last time a Republican presidential candidate won California was in 1988, and as a solidly blue state the 2012 presidential contest largely bypassed the Golden State. Some pundits worried that the lack of competition would ultimately depress turnout and impact the outcome of state and local races. At the same time, others suggested that if history were a teacher, Latino voters would continue to play a key

Figure 1. Percent Latino in California

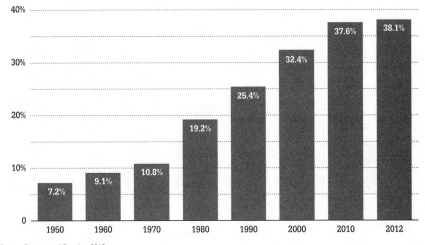

Source: Barreto and Ramírez 2013.

Figure 2. Percentage of Latinos in the California Electorate

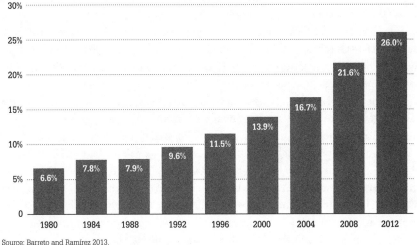

Source: Barreto and Ramírez 2013.

role in determining California's choice for president. To explore these possibilities, this chapter focuses on several indicators of influence over presidential elections in California, including Latinos' vote for president, their level of political participation, and mobilization efforts (see Barreto, Collingwood, and Manzano 2010). We also examine Latinos' enthusiasm for the election as it relates to their attitudes toward

Figure 3. Latino Elected Officials in California

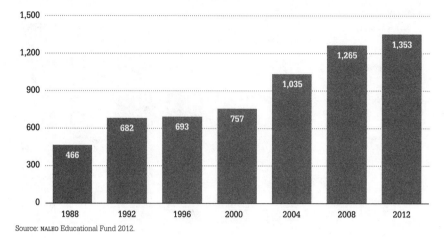

Source: NALEO Educational Fund 2012.

comprehensive immigration reform (CIR) and the candidates' platforms on the issue. Finally, we examine how Latinos played a role in the success and failure of three key propositions on the ballot, including Propositions 30, 32, and 38. In an effort to assess the political behavior and preferences of the Latino electorate in California, we rely on the impreMedia/Latino Decisions 2012 Latino Election Eve Poll. This poll, fielded in late October 2012, has a national sample of 5,600 Latino registered voters. We limit our analysis to 800 registered Latino voters sampled from California. The sample of 800 gives us a margin of error of ±3.5 percent.

In the 2012 presidential election, Barack Obama carried the state of California (and its 55 Electoral College delegates) with a comfortable 21 percentage point margin. To the extent that Latinos helped solidify Barack Obama's margin of victory, Latinos were overwhelmingly supportive of Obama's second bid for president. Table 1 shows that 77.68 percent of Latinos said that they either "voted" or "intended to vote" in favor of the president. Given this broad support, it is apparent that Latinos played a key role in keeping California a Democratic state. Our results further suggest that partisan attachments did not completely influence Latinos' vote for president. According to our California sample, 97.34 percent of Latinos who identified themselves as Democrat voted to keep Barack Obama in office for a second presidential term. Latino Republicans, however, were quite split over their decision for president. While 56.20 percent voted in favor of Governor Romney, a large percentage of Republicans (43.80 percent) voted for Barack Obama. At least for Latinos in California, therefore, partisanship only played a moderate role in the voting behavior of Latinos, as many Republicans crossed party lines to vote for a Democratic candidate.

Table 1. The Effect of Partisanship and Vote Choice in the 2012 Presidential Election (California)

	Vote for Mitt Romney	Vote for Barack Obama	Total
All Respondents	22.32%	77.68%	100%
Republican ID	56.20%	43.80%	100%
Democrat ID	2.66%	97.34%	100%

Source: impreMedia/Latino Decisions 2012 Latino Election Eve Poll.

PARTICIPATION AND MOBILIZATION

While Latinos were solidified in their vote for president, the ability to influence electoral outcomes also depends on the extent to which candidates receive a plurality of support from voters. In California, there has been a notable increase in the number of Latinos participating in presidential elections. Between 2000 and 2008, voter turnout increased from 1.6 million to nearly 3 million voters (NALEO 2012). In 2012, this number was expected to reach a record 3.9 million—a 32.1 percent increase from the previous presidential election (NALEO 2012). Voter turnout in California also reflects a larger nationwide trend where the number of Latinos participating in the presidential election increased by 22 percent (Taylor, Gonzalez-Barrera, Passel, and Lopez 2012). As noted before in this chapter, several demographic changes in California, including an expanding Latino electorate, have certainly contributed to these rising participation rates. However, population changes alone cannot entirely explain why Latinos decided to turn out in the 2012 presidential election.

It has been well established that mobilization is an important explanation of political participation (Rosenstone and Hansen 1993). Simply put, "people don't vote when no one asks them to" (Platkin 2012). Despite an increase in voter turnout, however, California was perhaps one of the most undermobilized states in the union. The 2012 Latino Election Eve Poll shows that only 30.97 percent of Latino voters were contacted by a campaign, political party, or community organization and asked to either vote or register to vote. As the chapter by Ramirez et al. in this volume notes, the amount of contact by a political party or organization in California was comparatively smaller than in other key battleground states, including Ohio, Nevada, New Mexico, and Colorado, where 48 to 59 percent of the respondents said that they had been contacted. Reports on national advertising further demonstrate the relative lack of attention to California. While supporters of both candidates spent a total of $892 million on advertising nationwide, the Campaign Media Analysis Group (CMAG) reported that a mere $330 was spent on two national ads—one in Bakersfield and the other in the Chico-Redding area (CNN 2012). The level of spending on television advertising was also comparable to the 2004 presidential election, in which national advertisements were diverted to other, more politically contentious states (Barreto, Ramirez, Fraga, and Guerra 2009, 15–16).

Still, California's sustained "blueness" can be better understood by the relative presence of the two major political parties. While 55.39 percent of the respondents reported having been contacted by Democrats, only 30.75 percent of our California sample said that they were contacted by Republicans. The comparatively lower levels of outreach by the GOP suggests that Republicans were willing to hedge their bets elsewhere, such as in Florida and Ohio, where they were believed to be more competitive. This strategy, however, may have left many Latinos in California, including Latino Republicans, feeling alienated by the Republican Party. Immediately following the 2012 presidential election, the California Republican Party leadership expressed concern over its inability to court Latino voters effectively. California Republican Party chair Tom Del Beccaro admitted that Republicans needed to change their appeal to Latino voters if they were to become electorally competitive (Gould 2012). These sentiments were also echoed by new Republican Party chair Jim Brulte, who has recently called upon party members to "venture outside of their traditional power base" and "increase [their] outreach to minority communities" (Edwards 2013; White 2013). Consequently, party strategists such as Hector Barajas have suggested that Republicans need to do more than simply rely on symbolic messages and hire mariachis to demonstrate their commitment to Latinos. Instead, Barajas suggested, Republicans should be knocking on doors and bringing their message face-to-face, which would allow them to engage Latinos in a more meaningful way (Mehta 2013).

To the extent that Republicans have changed their outreach strategies, the Republican National Committee (RNC) has called upon new communication directors (of Latin American descent) to improve coordination efforts with state and local party officials across seven key states: California, Florida, New Jersey, New Mexico, Pennsylvania, Texas, and Virginia (Richman 2013; Huang 2013). Clearly, this nationwide push to court the Latino vote is telling of Republicans' performance during the 2012 campaign. In California, the Republican Party officials hope to boost the GOP's level of engagement by building upon its grassroots infrastructure, establishing a year-round presence in the Latino community, and talking to business and community leaders (Richman 2013; Huang 2013). Still in the early stages of the program, however, it remains to be seen if Latinos will experience greater outreach, and if Latinos will be responsive to their efforts.

Next to the Democratic Party, civic organizations played the second largest role in mobilizing Latino voters. Among those who say they were contacted, 45.58 percent of our California sample said they were contacted by local community organizations, which is nearly 13 percentage points greater than the rest of the nation

(33 percent). This outcome is not surprising given the rich and deeply engrained presence of Latino organizations in California, and the disproportionate number of Latinos who continue to go unregistered in the state. In this volume, Ramirez et al. observes a nationwide effort among Latino civic associations to maximize outreach. In the ya es hora ¡Ve y Vota!, campaign, civic organizations such as the National Association of Latino Elected Officials (NALEO) and Mi Familia Vota canvassed California's neighborhoods, provided voter information and education, and organized voter-registration drives (Olson 2012). NALEO also created a voter and election hotline, which helped over seven thousand Latino voters in California with inquiries on registration, education, and voting (NALEO 2012). Finally, civic organizations extended their outreach beyond those who are already likely to vote to include the youth, rural and disadvantaged communities, and naturalized citizens ("Latino Youth" 2013; Daniel 2012; Olson 2012; NALEO 2012). In this regard, Latino-based civic organizations served as important mobilizing agents that supplemented the relative lack of attention by the two national parties.

Civic organizations, however, did not work alone, as they collaborated with the Spanish-language media to expand their outreach to Latinos. According to the 2012 Latino Election Eve Poll, a sizable percentage of our California sample reported getting their political news and information from Spanish newspapers (40 percent), radio (49 percent), and television (58 percent) either every day or a few times per week. While Latinos relied on several outlets to get their political information, we interpret this data to also mean that Latinos were exposed to civic organizations and their message despite having no direct contact. In California, for instance, Eliseo Medina—long-time civil rights activist and former secretary-treasurer for the Service Employees International Union—appeared on major Spanish television outlets, including Univision's Primera Edición and Telemundo to mobilize Latino viewers (SEIU Communications 2012). Indeed, the media is a useful and important resource because it provides opportunities to reach a wider audience. Thus, it is not surprising that civic organizations worked in collaboration with the Spanish-language media on national campaigns to inform viewers of important policy issues and encourage Latinos to register and vote.

ISSUE SALIENCY AND THE ROLE OF IMMIGRATION

The above results show that Latinos did not abandon the Democratic Party and that registered Latinos continued to participate in record numbers, despite experiencing comparatively lower levels of direct outreach. Still, Latinos were especially tuned into the 2012 presidential election. In the final weeks leading up to the election, a nationwide tracking poll by Latino Decisions suggested that enthusiasm for the

Table 2. The Role of Immigration on Vote Choice in the 2012 Presidential Election (California)

	Vote for Mitt Romney	Vote for Barack Obama	Total
Immigration Salient	18.27%	81.73%	100%
Know Someone Undocumented			
Yes	21.73%	78.27%	100%
No	23.28%	76.72%	100%
Enthusiasm for Obama			
More	8.37%	91.63%	100%
No Effect	38.53%	61.47%	100%
Less	58.87%	41.13%	100%
Enthusiasm for Romney			
More	81.52%	18.48%	100%
No Effect	33.09%	66.91%	100%
Less	11.01%	88.99%	100%

Source: impreMedia/Latino Decisions 2012 Latino Election Eve Poll.

2012 presidential election was quite high in the months leading up to the general election, as 87 percent of registered voters said that they were almost certain to vote in the upcoming presidential election (Latino Decisions 2012a). What explains this enthusiasm and continued support among Latino voters in California? We contend that the salience of immigration, coupled with candidates' attitudes towards immigration, helped to solidify Latinos' participation and ultimately choice for president. Table 2 shows the relationship between Latinos' attitudes towards immigration and vote choice. Among those who believed immigration to be an important issue, 81.73 percent voted in favor of Barack Obama. Less than 20 percent of Latino voters, however, said that they would cast their vote for Governor Romney.

Immigration policy has increasingly become more salient to Latinos. Next to the economy (39 percent), our California sample provided clear evidence that immigration was the second most important issue (24.5 percent) facing Latino voters. We believe that there are two factors driving this outcome. First, Republicans brought immigration into the national spotlight by initiating a series of anti-immigrant initiatives. In 2010, Arizona passed Senate Bill 1070, which (among other things) allowed local law enforcement to check the immigration status of detained individuals. Subsequent copycat legislation was also passed throughout other regions of the United States, including parts of the South and the Midwest (Lam and Morse 2012).

Since the law gave greater discretion to law enforcement authorities, many have argued that it could lead to racial profiling and anxiety among Latino citizens as well as the undocumented (Nuño 2011). A nationwide poll from Latino Decisions carried out in July demonstrated that 79 percent of Latino voters believed that it was likely that they would be pulled over by the police and asked about their immigration status (Latino Decisions 2012b). The Supreme Court would later overturn several of its provisions. However, the main provision of the law ("show me your papers") remains.

Second, the saliency of immigration has been reinforced by a majority of Latinos who say they currently have social connections with undocumented immigrants. For example, the 2012 Latino Election Eve Poll shows that 54 percent of Latinos in California know someone who is undocumented, including a family member, friend, or coworker. In comparison to the rest of the nation, California has the largest number of undocumented immigrants (2.5 million estimated) in the United States (Passel and Cohn 2011). Moreover, there is good reason to expect that many Latinos continue to live in ethnically homogeneous neighborhoods where undocumented immigrants are more likely to reside. For example, Logan and Stults (2011) find that the segregation of Hispanics tends to occur in major-metropolis cities, such as Los Angeles. Although these personal relationships add to our understanding of issue saliency, it is also plausible that these ties could increase the likelihood of voting for Barack Obama, who was viewed as the more immigrant-sympathetic candidate. The results in table 2, however, indicate that over 75 percent of respondents from both groups voted in favor of the president. Overall, this outcome implies that while knowing someone undocumented may be important for understanding issue saliency, the decision to vote for the president was based on more than just close personal relationships.

CANDIDATE PLATFORMS AND IMMIGRATION

In addition, the candidates' positions on immigration also played an important role in Latinos' decision for president. In June 2012, the president announced his plan for Deferred Action for Childhood Arrivals (DACA). In a last-minute effort to court the Latino vote, the president called for the Department of Homeland Security (DHS) to offer renewable work permits to the undocumented. The major provisions mandated that undocumented immigrants meet the following conditions: (1) arrived in the United States before the age of 16; (2) are under the age of 31; (3) have continuously resided in the United States since June 15th, 2007; (4) have not been convicted of a felony or significant misdemeanor; and (5) are enrolled in school, have graduated or obtained a certificate of completion from high school, or are an honorably discharged military veteran (Mayorkas 2012). Although the president's plan was far from comprehensive, it was nevertheless considered to be a positive gesture towards Latinos and the undocumented community. Given the size of the undocumented Latino population in the Southwest, the program was especially relevant to Californians. Recently, the USCIS announced that it has received over 110,000 applications from California alone—the most from any state since the initiation of Obama's plan (U.S. Citizenship and Immigration Office 2013).

In contrast to the president's immigration efforts, Governor Romney offered a much different plan by calling for undocumented immigrants to "self-deport" from the United States. The underlying logic to the plan was simple: make everyday life so intolerable that it would cause the undocumented to have no other choice but to leave the country. While Governor Romney's proposal lacked many of the specifics, its potential impact was far-reaching and reminiscent of former governor Pete Wilson's efforts to target Latinos in California.

In all, these divergent stances towards immigration resonated strongly with Latinos when they went to the polls. While 58.5 percent of Latinos responded enthusiastically to the president's outreach to Latinos, 32.5 percent said that the president's plan had no effect. We interpret this last finding to mean that either the level of enthusiasm was already high, or Latinos preferred an alternative, more comprehensive immigration plan to DACA. This argument is supported by a recent Latino Decisions poll that found Latinos overwhelmingly support comprehensive immigration reform (CIR) that would also include a pathway to citizenship (Barreto 2013). By contrast, Latinos were much less receptive to Mitt Romney and his call for self-deportation. After being informed of his immigration proposal, a clear majority (61.27 percent) responded by saying that they were less enthusiastic about the governor. This response was followed by 26.16 percent who said that the proposal had no effect at all on their attitudes towards the governor.

Although Latinos were somewhat divided over the president's proposal, table 2 shows a clear and positive trend between the level of enthusiasm for Obama and vote choice. For example, 91.63 percent of those who responded enthusiastically to the president's proposal also responded by saying they would vote for the president. While the results indicate a positive correlation between enthusiasm and voting for president, less enthusiasm for Obama did not substantially increase support for the governor. In fact, a sizable percentage (41.13 percent) continued to favor the president—even after saying they were less enthusiastic. Perceived enthusiasm for Governor Romney and his counterproposal, however, tells a somewhat different story. Table 2 demonstrates that the level of enthusiasm is positively associated with the decision to vote for the former governor. However, the results also suggest that Latinos' general lack of enthusiasm led to greater accountability and punishment at the polls. Among those who said they were "less enthusiastic" about Romney,

88.99 percent said they either intended to vote or had already voted for President Obama. Overall, the findings reinforce the notion that Latinos considered Barack Obama's proposal to be generally less hostile to Latinos. In the end, the evidence indicates that Latinos were pivotal in keeping California a solidly "blue" state. The relative lack of presence by the Republican Party, coupled with candidate's positions on CIR served to reinforce preexisting and negative attitudes towards Republicans. Not only did Latinos go out and vote, but they did so with overwhelming support for Barack Obama.

CALIFORNIA PROPOSITIONS

In addition to immigration policy, Latinos have demonstrated more liberal attitudes by showing greater support for government intervention in economic and social policy (Segura 2012). During the 2012 election, California voters were also asked to decide on a number of key propositions, including Propositions 30, 32, and 38, which focused on the role of unions in campaign spending and funding for public education. Among these three propositions, Propositions 30 ("Temporary Taxes to Fund Education, Guaranteed Local Public Safety Funding Initiative) and 38 ("Tax to Fund Education and Early Childhood Programs Initiative") garnered the most attention from the media. Sponsored by Democratic governor Jerry Brown, Proposition 30 sought to fund education by increasing taxes on individuals who earned over $250,000, and by increasing sales taxes by a quarter of a percent over the course of four years (California Secretary of State n.d.). Proposition 38, by contrast, intended to fund education and early childhood programs by increasing taxes on earnings using a sliding scale for twelve years. Sponsored by civil rights attorney Molly Munger, the proposition was viewed as an alternative to Proposition 30 that would increase taxes for most Californians, including those earning lower and middle incomes.

While both propositions were divided along party and ideological lines, Proposition 30 received the greatest attention in the media. Not only did Republicans and conservative groups reject Proposition 30 for targeting individuals having higher incomes, but they also questioned whether the funds would be diverted from public education and used for other means (Megerian 2012; Rainey 2012). Regardless, the proposition's financial impact on state education was rather significant. Assuming the proposition's failure, public schools and community colleges projected $5.4 billion in budget cuts, while the University of California and California State University systems were set to lose as much as $250 million each (Jones 2012). Moreover, the proposition's failure would have had a negative budgetary impact on the several Hispanic-Serving Institutions within the state. In all, the proposition

Table 3. The Role of California Politics on Vote Choice in the 2012 Presidential Election

		Vote for Mitt Romney	Vote for Barack Obama	Total
Prop 30	Yes	11.43%	88.57%	100%
	No	51.34%	48.66%	100%
Prop 32	Yes	32.87%	67.13%	100%
	No	18.84%	81.16%	100%
Prop 38	Yes	13.38%	86.62%	100%
	No	37.42%	62.58%	100%

Source: impreMedia/Latino Decisions 2012 Latino Election Eve Poll.

created a dilemma for voters to choose between increased taxes and funding for public education.

Ultimately, a majority of Californians preferred Proposition 30, with 55.4 percent of the vote (California Secretary of State n.d.). Both academics and pundits alike credited Latinos for the proposition's passage (Jones 2012). In an interview with the *Los Angeles Daily News*, Raphael Sonenshein, executive director of the Pat Brown Institute for Public Affairs at California State University, Los Angeles, reasoned that its passage could be attributed to a "transforming electorate who mobilized in the last few weeks" (Jones 2012). Our study confirms his assessment, as our California sample indicates that 71.30 percent of Latinos voted in favor of Proposition 30, whereas only 57.98 percent supported Proposition 38. While support for Governor Brown's proposal implies more liberal attitudes among Latinos, it is worth noting that many of the proposition's supporters also voted for Barack Obama. Table 3 shows that 88.57 percent of those who voted in favor of the proposition also voted in favor of Barack Obama. Meanwhile, a majority of Latinos voted in favor of the president regardless of their support for Proposition 38. In all, Latinos favored increasing taxes to fund public education. Moreover, they demonstrated greater support for the more liberal of the two propositions.

In addition to Propositions 30 and 38, another significant proposition was placed on the California ballot. Known as "Political Contributions by Payroll Dedication Initiative," Proposition 32 would prohibit unions from using payroll-deducted funds for political purposes. In an effort to combat the passage of Proposition 32, labor unions, such as the California Labor Federation (CLF), mobilized its support base by giving volunteer quotas to local unions, which yielded more than 30,000 campaign workers. The CLF also provided financial support to civic organizations to increase turnout among Latinos (Mishak 2012). According to one report, "Mi Familia Vota said that it expected to deploy 500 people on Election Day to knock on doors in Los Angeles to get voters to the polls" (Unified Against 2012). On the day of the election, a majority of Californians, including 70 percent of Latinos, ultimately rejected the proposition in favor of labor. However, our results in table 3 suggest no clear relationship between support for Proposition 32 and vote choice, as a majority of Latinos voted for Barack Obama regardless of their decision to vote for or against Proposition 32. Thus, the proposition did not spark the same ideological chord as the battle over public funding for education. Still, our results suggest that Latinos provided the decisive edge towards the proposition's failure.

Conclusion

Clearly, California has undergone a dramatic political transformation as a result of the growth of the Latino electorate and failure of the Republican Party to court their vote. Latinos in the state (as well as Latinos elsewhere) were often referred to as "the sleeping giant" because of their failure to transform their demographic growth into a political advantage. This is no longer the case in California, the state with the largest number of Latino voters. In an interview, Jaime Regalado, executive director of the Pat Brown Institute of Public Affairs, said, "No one is talking about the sleeping giant anymore. . . . The giant is here now, and Republicans aren't recruiting it" (Siders 2011). The failure of the GOP to reach out to Latinos in California has been politically disastrous for the party. The solid support for the Democratic Party among Latinos in California meant that the outcome of who was to win the 55 electoral votes was never in doubt. Consequently, the 2012 presidential candidates turned their attention to battleground states where the outcome was less certain. However, even in these battleground states (as noted in other chapters in this book) the GOP's lack of a Latino strategy proved costly.

The case of California is instructive because it provides a road map of the consequences of neglecting, perhaps even attacking, a minority population that was about to flex its political muscles. Yet, we believe Republicans could turn their Latino problem into an opportunity. After all, there are fears among some Latino leaders that the Democratic Party could take the Latino vote for granted. Arturo Vargas, executive director of the National Association of Latino Elected Officials, noted, "We absolutely need Latinos involved in both parties. The Latino community doesn't benefit from a partisan monopoly" (Wisckol 2011). How could Republicans turn their fortunes around? The 2012 Latino Election Eve Poll and other surveys allow us to outline two key lessons that could be used to develop a new Latino strategy that could provide a windfall for Republicans. These lessons are in no particular order. First, don't use immigrants as scapegoats for political gains—or as GOP assemblyman Rocky Chavez of Oceanside noted, "Why invite me to dinner but only let half my family in?" (Skelton 2013). As we have noted, the effects of attacking immigrants has been politically shortsighted and devastating for the Republican Party. Second, offer Latino noncitizens a pathway to political, social, and economic inclusion, e.g., the passage of a comprehensive immigration reform bill. In the mid-1990s, California became ground zero for what was to become a dramatic rupture between the GOP and Latinos and the beginnings of the Democratic Party *reconquista* of California. In the next decades, the GOP could begin their political *reconquista* of the state once it reengages the Latino electorate. Abandoning anti-immigrant rhetoric and policies, as well as the passage of a comprehensive immigration reform bill that puts the undocumented on a path toward citizenship are steps in the right direction.

REFERENCES

Barreto, Matt. 2013. "New Poll: Immigration Policy Stance Directly Tied to Winning the Latino Vote." *Latino Decisions*, March 5. Available at latinodecisions.com.

Barreto, Matt A., and Ricardo Ramírez. 2013. "Anti-Immigrant Politics and Lessons for the GOP from California." *Latino Decisions Research Report*, September 20. Available at latinodecisions.com.

Barreto, Matt A., Loren Collingwood, and Sylvia Manzano. 2010. "A New Measure of Group Influence in Presidential Elections: Assessing Latino Influence in 2008." *Political Research Quarterly* 63, no. 4: 908–921.

Barreto, Matt, Ricardo Ramírez, Luis Fraga, and Fernando Guerra. 2009. "Why California Matters: How California Latinos Influence the Presidential Election." In *Beyond the Barrio: Latinos in the 2004 Elections*, ed. Rodolfo de la Garza, Louis DeSipio, and David Leal. South Bend, IN: University of Notre Dame Press.

Barreto, Matt, Ricardo Ramírez, and Nathan Woods. 2005. "Are Naturalized Voters Driving the California Latino Electorate? Measuring the Impact of IRCA Citizens on Latino Voting." *Social Science Quarterly* 86: 792–811.

Bowler, Shaun, Stephen P. Nicholson, and Gary M. Segura. 2006. "Earthquakes and Aftershocks: Race, Direct Democracy, and Partisan Change." *American Journal of Political Science* 50: 146–59.

California Secretary of State. N.d. Available at sos.ca.gov.

CNN. 2012. "The 2012 Presidential Race: Ads, Money, and Travel." August 19. Available at cnn.com.

Daniel, Alice. 2012. "In Central Valley, Organizers Aim for Untapped Latino Vote." *KQED*, October 17. Available at kqed.org.

Edwards, Andrew. 2013. "California GOP Chair Jim Brulte Calls for Republicans to Leave Their Comfort Zones." *Inland Valley (CA) Daily Bulletin*, May 22. Available at dailybulletin.com.

Field Research Corporation. 2009. *California Opinion Index*. Vol. 2, *The Changing California*

Electorate. ISSN 0271–1095.

García Bedolla, Lisa, and Verónica N. Vélez. 2013. "Nativity and Latina/o and Asian American Online Voter Registration in California." *Center for Latino Policy Research,* June 4. Available at clpr.berkeley.edu.

Gould, Jens Erik. 2012. "Is California's Democratic Supermajority an Omen for the Rest of the U.S.?" *Time,* November 20.

Huang, Josie. 2013. "Republicans Launch Initiative Courting Latinos in California and Other Key States." *Southern California Public Radio,* October 11. Available at scpr.org.

Jacobson, Gary C. 2004. "Partisan and Ideological Polarization in the California Electorate." *State Politics and Policy Quarterly* 4: 113–39.

Jones, Barbara. 2012. "Young Voters, Democrats, Latinos and L.A. County Pushed Prop. 30 to Victory." *Los Angeles Daily News,* November 6. Available at dailynews.com.

Lam, Chau, and Ann Morse. 2012. "U.S. Supreme Court Rules on Arizona's Immigration Enforcement Law." *National Conference of State Legislatures,* June 25. Available at ncsl.org.

Latino Decisions. 2012a. "8 Percent of Latinos Have Already Voted Early, Enthusiasm Up Again in Final Week." October 29. Available at latinodecisions.com.

———. 2012b. "Poll: Latinos Overwhelmingly Oppose Supreme Court Decision to Uphold 'Show Me Your Papers.'" July 19. Available at latinodecisions.com.

"Latino Youth Civic Mobilization." 2013. Chicano/Latino Research Center Research Report No. 4. University of California, Santa Cruz. Available at circ.ucsc.edu.

Logan, John R., and Brian J. Stults. 2011. "The Persistence of Segregation in the Metropolis: New Findings from the 2010 Census." Census brief prepared for the Project US2010. Available at s4.brown.edu.

Mataconis, Doug. 2012. "The GOP Is Nearly Dead in California." *Outside the Beltway,* November 11. Available at outsidethebeltway.com.

Mayorkas, Alejandro. 2012. "Deferred Action for Childhood Arrivals: Who Can Be Considered." August 15. Available at whitehouse.gov.

McClatchy, David. 2011. "California GOP Not the Party It Was in Ronald Reagan's Day." *Modesto (CA) Bee,* September 7. Available at modbee.com.

Megerian, Chris. 2012. "Brown Found Path to Prop 30. Victory in a Divided California." *Los Angeles Times,* November 7. Available at latimes.com.

Mehta, Seema. 2013. "Republicans Announce $10-million Initiative to Lure Latino Voters." *Los Angeles Times,* October 10.

Mishak, Michael J. 2012. "Unified Against Proposition 32, Labor Works to Get Out the Vote." *Los Angeles Times,* November 6.

Nagourney, Adam. 2012. "Republican Party in California Is Caught in Cycle of Decline." *New York Times,* July 22.

NALEO Educational Fund. 2012. NALEO *2012 Latino Election Handbook.* Available at naleo.org.

———. 2012. "National Directory of Latino Elected Officials." Available at naleo.org.

"New Americans in California." 2012. Immigration Policy Center Report. January. Available at immigrationpolicy.org.

Nicholson, Stephen P. 2005. *Voting the Agenda: Candidates, Elections, and Ballot Propositions.* Princeton, NJ: Princeton University Press.

Nuño, Stephen. 2011. "Is Arizona 2010 Like California 1994?" *Latino Decisions,* May 24. Available at latinodecisions.com.

Olson, David. 2012. "Politics: Latino Organizations Not Resting after Election." *Press-Enterprise*, November 30. Available at pe.com.

Pantoja, Adrian D., Ricardo Ramirez, and Gary M. Segura. 2001. "Citizens by Choice, Voters by Necessity: Patterns in Political Mobilization by Naturalized Latinos." *Political Research Quarterly* 54: 729–50.

Passel, Jeffrey, and D'Vera Cohn. 2011. "Unauthorized Immigrant Population: National and State Trends, 2010." *Pew Hispanic Center.* Available at pewhispanic.org.

Pew Research Center. 2013. "State and County Databases: Latinos as Percent of Population, By State, 2011." *Pew Research Hispanic Trends Project*, August 29. Available at pewhispanic.org.

Platkin, Matt. 2012. "People Don't Vote When No One Asks Them To." *New York Times*, September 3. Available at nytimes.com.

Rainey, James. 2012. "Calif. Liberals Say Tax-Hiking Prop. 30 Could Be Model for U.S." *Los Angeles Times*, December 7.

Richman, Josh. 2013. "GOP Hires Hispanic State Director for California." *ContraCostaTimes.com*, October 10.

Rosenstone, Steven J., and John Mark Hansen. 1993. *Mobilization, Participation, and Democracy in America.* New York: Macmillan.

Segura, Gary M. 2012. "Latino Public Opinion and Realigning the American Electorate." *Daedalus* 141, no. 4: 1–16.

Segura, Gary M., Denis Falcon, and Harry Pachon. 1997. "Dynamics of Latino Partisanship in California: Immigration, Issue Salience, and Their Implications." *Harvard Journal of Hispanic Politics* 10: 62–80.

Sherry, Allison. 2010. "Latino Vote in 2012 May Hinge on Whether Dems Can Pass Immigration Reform." *Denver Post*, November 28.

SEIU Communications. 2012. "Rallying the Latino Vote on the Ground and the Airwaves." *SEIU. org* (blog post), October 12. Available at seiu.org.

Siders, David. 2011. "California's Republican Party Has Changed since Reagan's Time" *Sacramento Bee*, September 7.

Skelton, George. 2013. "Ugly Numbers for State GOP." *Los Angeles Times*, March 4.

Taylor, Paul, Ana Gonzalez-Barrera, Jeffrey S. Passel, and Mark Hugo Lopez. 2012. "An Awakened Giant: The Hispanic Electorate Is Likely to Double by 2030." *Pew Hispanic Center.* Available at pewhispanic.org.

U.S. Citizenship and Immigration Office of Performance and Quality. 2013. "Deferred Action for Childhood Arrivals Process." March 15. Available at uscis.gov.

White, Jeremy B. 2013. "John Burton, Jim Brulte Spar over Crime, Campaigns and Fate of GOP." *Sacramento Bee*, June 4.

Wisckol, Martin, 2011. "California's GOP Immigration Problem." *Orange County (CA) Register*, January 12. Available at ocregister.com.

TEHAMA LOPEZ BUNYASI

Brown Ballots
in the Buckeye State

FOR OVER A DECADE NOW, THE STATE OF OHIO HAS RECEIVED CONSIDERABLE attention as one of the nation's fiercest electoral battleground states. In this competitive field, the old adage "every vote counts" feels more true than trite to candidates and constituents alike. A shift in demographics, however, could potentially translate into a less malleable and more predictable state electorate. It is too early to know for certain how the rapid growth of a long-standing Latino population will affect this Midwestern state in future election cycles, but current data suggest that presidential candidates from here on out will have to take the Hispanic population into account if they want to be serious contenders.[1]

Only 0.7 percent of the country's Latino population reside in Ohio, but the roughly 355,000 Hispanics who call the Buckeye State their home are a vitally important part of the state's growth, and they are poised to be an even more consequential population in its future. According to the 2010 Census, 3.1 percent of the state's residents identified as Latino. Between 2000 and 2010, Ohio's entire population grew by 1.6 percent, which (as with other states in the Rust Belt) flagged well behind the national average of 9.7 percent. However, in the same ten-year period, Ohio's Latino population grew by 63.4 percent. In the first decade of the twenty-first century, Latinos were responsible for 75 percent of the state's growth, contributing 137,551 of the 183,364 new residents (Ennis et al. 2011). People of Mexican descent constitute the largest Latino subgroup in Ohio and total 1.5 percent of the state's population; Latinos of Puerto Rican descent are 0.8 percent, and those of Cuban descent are 0.1 percent. Ohioan Latinos with ancestral ties to other countries throughout the Caribbean and Central and South America are 0.7 percent of the entire state population (United States Census Bureau 2010).

To get an idea of what this population boom looks like on the ground, consider the growth rates in Ohio's ten largest cities. Between 2000 and 2010, Columbus's Latino population grew by 153.9 percent and it eclipsed Cleveland as the city with the largest number of Hispanics (44,359). Ohio's second- and fourth-largest Latino populations in Cleveland (39,534) and Lorain (16,177) grew by 13.8 percent and 12 percent, respectively. These cities are additionally noteworthy because they have the highest proportion of Latino residents, with Lorain at 25.2 percent and Cleveland at 10 percent. Toledo's Hispanic population (21,231), the third largest in the state, increased by 23.9 percent, and in Youngstown (6,207), now 9.3 percent Latino, it increased by 45 percent. Impressive growth rates of the Hispanic population in Dayton (59.2 percent), Akron (69.3 percent), Canton (88.8 percent), Cincinnati (96.4 percent), and Parma (120.3 percent) yield populations that are now between 2.1 percent and 3.6 percent Latino.[2]

To be sure, the Latino boom in Ohio is having a cultural impact on the state. You can find authentic Mexican cuisine up north in Oberlin, tune into the latest bachata hits on Columbus airwaves, and attend the Cincy-Cinco Latin Festival in the southern city of Cincinnati, where in 2006, organizers built and busted the world's largest piñata. But, what are the political characteristics of this growing population and how is it affecting electoral outcomes? To answer these questions, I examine data from the Ohio subsample of the impreMedia/Latino Decisions 2012 Latino Election Eve Poll fielded between November 1 and 5, 2012. After first providing a demographic profile of the Latino electorate, I analyze the survey responses of 400 Latino voters to explain their evaluation of the candidates, vote choice, and policy preferences for the issues that matter most to them. Throughout the analysis, I look closely at the various segments of the Latino electorate so as to identify the population cleavages and trends that candidates will likely capitalize on or maneuver around in coming elections. I conclude with a discussion of statewide responses to the Latino population and what these trends may mean for future politics in Ohio.

Ohio's Latino Electorate

In 2012, Latinos were an estimated 2.5 percent of all eligible voters in Ohio, and 2.2 percent of all registered voters (Barreto 2011). Relative to other states, Ohio's proportion of eligible Latino voters is modest, and ranks fortieth in the nation for its Latino share of the state's voting-eligible population. However, with 47 percent of all Latinos in the state being eligible to vote, Ohio has the thirteenth-highest percentage of eligible Latino voters in the country (Motel and Patten 2012).

The diverse representation of ancestral origin within Ohio's Latino eligible voting population is quite unique. Ohio is the only state in the country whose Latino electorate is at least one-third Puerto Rican (33.2 percent) *and* one-third or more Mexican (44.3 percent). Also of note is the sizable proportion (16.7 percent) of the Latino eligible voting population that claims an origin other than the top five most represented in the United States: Mexican, Puerto Rican, Cuban, Salvadoran, or Dominican. Of all eligible voters in Ohio, Latinos are the youngest; 32.2 percent of Latino eligible voters are between eighteen and twenty-nine years old, compared to 24.1 percent of black eligible voters, 19.2 percent of white eligible voters, and 18.9 percent of Asian eligible voters (Motel and Patten 2012). With 38 percent of the Hispanic population under the age of eighteen, the Latino electorate in Ohio is just beginning to realize its full potential at the voting booth.[3]

Among those voters polled by impreMedia/Latino Decisions, 57 percent said they were Democrats, 9 percent think of themselves as Republicans, and 27 percent said they identified as Independents. When compared to other states included in the multi-state survey, Ohio has the second highest percentage of Latinos who consider themselves Independents (after North Carolina [30 percent]). When Latino Ohioans were asked why they turned out to vote during the November 2012 election, 44 percent said they wanted to support the Democratic candidate, 10 percent were casting their ballot to endorse the Republican candidate, and 34 percent said they were voting to represent the Latino community.

When we look at reasons for voting at a more detailed level, we find only modest differences between women and men. More remarkable was the variance in responses given by native-born and naturalized citizens. A whole 53 percent of those born in the United States turned out to vote primarily as a way of supporting the Democratic candidate, compared to 34 percent of the naturalized population, which was most motivated to vote to support Latinos (44 percent). Reasons for voting are also worth examining along lines of ancestral origin. People of Mexican ancestry were most likely to vote because they wanted to support the Democratic Party (53 percent), Puerto Ricans were most motivated to vote as a way of supporting

Figure 1. Reasons for Voting (percent)

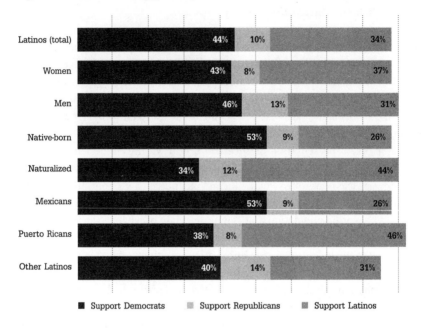

Note: Data from the Ohio subsample of the impreMedia/Latino Decisions Election Eve Poll. Percentages may not total 100 percent because unspecific responses such as "DK" were omitted from the figure.

Latinos (46 percent), and Latinos of other ancestral origins, like those of Mexican descent, were most likely to report that they wanted to vote as a way of supporting the Democratic Party (40 percent). Less than 15 percent of any ancestral origin group stated that they were voting in order to support the Republican Party.

Latinos Cast Their Votes

It was clear from the get-go that both presidential candidates would need to be aggressive in their bid for Ohio's 18 electoral votes, as winning the state was critical to just about any victorious scenario each could realistically imagine. In hopes of besting one another throughout the 2012 campaign season, the four presidential and vice-presidential candidates visited the Buckeye State almost every other week (West 2012). By the end of the campaign, the *Columbus Dispatch* counted eighty-three visits in a single year between Barack Obama and Mitt Romney—"a record at least in modern history" (Rowland 2012). By most polls' accounts, Obama held a slight lead over Romney throughout the campaign, but given the importance of Ohio to each team's calculus, the numbers were always too close for either side to let up and divert resources elsewhere.

In 2008, then-Senator Obama took Ohio with a lead of 4.6 percentage points, propelling him to victory over Senator John McCain. To signal his recognition of Ohio's importance, President Obama kicked off his reelection campaign on Ohio State University's campus in May 2012. Throughout the summer and fall, he and Vice President Joe Biden visited frequently to articulate their commitment to improving the nation's economy, and to insist that their administration exemplified that commitment in 2009 by bailing out the American automobile industry (which is related to one in eight jobs in Ohio). Much of their time was spent in the northern region of the state, which is historically blue-collar and votes heavily in favor of the Democrats. In one last effort to mobilize his statewide coalition of working-class whites, people of color, and Millennials of all races, Obama returned to Columbus the day before the election, with musical artists Bruce Springsteen and Jay-Z rallying at his side.

Mitt Romney and Paul Ryan visited Ohio with as much frequency and vigor, undoubtedly aware that no Republican has ever taken the White House without Ohio's electoral votes. In their time on the ground, the two Republicans worked to deemphasize Romney's earlier position to let American automobile manufacturers go bankrupt, by talking up fair trade with China and claiming that he would protect American automotive jobs from moving overseas.[4] While it was necessary to stump in urban manufacturing areas of the state, Romney kept his campaign trail closely linked to the rural and southern regions that were both supportive of and vital to his recent predecessors. To mark their final push of the season in the "battleground of the battlegrounds" (Haake and Moe 2012), Romney and Ryan spoke to tens of thousands at a rally in House majority leader John Boehner's district alongside elite members of the Republican Party such as Senator McCain and Texas governor Rick Perry.

When the candidates were not themselves in the state, their ads and small armies of campaign volunteers were constantly delivering their message on their behalf. By October 2012, the Romney campaign boasted 40 campaign offices around the state, but this organizing effort paled in comparison to Obama's five-year-old ground operation of 131 offices (Ball 2012). In addition to their ground game, both Romney and Obama put more campaign ads on Ohio television than in any other state (West 2012). While the lion's share of commercials were created for an English-speaking audience, each candidate spent money in Ohio on Spanish ads. Romney's "País de Inmigrantes" emphasized his family's ties to Mexico, and Obama's "Buen Ejemplo" affirmed the DREAMers as quintessentially American. Ohio's Hispanic population was understandably too small in 2012 to create Spanish or English ads with state-specific appeals to the Latino electorate, but Obama's "De Eso Nada" with talk-show host Cristina Saralegui focused on the economy and included a scene with the president hugging an employee in front of a car assembly line, which may be read as a subtle nod to the region's manufacturing identity.

With all votes tallied, Barack Obama won the swing state of Ohio for a second time with support from 50.7 percent of the state's entire electorate, edging out Mitt Romney's share of the votes by 3 percentage points (Husted 2012). Obama's statewide victory was decisive, but his win among the Latino electorate was nothing short of a landslide, with 82 percent of the vote cast for the president. According to the 2012 Latino Election Eve Poll data, Latinos in Ohio gave Obama the third highest proportion of any state's Latino electorate after Massachusetts (89 percent) and Colorado (87 percent).

Obama did especially well among Hispanic women, who supported him at a rate of 86 percent, 8 percentage points higher than their male counterparts, and the native-born and naturalized populations gave the president nearly the same proportion of their vote, 83 percent versus 81 percent, respectively. Obama received 90 percent of the Puerto Rican vote, 86 percent of the Mexican vote, and 70 percent of the vote cast by people belonging to other Latino groups. Overall, the Latino electorate gave Barack Obama a 1-point lead over Mitt Romney.

When Hispanic voters in Ohio were asked to evaluate how the presidential candidates felt about the Latino community, 71 percent said that Obama truly cared about Latinos, 21 percent thought Obama didn't care too much, and 2 percent said Obama was hostile to Latinos. Only 13 percent of Hispanics polled in Ohio believed that Mitt Romney cared about their ethno-racial group, 57 percent said Romney didn't care too much, and 20 percent said Romney was actually hostile to Latinos.[5] Overall, most Latinos perceived Romney as indifferent to their group, but saw Obama as invested in the well-being of Latinos. The perceived care one has for Latinos seemingly works to garner electoral support among Latinos, as the states with the highest level of support for Obama also ranked as the top three states whose voters believed the president cared about their group.[6]

In one of the nation's most competitive senatorial races, Republican state treasurer Josh Mandel fought to unseat Democratic incumbent Sherrod Brown. The two candidates took opposing views on economic policy and used those differences as the cornerstone of their attacks against one another. Mandel criticized Brown's support of the Dodd-Frank Wall Street Reform and Consumer Protection Act because he believed the bill "painted with a broad black brush anyone who works in the system [of financial institutions]" (Shaffer 2012). During their first face-to-face debate, Brown took a swipe at Mandel for signing the Taxpayer Protection Pledge[7] when he quipped, "Signing a pledge to a fat-cat lobbyist like Grover Norquist is essentially giving away

Figure 2. Candidate Latino Outreach

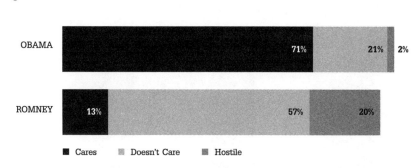

OBAMA   71%   21%   2%

ROMNEY   13%   57%   20%

■ Cares   ▨ Doesn't Care   ▨ Hostile

Note: Data from the Ohio subsample of the impreMedia/Latino Decisions Election Eve Poll. Percentages may not total 100 percent because unspecific responses such as "DK" were omitted from the figure.

your right to think" (LaRosa 2012). At the heart of the debates, however, were their starkly different positions on the president's auto-industry bailout. Mandel called the plan "un-American" and blasted the senator's vote in favor of the program, arguing that the federal government should have permitted General Motors and Chrysler to go through a regular bankruptcy (Shaffer 2012; Boles 2012). Brown, for his part, proudly affirmed his support for the bailout and claimed that it helped keep Ohio's unemployment rate below the national average.

Although Mandel received tens of millions of dollars from out-of-state donors (Sullivan 2012), Brown and his supporters successfully portrayed Mandel as infrequently attendant to his primary duties as treasurer and gravely out of step with blue-collar Ohioans who depend on the auto industry and other manufacturing companies for their livelihood. Brown kept his seat in Ohio with support from 50.7 percent of the entire state electorate, while Mandel received 44.7 percent of the vote (Sullivan 2012). Among Latinos, Brown did almost as well as Obama, shoring up 80 percent of Hispanic support against his opponent.[8]

In the aforementioned statewide elections, Ohio voters sent Democrats back to the White House and the Senate, but in the more regional contests for the 113th Congress, only four of the sixteen seats in the House of Representatives went to Democrats. After the 2010 Census, Ohio lost two House seats, and a new map was signed into law in September 2011, making the races just that much more competitive. The best-known of the twelve Republican congressmen and women, House Speaker John Boehner of the 8th District, appeared relatively immune from the newly devised districts as he ran virtually unopposed to win his twelfth term. Although Democrats running for the House of Representatives did not win even half of the congressional seats, they did do well among Latinos, accumulating 80 percent

Figure 3. Latino Vote for President, Senate, House

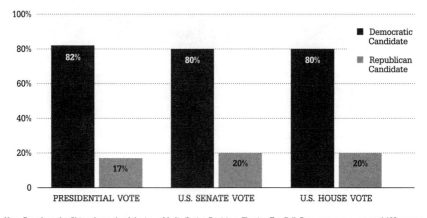

Note: Data from the Ohio subsample of the impreMedia/Latino Decisions Election Eve Poll. Percentages may not total 100 percent because unspecific responses such as "DK" were omitted from the figure.

of the Latino vote. Not surprisingly, these elected officials come from the 3rd, 9th, 11th, and 13th Districts, which include parts of Columbus, Lorain, Cleveland, and Youngstown, some of the state's most heavily populated Latino regions.[9]

The Issues

When Latinos in Ohio were asked to name the most important political issues facing the Latino community, 54 percent said the economy and jobs were the most salient issue, 31 percent named immigration as the most pressing matter, and 13 percent claimed that health care was the issue most important to them. The prominence of the economy is well understood given the national economic downturn in 2008. But the ideological divisions about the rights of laborers and unions took center stage in Ohio during the interim between the 2008 and 2012 elections. In a bold attempt to balance the state budget, newly minted Republican governor John Kasich championed anti-collective bargaining legislation in the form of Senate Bill 5,[10] a law that would, among other things, restrict the rights of 360,000 public workers to negotiate contracts, ban public-sector strikes, and do away with binding arbitration of labor–management disputes. On March 2, 2011, the bill passed narrowly in the State Senate on a 17–16 vote with six Republicans standing opposed alongside a unified Democratic front. When the bill arrived in the House, a bipartisan opposition of 60 people stood against the measure, but they were outvoted.

After Kasich signed SB 5 into law in late March, Ohioans had ninety days to get 231,149 people (6 percent of the vote in the 2010 gubernatorial election) to sign a petition to halt the bill's implementation and put the legislation to a referendum vote in November 2011. We Are Ohio, a coalition of public and private sector employees, collected over one million more signatures than required. On November 2, 2011, some 2.1 million voters turned out to the polls in an off-election year and overturned SB 5 by voting no on Issue 2 by a 62–38 percent margin.

A poll taken by the AFL-CIO in November 2012 suggests that their Ohio union members were about as enthusiastic about Barack Obama during his second run for office as they were during his first campaign, but others argue that the SB 5/Issue 2 controversy galvanized unions, public employees, and sympathetic activists—many affiliated with Obama for America—into an organizing frenzy that mobilized voters for 2012 (Bloom 2012; Quinnell 2012). To be sure, Ohio's battle over collective bargaining, along with similar struggles in Wisconsin and New Jersey, showcased conservative attempts to regain control over the economy and set the stage for a 2012 election that advanced presidential candidates with drastically different approaches to economic policy.

With the political drama of SB 5/Issue 2 only one year behind them, Ohioan Latinos were asked how the country should go about reducing the deficit. The largest proportion (39 percent) supported the idea of only raising taxes on the wealthy; the second largest proportion (35 percent) said Congress should both raise taxes on the wealthy and make cuts to existing programs; and the smallest group (13 percent) supported the idea of cutting existing programs only. Ten percent said that they didn't know what they preferred to do, and the last 3 percent said either "none of these" or "something else." The policy preferences between naturalized and U.S.-born citizens were only 2 percentage points apart for each item, with 38 percent of naturalized citizens and 40 percent of U.S.-born citizens wanting to raise taxes on the wealthy, and 37 percent of naturalized citizens and 35 percent of the U.S.-born preferring a combination of raising taxes and cutting programs. The two largest subgroups, Mexicans and Puerto Ricans, were almost identical on each item, lending most of their support (40 percent of Mexicans and 41 percent of Puerto Ricans) to raising taxes on the wealthy. The largest policy differences were between men and women; 45 percent of men and 33 percent of women supported raising taxes on the wealthy, 16 percent of men and 10 percent of women supported cutting existing programs, and 29 percent of men and 41 percent of women preferred a combination of both deficit-reducing methods.

The second most urgent political matter for Ohioan Latinos after the economy was immigration. Two of the figures most responsible for keeping the immigration issue in the Ohio news cycle are former state representative Courtney Combs (R) of Hamilton (2004–2012) and Butler County sheriff Richard K. Jones. Since the days of the George W. Bush administration, Jones has worked to recast the problem of undocumented immigration as one that predominantly affects border states to one that profoundly touches America's heartland. Up until the Obama presidency, Jones was well known as the Ohio sheriff who unsuccessfully billed the Federal Bureau of Immigration and Customs Enforcement (ICE) for prisoners believed to be "undocumented aliens" housed in his Butler County Jail. In 2005, Combs joined Jones and Butler County commissioner Mike Fox when they announced their intentions to create a state law making it illegal for undocumented immigrants to enter the state of Ohio.[11]

In 2010, Ohioans of various political stripes watched intently as the state of Arizona passed its controversial law, Senate Bill 1070, authorizing police to question an individual's immigration status if that person has been stopped, detained, or arrested on another crime, and if the police have "reasonable suspicion" to believe that such person is an undocumented immigrant. Shortly after Arizona passed its contentious bill, Combs and Jones made new headlines when they initiated a campaign to place their version of Senate Bill 1070, the Ohio Immigration Reform Initiative, on the 2011 ballot. Then-governor Ted Strickland (D) responded by promising to veto any Arizona-like bill to come across his desk (Hershey 2010). Combs and Jones halted the campaign to await the Supreme Court's decision on *Arizona v. United States*, and the two continued to work both separately and in tandem on a number of initiatives to curb undocumented immigration in Ohio up until 2012, when Combs stepped down as the 54th House District representative to seek a seat on the Butler County Commission. In his last year as House district representative, Combs proposed legislation that would implement the now upheld portion of the Arizona law requiring police to ask any person they stop for any cause to show proof of their American citizenship (Weiner 2012).

State senators on the other side of the aisle—Tom Sawyer (D) of Akron, the ranking member of the Senate Education Committee, and Charleta B. Tavares (D) of Columbus—cosponsored Senate Bill 357, the Tuition Equity Act, in the summer of 2012. As Ohio's version of the DREAM Act, this law would make the children of undocumented immigrants eligible for financial aid and in-state tuition at Ohio state colleges and universities (Atkinson 2012). As part of the run-up to the 2012 election, members of the Ohio Republican and Democratic Parties clearly staked out their territory on the immigration issue for their constituents to see and hopefully rally around.

With immigration gaining more attention at the state level, pollsters asked Latinos whether each presidential candidate's immigration policy made them feel more enthusiastic about the candidate or less enthusiastic, or whether the candidate's

Figure 4. Latinos' Feelings About Candidates Based on the Candidates' Position on Immigration

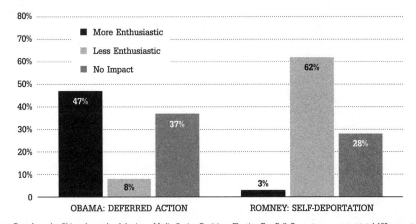

Note: Data from the Ohio subsample of the impreMedia/Latino Decisions Election Eve Poll. Percentages may not total 100 percent because unspecific responses such as "DK" were omitted from the figure.

immigration policy did little to change their feelings about the candidate. Before gauging each respondent's level of enthusiasm, interviewers reminded voters of each candidate's stance. In June 2012, Barack Obama implemented his Deferred Action for Childhood Arrivals (DACA) and announced a new Department of Homeland Security policy to stop the deportation of any undocumented youth who attends college or serves in the military. His plan, furthermore, provides undocumented youth with a renewable legal work permit. When asked how they felt about deferred action, 47 percent of Latino voters (49 percent of naturalized voters and 45 percent of the native-born voters) said they were more enthusiastic about Obama because of his position on immigration. Another 37 percent of all Latinos (36 percent of naturalized voters and 40 percent of native-born voters) thought no differently about Obama because of his policy. A mere 8 percent of Latino voters in Ohio said they were less enthusiastic about Obama because of deferred action, and 8 percent said they didn't know, or that their opinion depended on some unspecified reason.

As the Republican nominee, Mitt Romney said that the country needs a nationwide system in place so that undocumented immigrants are prevented from being hired in the United States. He added that if undocumented immigrants can't work in the United States, they should deport themselves. Unlike Obama, Romney said he would not grant any new work permits to undocumented immigrant youth. When asked how they felt about self-deportation, 62 percent of Latino voters in Ohio (65 percent of naturalized voters and 62 percent of native-born voters) said that Romney's self-deportation policy made them less enthusiastic about him as a candidate, and 28 percent (29 percent of naturalized voters and 28 percent of native-born voters) said it made no impact on their assessment of Romney. Only 3 percent of Latinos liked Romney's plan; not surprisingly, not a single naturalized citizen polled in Ohio favored Romney because of his policy.

These data indicate that Romney's self-deportation policy did more to hurt him in the eyes of Latino voters than the deferred-action plan did to help Obama. When compared to the other ten states oversampled in the Election Eve Poll, Ohio had the lowest percentage of Latino voters (3 percent) who were enthusiastic about Romney's candidacy based on his immigration plan. Ohio ranked second in the poll (tied with California at 62 percent, and behind Colorado's 68 percent) for having the highest percentage of Latino voters that were put off by Romney's self-deportation stance. Ohio's relative aversion to Mitt Romney's unaccommodating policy is all the more interesting given that Ohio has the smallest percentage (40 percent) of Latinos who said they knew an undocumented immigrant who would be directly affected by such a policy. It is also important to note that nativity made little difference when it came to evaluating the candidates' positions on immigration.

Health care was the third most important issue to the Latino electorate in Ohio. When asked whether Obamacare should be left to stand as law, or whether it should be repealed, a clear majority of 63 percent said it should remain federal law, and 28 percent said it should be nullified. Six percent of voters said they didn't know how they felt about the matter, and 4 percent either said "none of these" or "something else." While there was almost no difference between the attitudes of U.S.-born citizens and naturalized citizens, there was a noteworthy difference between Latinos of different subgroups, and on the basis of gender. Ohioans of Mexican ancestry led the Latino electorate in their support for Obamacare, with 76 percent in favor of the law, to be followed by support from 63 percent of the Puerto Rican population, and 50 percent of the remaining array of Latino subgroups; women showed more support for universal health care than did men (70 percent versus 55 percent). On this issue, the majority of Ohioan Latinos are seemingly out of step with the majority of Ohio voters (66 percent) who in 2011 voted yes to Issue 3, a mostly symbolic amendment that declared there would be no law compelling any person, employer, or health-care provider to participate in a health-care system (Husted 2011).

In another question, voters were asked whether the federal government should play a role in ensuring that all people have access to health insurance, or whether people should be responsible for getting their own health insurance. This general question elicited even more support than the question specifically about the Afford-able Care Act: 70 percent of Latino voters said the government should play a role, while 23 percent of voters said people should get their own health insurance. Once again, the native and foreign-born voters were in sync with their attitudes, with 71

Table 1. Economic and Health-Care Policy Preferences by Percent

	Raise taxes on wealthy	Combination of higher taxes and spending cuts	Only spending cuts	Keep Obamacare	Repeal Obamacare	Gov't should ensure healthcare	People should provide their own healthcare
Latinos (total)	39	35	13	63	28	70	23
Women	33	41	10	70	19	71	20
Men	45	29	16	55	38	69	27
Native-born	40	35	14	64	28	71	26
Naturalized	38	37	12	63	28	71	20
Mexicans	40	36	11	76	18	61	33
Puerto Ricans	41	35	11	63	24	83	6
Other Latinos	36	35	18	50	41	67	29

Note: Data from the Ohio subsample of the impreMedia/Latino Decisions Election Eve Poll. Percentages may not total 100 percent because unspecific responses such as "DK" were omitted from figure.

percent of each group supporting governmental intervention. Puerto Ricans led the electorate with 83 percent in support; 61 percent of people of Mexican descent supported governmental intervention, as did 67 percent of other Latino groups. About 33 percent of Mexicans, 6 percent of Puerto Ricans, and 29 percent of other Latino groups said that Americans should get their own health insurance. When the health-care question was framed in this more general way, men and women were virtually of the same mind, with 71 percent of women and 69 percent of men stating that the government should ensure that all people have access to health insurance.

After examining the policy preferences of the Ohio Latino electorate, it is evident that they are lending heavy support to Democratic candidates because the Democratic platform best matches their economic, immigration, and health-care policy preferences. It is important to note the similarity of preferences between native-born and naturalized citizens. In Ohio, there is no substantial gap between the two groups, which suggests that politicians will have little incentive to divide the Latino population along lines of nativity. Both groups believe the federal government should play an important role in providing health care to all Americans, and they are also closely alike in their inclination to promote tax increases for the wealthiest Americans and avoid cuts to existing programs. The most pronounced divides in opinion within the Latino electorate run along lines of gender and subgroups, but these fissures may be too difficult to exploit for partisan advantage because the majority of each group breaks to the left. These policy preferences seemingly put most of the Latino electorate in Ohio beyond the natural reach of a Republican Party that is committed to less government and no new taxes. To further demonstrate the better-suited match between the Democratic Party and Ohioan Latinos, we should consider what voters had to say after being presented with a hypothetical situation where Republicans took a leadership role in both supporting and passing comprehensive immigration reform with an eventual pathway to citizenship for undocumented immigrants. In this scenario, only 26 percent of Latinos in Ohio said they would be more likely to vote Republican, and a whole 50 percent said it would not affect their evaluation of the party. This scenario further suggests that Latinos in Ohio are voting for Democrats at the executive and congressional levels because their policy preferences on a host of issues—not just immigration—are best reflected by the Democratic Party platform.

Discussion and Conclusion

Latinos in Ohio constitute a small but quickly growing segment of the state's population. In the coming years, Latinos will likely become increasingly influential within the state's electorate as today's underage population matures and reaches voting age. Their influence will not only increase, but it will presumably grow more partisan. For decades, Americans of Mexican and Puerto Rican descent have expressed their affinity for the Democratic Party (de la Garza 2004; DeSipio 1996; Hero 1992), and the data presented here suggest that this tendency remains rational given these two groups' issue positions. If the Latino electorate in Ohio continues to grow and reflect the three-fourths Mexican and Puerto Rican demographic recorded in 2010, we should anticipate that a highly mobilized Latino electorate could help the Democratic Party secure victories during neck-and-neck federal elections. The election of 2012 gave the GOP much to consider. With the Latino population growing, the white population shrinking, and the black electorate overperforming and turning out at a higher rate than whites for the first time ever (Taylor and Lopez 2013), the GOP must realize the need to refigure their platform and devise new strategies for appealing to minority voters rather than exclusively relying upon the white rural and suburban voters for their victories.

The near-future impact of the Latino electorate, however, could have as much to do with structural forces at the state level as it does with fertility rates. In some areas of the state, such as Butler County just north of Cincinnati, notable public officials are fiercely intent on curbing undocumented immigration that inevitably affects some portion of the Latino community. In other parts of the Buckeye State, politicians and business owners are being conscientious and ambitious about recruiting authorized immigrants to their cities as a strategy of saving their region from job loss and population decline. In reaching out to newcomers, these cities are leaving the policing of undocumented immigration to the federal government.

The western city of Dayton became an exemplar for attracting immigrants when in October 2011, the Dayton City Commission approved the "Welcome Dayton" plan, "a community-wide initiative designed to attract immigrant groups that can help the city grow jobs, businesses and population." City manager Tim Riordan explained the city's embracing posture by noting, "Immigrants are more than twice as likely as other citizens to become entrepreneurs and create jobs. We want to make every effort we can to not only attract more of these creative and industrious people, but also to encourage them to stay in our community and plant deep roots for the future" (Welcome Dayton 2013).

The city of Cleveland is also intent on recruiting immigrants to come live and work in northeast Ohio so that they might recover from the 17 percent drop in population incurred between 2000 and 2010 (U.S. Census Bureau 2011). The Global Cleveland Initiative, a nonprofit organization that focuses on economic development through an active recruitment of newcomers, is working with employers, community organizations, and institutions of higher learning to increase the urban population. Their plan, El Futuro de Cleveland, is particularly committed to retaining local Latino talent by offering paid internships to college students (Global Cleveland).

Where might Republicans gain traction in a state where cities are hopeful about and, in some cases, explicitly welcoming of a growing number of immigrants? According to the 2012 Latino Election Eve Poll, only 10 percent of Latino voters said they were motivated to vote to support the Republicans, but almost three times as many people (34 percent) indicated that they voted to support the Latino community. If the Republican Party can convince this portion of the Latino electorate that it cares about the overall Latino community and commits itself to securing comprehensive immigration reform with a pathway to citizenship for undocumented immigrants, it may be able to gain favor with the quarter of Ohioan Latinos who indicated a willingness to vote Republican in the future if the party changed its tune on the issue. In the wake of another Obama victory, Ohio's most visible Republican, House Speaker John Boehner, appears to be pushing his party in a more proactive direction to seek future Latino votes by prioritizing comprehensive immigration reform (Wolf 2012). If his party takes heed, the GOP may still have a fighting chance to gather enough brown ballots in the Buckeye State to keep their party competitive in their bid for the White House for some years to come.

While the rapid growth of the Latino population would seem to guarantee a powerful Latino electorate in the near future, more immediate structural influences in the form of voter suppression may work to attenuate the impact of the Latino electorate. On February 21, 2014, Governor Kasich signed into law two Republican-sponsored bills that are causing alarm among voting-rights activists. Senate Bill 238 reduces the time allowed for early voting from thirty-five to twenty-nine days, and it eliminates "Golden Week," a six-day period when Ohio citizens were once able to both register to vote and cast an in-person absentee ballot. Senate Bill 205 alters how absentee-voter applications are distributed throughout Ohio such that the secretary of state will only be able to send unsolicited, non-prepaid ballot applications if the General Assembly specifically funds it, leaving voters uncertain as to whether they might receive an absentee-ballot application. The bill, furthermore, restricts the distribution of such applications to even-numbered election years, bans all other government agencies (including local boards of elections) from issuing unsolicited absentee-ballot applications, and allows boards of elections to toss out votes with "incomplete" identification envelopes, which left to interpretation may disenfranchise those voters who forget to write their middle initials or zip codes. While the primary sponsors of SB 205 (R-Bill Coley) and SB 238 (R-Frank LaRose) claim that these bills will standardize processes of registration and voting throughout the state, Democratic opponents argue that the legislation will create more barriers for all Ohioans, and will be especially detrimental to women voters, low-income voters, minority voters, and elderly voters.

By embracing comprehensive immigration reform, the Republican Party could possibly attract enough of the Latino electorate to be competitive in the next several presidential elections. Taking such a position would likely upset their current base of supporters, but the sacrifice might be worthwhile in the long term if the party is able to recruit a segment of the rapidly growing Latino population. However, it would appear that in the absence of nationwide, bipartisan negotiations on immigration reform, the GOP's state-level officials in Ohio are trying to demobilize a growing voting-eligible population that looks less like their suburban and rural white base, and more like the future majorities of America.

NOTES

1. The terms "Latino" and "Hispanic" are used interchangeably.

2. See http://factfinder2.census.gov.

3. See www.prb.org. The proportion of other racial groups under the age of eighteen years old is as follows: blacks (28.5 percent), Asians (23.7 percent), whites (21.6 percent), and American Indians (20.1 percent).

4. When speaking to a large General Motors crowd in Defiance, Romney said, "I saw a story today that one of the great manufacturers in this state, Jeep—now owned by the Italians—is thinking of moving all production to China. I will fight for every good job in America. I'm going to fight to make sure trade is fair, and if it's fair America will win." A Chrysler spokesperson quickly responded by saying, "Jeep has no intention of shifting production of its Jeep models out of North America to China," and that Romney's misinterpretation of a Bloomberg report was "a leap that would be difficult even for professional circus acrobats" (Miller 2012).

5. Women were more likely than men to believe Barack Obama cared (78 percent versus 64 percent), and those who were born in the United States were more likely than naturalized citizens to believe the same (75 percent versus 68 percent). Men were more likely than women to say that Romney truly cared (17 percent versus 9 percent), and they were also more likely than women to say that Romney was hostile (22 percent versus 18 percent); 60 percent of women and 55 percent of men believed that Romney was indifferent to Latinos. The naturalized population was more inclined than the native-born to say that Romney cared (15 percent versus 11 percent), and native-born Latinos were more likely than naturalized citizens to believe Romney was hostile to their ethno-racial group (25 percent versus 15 percent).

6. Ohio comes in third for the highest level of believing that Obama truly cares about Latinos, this time with Colorado being first (80 percent) and Massachusetts being second (77 percent).

7. Those who sign the pledge promise to oppose any increase to marginal income-tax rates for individuals and/or businesses, and to oppose any net reduction or elimination of deductions and credits, unless matched dollar for dollar by further reducing tax rates.

8. More women than men voted for Brown (84 percent versus 77 percent), and more men than women voted for Mandel (23 percent versus 16 percent). More native-born Latinos voted for Brown than did those who were naturalized (82 percent versus 77 percent), and slightly more of the naturalized population voted for Mandel than did those who were native-born (23 percent versus 18 percent). Sherrod Brown netted 83 percent of the Puerto Rican vote, 86 percent of the Mexican vote, and 71 percent of the vote cast by people belonging to other Latino groups, while Josh Mandel received 17 percent of the Puerto Rican vote, 14 percent of the Mexican vote, and 29 percent of the vote belonging to other Latino groups.

9. A full 87 percent of Hispanic women and 73 percent of men voted for the Democrat running in their district, whereas 27 percent of men and 13 percent of women voted for the Republican candidate. Native-born Latinos, again, showed a slight bit more support for Democratic candidates than did those who were naturalized (82 percent versus 78 percent), and the Republican candidates, who received one-fifth of the Latino vote, saw more support from the naturalized population than the native-born (22 percent versus 18 percent). Democrats running for the House of Representatives received 80 percent of the Puerto Rican vote, 87 percent of the Mexican vote, and 72 percent of the vote cast by people belonging to other Latino groups. Republican candidates received 20 percent of the Puerto Rican vote, 13 percent of the Mexican vote, and 28 percent of the vote belonging to other Latino groups.

10. SB 5 was introduced to the state Senate on February 8, 2011, by Republican senator Shannon Jones of Springboro.

11. See http://www.butlersheriff.org/phpBB/viewtopic.php?p=34&sid=b43991a90cf0f61133c7a 29ddf37e537.

REFERENCES

Atkinson, Marcus. 2012. "Ohio Introduced Tuition Bill for DREAMers." *Hispanic Ohio.com*, June 27. Available at hispanicohio.northcoastnow.com.

Ball, Molly. 2012. "Obama's Edge: The Ground Game That Could Put Him over the Top." *Atlantic*, October 24.

Barreto, Matt. 2011. "Where Latino Votes Will Matter in 2012." *Latino Decisions Blog*, March 31. Available at latinodecisions.com.

Bloom, Molly. 2012. "Map: How Issue 2 in 2011 Helped Obama Win Ohio in 2012." *State Impact NPR*, November 12. Available at stateimpact.npr.org.

Boles, Corey. 2012. "Democrat Sherrod Brown Wins Ohio Senate Seat." *Wall Street Journal*, November 6. Available at blogs.wsj.com.

Cook, Dave. 2012. "What Did John Boehner Actually Say about GOP and Minority Voters?" *Christian Science Monitor*, August 28.

de la Garza, Rodolfo O. 2004. "Latino Politics." *Annual Review of Political Science* 7: 91–123.

DeSipio, Louis. 1996. *Counting on the Latino Vote: Latinos as a New Electorate.* Charlottesville: University of Virginia Press.

Ennis, Sharon R., Merarys Ríos-Vargas, and Nora G. Albert. 2011. "The Hispanic Population: 2010: 2010 Census Briefs. Report No. C2010BR-04." May. Washington, DC: Department of Commerce. Available at census.gov.

Global Cleveland Initiative. "Global Cleveland Is Saying 'Mi Cleveland es su Cleveland!'" Available at globalclevelandinitiative.com.

Haake, Garrett, and Alex Moe. 2012. "Romney Launches Final Election Push with Massive Ohio Rally." *NBC News.com*, November 2. Available at firstread.nbcnews.com.

Hero, Rodney. 1992. *Latinos and the U.S. Political System: Two-Tiered Pluralism.* Philadelphia: Temple University Press.

Hershey, William. 2010. "Supporters of Arizona-like Immigration Law Focus on 2011." *Dayton Daily News*, May 11.

Husted, Jon. 2011. "State Issues Results: Excel Spreadsheet. General Election November 8, 2011." Available at sos.state.oh.us.

———. 2012. "Official Results for 2012 General Election. Available at sos.state.oh.us."

LaRosa, Michael. 2012. "Brown, Mandel Clash in Ohio Debate." *MSNBC News.com*, October 15. Available at tv.msnbc.com.

Mayer, Det. Monte. 2005. "Sheriff Bills I.C.E. for Aliens 10–26–2005." *Butler County Sheriff's Office*, October 26. Available at www.butlersheriff.org.

Miller, Jake. 2012. "Romney Cites Incorrect Auto Manufacturing Claim in Ohio." *CBS News.com*, October 26. Available at cbsnews.com.

Motel, Seth, and Eileen Patten. 2012. "Latinos in the 2012 Election: Ohio." *Pew Hispanic Research Center*, October 1. Available at pewhispanic.org.

Quinnell, Kenneth. 2012. "Ohio Union Members Energized to Re-Elect President Obama and Sen. Sherrod Brown." *AFL-CIO*, November 6. Available at aflcio.org.

Rowland, Darrel. 2012. "Dispatch Poll: Ohio's a Toss-up." *Columbus Dispatch*, November 4.

Shaffer, Cory. 2012. "Josh Mandel Says Sherrod Brown Should Be 'Ashamed of Himself' for Auto Bailout at Strongsville Fundraiser." *Cleveland.com*, August 31. Available at cleveland.com.

Sullivan, Sean. 2012. "Washington Post Poll: Brown Leads Mandel in Ohio Senate Race." *Washington Post*, September 25.

Taylor, Paul, and Mark Hugo Lopez. 2013. "Six Take-aways from the Census Bureau's Voting Report." *Pew Research Center*, May 8. Available at pewresearch.org.

U.S. Census Bureau. 2010. "Profile of General Population and Housing Characteristics: 2010. 2010 Demographic Profile Data." Available at factfinder2.census.gov.

———. 2011. "U.S. Census Bureau Delivers Ohio's 2010 Census Population Totals, Including First Look at Race and Hispanic Origin Data for Legislative Redistricting." Available at census. gov.

Weiner, Richard. 2012. "Ohio Lawmakers Proposing New Legislation on Immigration." *Akron Legal News*, July 20. Available at akronlegalnews.com.

Welcome Dayton: Immigrant Friendly City. 2013. "Summary." Available at welcomedayton.org.

West, Paul. 2012. "President Obama Hits Battleground State of Ohio Hard." *Los Angeles Times*, August 2.

Wolf, Z. Byron. 2012. "PM Note: Boehner off Obamacare, on Immigration, Romney and Demography, How GOP Can Recover with Latinos." *ABC News.com*, November 8. Available at abcnews.com.

D. XAVIER MEDINA VIDAL

The New *Virginiano* Electorate and the Politics of Immigration in Virginia

THE GROWING IMPACT OF VIRGINIA HISPANICS ON SOCIAL AND ECONOMIC life in the Old Dominion is reflected in the rapid growth of this diverse community and its significant contributions to the state's work force. The 2012 presidential election, which captured a great deal of analysts' interest in the role that Hispanic voters and voters in the swing states would have on the election, situated the voting behavior of Virginia's and North Carolina's Hispanic electorates in a privileged position for the first time in U.S. electoral politics. With so many eyes and ears tuned in to learn whether Virginia and North Carolina would swing back to the GOP column after falling in behind Democrat Barack Obama in his historic 2008 victory, and whether this would be Latinos' year of influence on electoral politics on the national stage, many looked to these neighboring southern states, in anticipation of their young and rapidly growing Latino electorate, for answers. The tale of the Virginia Hispanic electorate and its present and future potential to shape electoral politics in the commonwealth has two important lead lines worthy of any analyst's attention: (1) a heterogeneous Hispanic electorate bolstered by a strong growth trajectory of the Hispanic population as a whole, and (2) experience with Arizona-style anti-immigrant legislation that built a wall between the Virginia GOP and the commonwealth's Hispanic voters. The following pages are an analysis of these two complementary phenomena that draws on a number of sources, chief among them the 2012 Latino Election Eve Poll conducted by impreMedia/Latino Decisions.

Hispanic Demographics in Virginia

Northern Virginia (in and around the Virginia suburbs of the nation's capital) is home to a rapidly growing, vibrant, and complex population comprised of individuals who have come to the region from a number of different Latin American countries. Most Latino migrants to Virginia have ancestral homes in Mexico, El Salvador, and Puerto Rico, but they come from almost every corner of Latin America. Table 1 reports a general racial and ethnic demographic portrait of Virginia according to Census figures and other projections. Note that Latinos in Virginia were about 8 percent of the state population in 2012, and by 2020 they are expected to be over 11 percent if current population trends hold in the next few years.

Perhaps the most telling story of table 1 is that trend. According to Census records, Virginia's Hispanic population grew by 92 percent between the 2000 and 2010 Census counts, a rate ten times that of non-Hispanic Virginians. Relative to other racial and ethnic minority groups in the commonwealth, Latino growth is incredibly strong. While the nonwhite, non-Hispanic population in Virginia is still firmly in the minority, Latino growth appears to be the engine behind the growth of racial and ethnic minority group presence in the commonwealth. Other groups in the state have dissimilar growth trajectories from Latinos. While the Asian American population grew by 69 percent—a rate nearly as impressive as the Latino growth rate—the proportion of African Americans in Virginia (19 percent in 2010) is not expected to change by 2020. The strong growth of the Hispanic population relative to other groups in Virginia points to a present and future of minority political representation, incorporation, and behavior with the potential to raise thought-provoking questions about the role Latinos will have in shaping Virginia politics going forward.

Virginia's Hispanic Electorate

A question that many Beltway observers asked in the months before and after Election Day was whether or not the Hispanic vote would play a critical role in shaping the presidential race in the swing states. The growth of the U.S. Hispanic population and the Latino community's growing potential to impact election outcomes in a number of different states have not been a subtly developing phenomenon by any means, but

Table 1. Virginia Demographic Profile (2010)

Race & Ethnicity	Population 2010	Percent of Population 2010	Percent Increase 2000–2010	Percent Projection 2020*
Hispanic or Latino	631,825	7.9	91.7	11.1
Not Hispanic or Latino	7,369,199	92.1	9.2	88.9
White	5,486,852	68.6	7.2	65.3
African American	1,551,399	19.0	11.6	19.0
American Indian	29,225	0.4	38.0	—
Asian	439,890	5.5	68.5	6.9
Native Hawaiian, P.I.	5,980	0.1	51.5	—
Some other race	254,278	3.2	83.1	8.8
Two or more races	233,400	2.9	63.1	—

Source: Census 2010.
*Weldon Cooper Center for Public Service

what emerged in 2012 offered a special set of circumstances for keen Beltway observers. In the closing months of the 2012 election, a perfect Latino-election-influence storm kicked up in Virginia. This storm consisted of the commonwealth's swing-state status in the presidential race, an increasingly contentious contest for an open U.S. Senate seat, and budding speculation that a state with a small but rapidly growing Latino electorate could determine the fate of this important national election.

Latino-politics analysts and political pundits of all persuasions had long been looking south to Latino-influence states like Florida (2000, 2004, 2008), and west to Illinois (1996), Colorado (2000, 2004), and New Mexico (2000, 2004, 2008). To be sure, the potential of Hispanic electoral power in these places has been well documented for over two decades in volumes widely cited by scholars and Washington, DC, pundits alike (e.g., García 1997; de la Garza and DeSipio 1997, 2005). Though our interest in and understanding of the Latino population's impact on electoral politics has only grown in recent years, in 2012 analysts and pundits inside the Capital Beltway had to look just across the Potomac to Virginia to see Hispanics shaping U.S. electoral politics.

The impact of demographic changes in Virginia that will situate Hispanics in a prominent and decisive role in Virginia politics will depend on whether and how the group wields its influence at the polling place, and on whether voting Latinos have the interests of noncitizen Latinos and all immigrants in mind when they go to the polls. About one-third (34 percent) of Virginia Hispanics are eligible to vote, ranking Virginia 36th nationwide in the share of the Hispanic population that is eligible to vote (U.S. Census 2010; Pew Hispanic Center 2012). By contrast, more than three-quarters (78 percent) of the state's white population is eligible to vote. Census estimates and data from the Hispanic eligible voters in Virginia create a different Hispanic-origin profile from that of Hispanic eligible voters nationwide. About one in four (26 percent) are of Mexican origin. More than two in ten (21 percent) are Puerto Rican, 13 percent are Salvadoran, and 40 percent are of other Hispanic origin—a category that includes large numbers of Latino voters of South American origin (U.S. Census 2010; Pew Hispanic Center 2012).

The countries of origin of the 2012 Latino Election Eve Poll likely voter respondents also reveal the diversity of Virginia's Hispanic population. A plurality (28.5 percent) of the 400 Latino likely-voter interviewees traced their ancestry to South American countries, 20 percent to the Caribbean, 16.5 percent to North America, and 14.3 percent to Central America. The largest single Latino-origin groups were Mexican (14.5 percent), Puerto Rican (11.5 percent), and Salvadoran (10 percent). In many U.S. states, majority Latino-origin groups tend to dominate the political discourse (e.g., Mexican American voters in California and Texas, and Caribbean-origin voters in Florida and New Jersey). In Virginia, where the plurality of Latinos are by most accounts neither of Puerto Rican, Mexican, nor Cuban descent, no single national-origin group comes close to overshadowing the interests of other Latino subgroups. Likewise, no single national-origin group was targeted by the Latino outreach campaigns in 2012.

Differences among foreign-born Hispanics, U.S.-born Hispanics, and non-Hispanics in Virginia in terms of their economic status and educational attainment are important to our understanding of Virginia's Latino voters in 2012. While U.S.-born Virginia Latinos resemble their non-Hispanic counterparts in these dimensions, foreign-born Latinos continue to experience different sets of needs and limitations to their economic success. Twice as many foreign-born Hispanics (44 percent) than U.S.-born Hispanics (22 percent) and non-Hispanic (24 percent) households are likely to be considered "income inadequate." In terms of educational attainment, over three times as many foreign-born Hispanics over age twenty-five (39 percent) have less than a high school education compared to their U.S.-born Hispanic (12 percent) and non-Hispanic (12 percent) counterparts (Clapp 2011). Economic insecurity in times of economic crisis is an issue unifying most Americans, and Virginia Latinos are no exception. When asked what issues facing the Hispanic/Latino community politicians should address in the 2012 election, 43 percent of Hispanic Virginians surveyed in the 2012 Latino Election Eve Poll said that creating more jobs/ fixing the economy was their top concern. U.S.-born Hispanics and foreign-born Virginia Hispanics, however, tend to work in different types of jobs, which leads to these two groups having potentially different experiences with economic insecurity. The most common occupations for U.S.-born Hispanics in Virginia—cashiers, retail salespersons, military personnel, managers, secretaries, and administrative assistants—vary from the top jobs as maids and housekeeping cleaners, cooks, construction laborers, carpenters, janitors, and building cleaners claimed by foreign-born Virginia Hispanics (Clapp 2011). Irrespective of these different occupations and associated economic status, economic insecurity and agreement about the most important issues facing the Hispanic community are what unified Latino voters in 2012.

Equipped with an understanding that Latino voters and nonvoting immigrant Latinos in Virginia are both unified and divided in terms of important socioeconomic indicators of civic engagement, our explanations of the preferences and behaviors of Virginia's Latino electorate draws on the degree to which all Virginia Latinos are united on the important contemporary political questions. Indeed, a sense of group consciousness and in-group affinity among all Virginia Hispanics, coupled with their dissimilarities to Virginia's non-Hispanic population, are most readily observable along political—rather than economic—dimensions.

Citizenship and immigration patterns among Virginia's population reveal some important information about Virginia's Latino voters. Just over half of Virginia Hispanics were born in the United States. Among foreign-born Virginia immigrant Latinos, approximately 25 percent are naturalized citizens and 75 percent are noncitizen residents (Clapp 2011). These figures begin to get us to an understanding of the influence that voting-eligible Latinos potentially have on elections in Virginia. The timing of the arrival of Hispanic immigrants in Virginia likewise affects the policy issues Virginia Latinos deem important as they engage in electoral politics. Of noncitizen Hispanics in Virginia, approximately 65 percent have lived in the United States for less than ten years, 24 percent between eleven and twenty years, and 10 percent for over twenty-one years (Clapp 2011). These data are a not-so-subtle hint that issues affecting immigration policy and the lives of immigrants are chief in the hearts and minds of Virginia immigrant and noncitizen Hispanics. Given the in-group heterogeneity of Virginia Latinos discussed above, with no single national-origin group dominating the state's Latino politics, immigration-policy preferences and how they translate to electoral preferences are a good test of whether Latino group consciousness (Sanchez 2006) and "linked fate" (Dawson 1995)[1] affect the vote preferences of Latino voters in 2012.

Immigration Policy a Top Concern for Virginia Hispanics in 2012

To begin an examination of the issues around which Virginia Latinos are developing their sense of group affinity, we turn to the 2012 Latino Election Eve Poll for evidence of Latino voter preferences and orientations. When asked to think about the most

Figure 1. Issues Important to Virginia Hispanics Voting in 2012 (percent ranking issue as top priority)

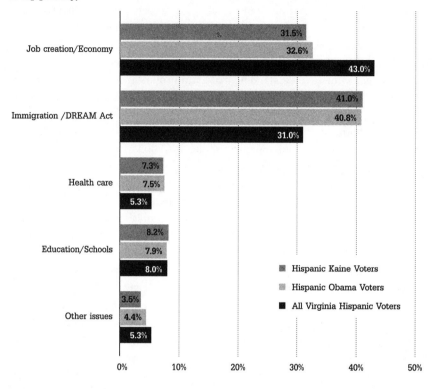

Source: Latino Election Eve Poll (400 Virginia respondents)

important issues facing the Hispanic/Latino community going into the 2012 elections that our politicians should address, 43 percent of all Virginia Hispanic voters surveyed cited job creation and the economy as their top concern, and 31 percent of all Hispanic voters cited immigration policy and the DREAM Act as their top concern (figure 1). In all, nearly three in four Virginia Latinos ranked these two policy areas as highest in salience. Hispanics who expressed support for both President Obama and Tim Kaine (the Democratic candidate for the open Virginia U.S. Senate seat) agreed that the economy and immigration policy were top concerns. However, these respondents felt that immigration policy was even more important than fixing the economy through job creation.

As in most of the United States, immigrant rights and immigration policy have been a top concern for much of the population of Virginia Latinos in recent years. Many observers and analysts of Latino politics and the national push for immigration policy reform point to Arizona's draconian "SB 1070" law (enacted in 2010) as the initial flashpoint that has structured contemporary debate around immigration reform. While the SB 1070 law and subsequent versions of the law appearing in other states is by every measure significant to our understanding of the effects of local enforcement of federal immigration laws, Virginia Latinos and immigrant-rights advocates have experience with SB 1070–style issues dating back to July 2007. That year, anti-immigrant activists (under the banner of "Help Save Manassas"), disturbed by the rapid growth in the Virginia Latino community in the large urban and suburban centers of Northern Virginia, and by the growing economic insecurity amidst a global financial crisis, formed one of the most vitriolic assaults on the rights of immigrant Latinos to live and work peacefully in the Old Dominion. Virginia's own flashpoint moment in the politics of immigration came when the board of supervisors of Prince William County, one of several suburban Northern Virginia counties with significant and fast-growing numbers of Hispanic residents, passed a "probable cause" mandate that empowered local police to check the immigration status of anyone they suspected of being undocumented. Claims as radical and nonsensical as those that the Zapatista Army of National Liberation (EZLN) were invading Prince William County were taken seriously by key Republican members of the PW County board of supervisors and resulted in the passage of the most blatant authorizations of racial profiling in recent history.

Thanks to pressure from the "9500 Liberty" movement spearheaded by Latino activists (who used public art and billboard-sized messages of inclusion and tolerance), along with local activists (with popular blogs that countered those of the Help Save Manassas anti-immigrant group), and support from the U.S. Commission on Civil Rights, the "probable cause" mandate that had made Prince William County, Virginia, a beacon of intolerance was repealed in April 2008 after eight weeks of the law's full effect (Park and Byler 2009).

Recalling the economic insecurity that prompted anti-immigrant groups to mobilize communities around the premise that immigrant Latinos were taking jobs and American culture away from Virginians, public support for Help Save Manassas and the "probable cause" mandate dissipated in light of another economic crisis. When local residents and tax coffers began to feel the economic impact of a sudden exodus of workers, businesses, and consumers to Prince William County's neighboring counties in Northern Virginia and Maryland, the tone of immigration politics in this Northern Virginia county changed enough to push local lawmakers toward a repeal of the "probable cause" mandate. Because of the Help Save Manassas movement's ties to the Federation for American Immigration Reform (FAIR) and the national anti-immigrant movement, the same basic framework of Prince William

County's "probable cause" resolution resurfaced in 2010 as the "Support our Law Enforcement and Safe Neighborhoods Act," which came to be known as Arizona's SB 1070. Prince William County's trials with immigration politics in 2007 and 2008 are documented in *9500 Liberty*, an interactive documentary on YouTube and a full-length documentary of the same name, both by filmmakers Annabel Park and Eric Byler (Park and Byler 2009).

This period in Virginia's recent history alerted Virginia's political leadership to the fact that Latinos were already having an important economic impact on the commonwealth, and that Hispanic-led community organizations were a force to be reckoned with going forward (Aranda-Yanoc 2013). In short, the reaction to Help Save Manassas and the repeal of "probable cause" in Prince William County secured a space for Latinos in the minds of Virginia's political leadership and brought immigration policy to the top of the list of policy concerns Latinos would be taking with them to the polls in subsequent elections.

Important historic, though countervailing, events related to race and ethnic politics in Virginia took place in 2008: the election of Barack Obama, and the Help Save Manassas/9500 Liberty events. Since that year, the Virginia General Assembly has taken up the issue of immigration policy a number of times via legislation aimed at the incorporation of immigrant Virginians. In the same period, Virginia's legislature has been consistently siding with anti-immigrant opinion in the commonwealth's politics. It is clear that Hispanic Virginians, immigrant and native-born alike, are making an imprint on policy agendas in the commonwealth. In recent years, the Virginia General Assembly has heard several measures calling for in-state college tuition eligibility for immigrant students. In 2013, a bipartisan effort led by two Northern Virginia delegates, Alfonso López (an Arlington Democrat) and Tom Rust (a Herndon Republican), saw legislation allowing certain undocumented students access to in-state tuition advance farther than previous legislative attempts. Nonetheless, with a divided House of Delegates, a Republican-controlled Virginia Senate, and a decidedly hostile Republican governor, the prospects for successful passage in the 2014 state legislature will require much more GOP buy-in than legislators have been able to muster in recent years.

Achieving higher levels of buy-in on the advancement of Virginia immigrant issues depends largely on the work of advocacy and mobilization groups. Led by the Virginia Coalition of Latino Organizations (VACOLAO), such community groups have come to the defense of Virginia's Hispanic community by expressing dissatisfaction with GOP-led efforts to marginalize Virginia's immigrant Latinos through legislating draconian and targeted policing of Latino communities. As Congress moves forward on comprehensive immigration reform, experts and analysts will certainly be evaluating efforts in states like Virginia and evidence of a changing political tide—one led by immigrant and U.S-born Latinos—for guidance.

Partisan Outreach and Partisan Differences on Immigration Policy

Republican members of Congress, feeling recalcitrant about the need for a reasonable set of immigration policy reforms, will have to evaluate seriously the impact of the Latino-led political tide on 2012 election outcomes. Doing so requires an assessment of important differences between Democratic and Republican candidates in the 2012 campaign in Virginia. For eight consecutive presidential contests (1976–2004), Virginia's Electoral College votes were cast for Republican presidential candidates. Barack Obama's 2008 victory thus ushered in swing-state status for the commonwealth.

Bolstered by Virginia's swing-state status, the growing number of needs of the Latino community, and demands that those needs be met, Latinos living and working in urban and suburban Virginia were aggressively pursued by partisan and community organizing get-out-the-vote (GOTV) efforts during the 2012 election cycle. Thus, Virginia's Hispanic electorate in 2012 can most plausibly be cast in terms of the "pivotal vote thesis" (de la Garza and DeSipio 1992, 1997, 2005; Gross and Barreto this volume). To be sure, with the Latino population nearly doubling between 2000 and 2010 according to Census figures, the absolute growth of the Hispanic electorate also suggests that sheer demographic growth paved the way for Virginia Latinos to have a real impact on the 2012 election (see, e.g., Bowler and Segura 2011). The last months of the 2012 election were painted by news media, analysts, and pundits as an election about demographics. Thus, many eyes turned to how Latinos in the swing states like Virginia might affect a presidential contest that was perceived as increasingly competitive. Spanish-language and other media-based appeals to potential Virginia Latino voters were not significantly different from previous election cycles. However, swing-state status and potential Latino impact on election outcomes in Virginia did result in higher levels of direct outreach to Virginia Latinos compared to the rest of U.S. Latinos. According to the 2012 Latino Election Eve Poll, 49 percent of Virginia's Hispanic likely voters were contacted for the purposes of registering to vote or to get out to vote compared to 42 percent of all U.S. Hispanics surveyed (see figure 2). Compared to their counterparts in other states, Virginia Hispanics received more attention directly from party organizations than from community organizations, and the Democrats were the source of most of the contacts Virginia Latinos received.

Figure 2. Hispanics Contacted during the 2012 Campaign to Register to Vote or Get Out to Vote (percent)

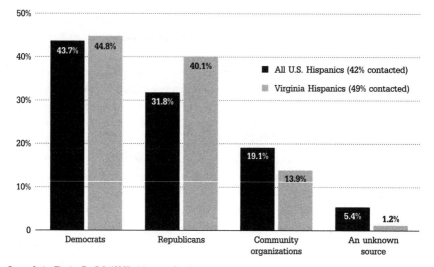

Source: Latino Election Eve Poll (400 Virginia respondents)

The mobilization of this potentially influential group in this unpredictable swing state was certainly taken seriously by both political parties, but as respondents in the 2012 Latino Election Eve Poll reported, the Republicans were significantly more active in courting Latino votes in Virginia than elsewhere (40.1 percent GOP contact in Virginia compared to just 31.8 percent GOP contact among all U.S. Latinos). Still, Virginia Latinos were contacted more by Democrats than Republicans to register to vote or to vote on Election Day.

Different rates of partisan outreach perhaps also played a role in the motivation of Hispanics to get out to vote in the general election. When asked on Election Eve about their motivations for voting, 38.8 percent of Latino voters in the swing state said they were voting because they wanted to support the Democratic candidate, while only 22.8 percent said they were voting to support Republicans (see figure 3). Support for Democrats, the most frequently reported reason Virginia Latinos cited for voting in 2012, is the same factor motivating Latinos in other U.S. states. In spite of the high level of voter outreach conducted by both Democrats and the GOP however, U.S. Latinos generally were not necessarily motivated to vote to support the Republicans at the polls. Instead, Latinos cited support for the Latino/Hispanic community as the second leading reason for voting. While Hispanic Virginians ranked their motivations for voting in the same way as the average U.S. Hispanic

Figure 3. Motivation for Voting in 2012 (percent)

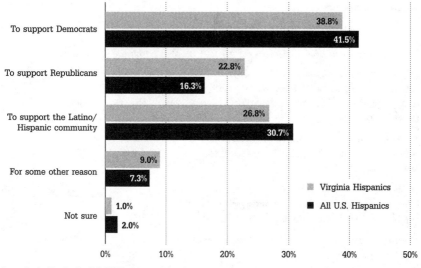

To support Democrats — 38.8% (Virginia Hispanics), 41.5% (All U.S. Hispanics)
To support Republicans — 22.8% (Virginia Hispanics), 16.3% (All U.S. Hispanics)
To support the Latino/Hispanic community — 26.8% (Virginia Hispanics), 30.7% (All U.S. Hispanics)
For some other reason — 9.0% (Virginia Hispanics), 7.3% (All U.S. Hispanics)
Not sure — 1.0% (Virginia Hispanics), 2.0% (All U.S. Hispanics)

■ Virginia Hispanics
■ All U.S. Hispanics

Source: Latino Election Eve Poll (400 Virginia respondents)

voter, support for the GOP was a stronger voting motivator for Virginia Latinos than for U.S. Latinos in general. It appears that Democratic and Republican attention to Virginia's Latinos—whether because they are Latino or because they are likely voters in a swing state—had an impact on shaping Latino voters' motivations for voting. Still, the well-being of the Hispanic/Latino community is what motivated 26.8 percent of Latinos to get out to vote. This is likely a sign of a strong and—until Election Day—latent sense of group consciousness among the relatively small numbers of voting Latinos and noncitizen Latinos in an election in which immigration policy and immigrant Latinos were front and center for voters of all stripes in Virginia.

Given the boot print left by Prince William County's 2007/2008 engagement in the politics of immigration, the rights of immigrants and the need for immigration policy reforms were indeed highly salient issues for Virginia Latinos in the 2012 election. This fact was not lost on President Obama nor on his Republican challenger, Mitt Romney, who were both cast in the lead roles for their parties on the issue of immigration policy reform. The race for an open seat representing Virginia in the U.S. Senate likewise could not escape the inevitability of the immigration debate being important to Virginia voters (having been a critical part of political discourse for many since at least 2007, when it was taken up in Prince William County). Nationally, the attitudes of the presidential candidates toward immigrants

Table 2. Effects of 2012 Presidential and U.S. Senate Candidate Attitudes toward Immigrants and Immigration Policy on Virginia Latinos' Enthusiasm for Their Candidacies

Statements about immigrants and immigration policy	More Enthusiastic (%)	Less Enthusiastic (%)	Have No Effect (%)
*Obama (D): "Stop deportation of undocumented immigrant youth who attend college or serve in the military and provide them with a legal, renewable work permit"	55.9	9.1	35.0
*Romney (R): "We need a nationwide system in place so that undocumented immigrants are not allowed to work here…if they can't work here, immigrants should self-deport"	9.0	59.9	31.1
†Kaine (D): "I support the DREAM Act so that students brought to the U.S. by their parents are not penalized, but instead given a meaningful opportunity to pursue the American dream"	65.0	6.0	26.0
†Allen (R): (In opposition to President Obama's decision to provide legal work status to undocumented immigrant youth): "If the government rewards illegal behavior, we will encourage more illegal behavior"	8.0	49.0	36.0

*2012 Latino Election Eve Poll
†Latino Decisions/America's Voice Virginia Latino Voter Survey (October 15, 2012)

and immigration policy made up a significant part of campaign rhetoric, and for Latino voters attentive to the campaign, these attitudes were prominent. President Obama's June 2012 announcement that the Department of Homeland Security would put an end to deportations of undocumented immigrant youth who were pursuing college educations or military service made 55.9 percent of Virginia Hispanics more enthusiastic about President Obama's candidacy. High issue saliency of immigration policy/DREAM Act, along with Virginia's strong traditions of military service, and an economy tied intimately to military-related industries, likely contributed to this sentiment among Virginia's Latino electorate.

Governor Mitt Romney had even more success in influencing Latino voters' enthusiasm during the campaign. However, Romney's views on immigration drove Latinos away from his candidacy. During the campaign, he called for undocumented immigrants to "self-deport," a sentiment shared perhaps by the most conservative members of the GOP but not, obviously, by Virginia's Latino electorate. Romney's call for self-deportation made nearly 60 percent of Virginia Hispanics less enthusiastic about his candidacy.

The national debate about the need for comprehensive immigration reform also drew the attention of the aspirants for the open U.S. Senate seat in Virginia. Democrat Tim Kaine and Republican George Allen, both former governors of the commonwealth, entered the immigration-politics fray with starkly different views on the issues facing immigrants. According to the Latino Decisions/America's Voice Virginia Latino Voter Survey, George Allen's opposition to President Obama's decision to provide legal work status to undocumented immigrant youth, on grounds that it would encourage more illegal behavior, drew 49 percent of likely Hispanic voters away from his candidacy. Tim Kaine's views, more than any other candidate at the top of the ticket in Virginia, tapped into the specific policy (the DREAM Act) that most casual observers of the immigration debate are familiar with. Kaine, with his expression of support of the DREAM Act in terms of its links to opportunity and pursuit of the American dream, was more successful in building enthusiasm for his own candidacy—drawing 65 percent of Latino likely voters in his favor—than any other statewide candidate in Virginia in 2012.

The links between Virginia's changing racial and ethnic demographics and the prominence of immigration issues in the minds of Latino voters, and the connections Hispanic voters make between parties' and candidates' immigration-policy positions, all point us toward wondering if Latinos who voted in 2012 might translate these phenomena into meaningful influence on future election outcomes.

Hispanic Influence on the 2012 Election

Though a number of different perspectives on how to determine Hispanic influence on any electoral outcome are discussed elsewhere in this volume, for our assessment of Virginia Hispanics' influence on the 2012 election, I review some important demographics and compare these to support for presidential and Senate candidates expressed by 2012 Latino Election Eve Poll respondents, actual vote margins, and Latino Decisions's voter-turnout predictions.

Going into the 2012 presidential election, Virginia joined the ranks of the all-important handful of swing states predicted to wield disproportionate influence on the presidential election outcome. In the months leading up to the 2012 general election and drawing from 2010 Census data, the Pew Research Hispanic Center estimated Virginia Hispanics to be 3.7 percent of the commonwealth's electorate (Pew Hispanic Center 2012), which amounts to approximately 214,000 eligible Latino voters.

Building a model of the impact of these 214,000 eligible Latino voters on the 2012 general election calls for an understanding of a few key factors. First, we take into account citizenship rates and voting-age eligibility to vote. Census estimates placed the number of Virginia Hispanics eligible to participate in the 2012 general election at around 214,000, or 34 percent of all Virginia Hispanics (U.S. Census Bureau 2012; Pew Hispanic Center 2012). Second, in the final week leading up to the election, the final week of the Latino Decisions Tracking Poll (Week 11), data indicated that 77 percent of registered Latino voters were almost certain they would vote. Coupled with our understanding of trends in Latinos' electoral participation in Virginia elections between 2000 and 2010 (an increase of 76 percent according to Census figures), this Hispanic-turnout prediction reflected a relatively high level of enthusiasm for the 2012 election among Hispanic voters. The effect of strong enthusiasm and Latinos' intentions of voting tempered expectations of lower Latino turnout and lower levels of support for President Obama relative to 2008, and gave us a good barometer with which to gauge Hispanic participation in 2012.

Next, the 2012 Latino Election Eve Poll (which surveyed the attitudes, voter preferences, and political orientations of 400 Virginia Hispanics) recorded 66 percent of Virginia Latino voters supporting the reelection of President Obama. Only 31 percent of Virginia Latino voters were likely to cast votes for Mitt Romney (4.9 percent margin of error). The 2012 Latino Election Eve Poll also captured and reported Latino support for Democratic U.S. Senate candidate Tim Kaine (70 percent) and Republican candidate George Allen (29 percent). These elements of Latino support build on the potential impact Hispanics had on the presidential and U.S. Senate contests in the swing state of Virginia and yield the figures presented in table 3 as Hispanic influence on the presidential race, and in table 4 as influence on the U.S. Senate race.

President Obama's reelection did, as predicted, come down to key victories in key swing states. In Virginia, his margin of victory over Romney was a slim 3.9 percent (149,298 votes). In table 3 we take into account Latinos' expressed support for Obama's reelection with an understanding of their share of the electorate. If those Latinos who expressed a strong likelihood of voting for Obama actually turned out to vote on Election Day (77 percent turnout), then the Latino share of Obama's statewide margin of victory over Romney is nearly three-fourths (72.8 percent). A more conservative estimate of 50 percent Hispanic turnout suggests that Hispanics accounted for nearly half (47.3 percent) of Obama's margin of victory over Romney.

In the U.S. Senate race, in which Tim Kaine enjoyed even higher levels of support from Latinos, the Democrat had a more decisive margin of victory (5.9 percent) over Republican George Allen. In table 4 we can see how, under the same Latino turnout scenarios of 50 percent and 77 percent, Hispanics' contributions to Kaine's margin over Allen were somewhat smaller than Obama's over Romney. One-third (33.4 percent) of Kaine's margin over Romney is attributable to Hispanics if 50 percent of eligible voters turned out, while Hispanic influence on the Senate race

Table 3. Hispanic Influence on the 2012 Presidential Race in Virginia

| | Hispanic Population (%) | Hispanic Voting-Age Population | Hispanic Eligible Voters | Total Vote for Obama (51.2%) | Total Vote for Romney (47.3%) | Margin (Obama-Romney) | Hispanic Support for Obama: 66% (LEE Poll) | | | |
| | | | | | | | 50% Hispanic Turnout | | 77% Hispanic Turnout | |
							Hispanic Vote for Obama	Share of Obama Margin (%)	Hispanic Vote for Obama	Share of Obama Margin (%)
Virginia	8.2	426,857	214,000	1,971,820	1,822,522	149,298	70,620	47.3	108,755	72.8
High-Density Hispanic Localities										
Manassas Park City	33.5	3,003	1,744	2,879	1,699	1,180	576	48.8	886	75.1
Manassas City	31.5	7,356	4,208	8,478	6,463	2,015	1,389	68.9	2,139	106.1
Prince William County	20.5	52,354	29,153	103,331	74,458	28,873	9,620	33.3	14,815	51.3
Alexandria City	16.4	16,867	8,061	52,199	20,249	31,950	2,660	8.3	4,097	12.8
Fairfax City	16.2	2,595	1,238	6,651	4,775	1,876	409	21.8	629	33.5
Harrisonburg City	16.2	5,066	2,755	8,654	6,565	2,089	909	43.5	1,400	67.0
Fairfax County	15.8	118,944	59,121	315,273	206,773	108,500	19,510	18.0	30,045	27.7
Winchester City	15.8	2,536	1,428	5,094	4,946	148	471	318.3	726	490.2
Arlington County	15.2	24,100	11,150	81,269	34,474	46,795	3,679	7.9	5,666	12.1
Galax City	13.5	553	320	900	1,332	−432	106	—	163	—
Loudoun County	12.6	25,467	13,886	82,479	75,292	7,187	4,582	63.8	7,057	98.2
Fredericksburg City	11.0	1,763	960	7,131	4,060	3,071	317	10.3	488	15.9
Stafford County	9.5	7,253	4,247	27,182	32,480	−5,298	1,402	—	2,158	—
Falls Church City	9.1	771	393	5,015	2,147	2,868	130	4.5	200	7.0
Culpeper County	8.9	2,614	1,430	8,285	11,580	−3,295	472	—	727	—

Sources: 2010 Census Summary File, Virginia State Board of Elections, impreMedia/Latino Decisions Weekly Tracking Poll (Week 11), and 2012 Latino Election Eve Poll

Table 4. Hispanic Influence on the 2012 U.S. Senate Race in Virginia

| | Hispanic Population (%) | Hispanic Voting-Age Population | Hispanic Eligible Voters | Total Vote for Kaine (52.9%) | Total Vote for Allen (47.0%) | Margin (Kaine-Allen) | Hispanic Support for Kaine: 70% (LEE Poll) | | | |
| | | | | | | | 50% Hispanic Turnout | | 77% Hispanic Turnout | |
							Hispanic Vote for Kaine	Share of Kaine Margin (%)	Hispanic Vote for Kaine	Share of Kaine Margin (%)
Virginia	**8.2**	**426,857**	**214,000**	**2,010,067**	**1,785,542**	**224,525**	**74,900**	**33.4**	**115,346**	**51.4**
High-Density Hispanic Localities										
Manassas Park City	33.5	3,003	1,744	2,829	1,752	1,077	610	56.7	940	87.3
Manassas City	31.5	7,356	4,208	8,322	6,550	1,772	1,473	83.1	2,268	128.0
Prince William County	20.5	52,354	29,153	102,859	74,809	28,050	10,203	36.4	15,713	56.0
Alexandria City	16.4	16,867	8,061	52,502	19,498	33,004	2,821	8.5	4,345	13.2
Fairfax City	16.2	2,595	1,238	6,728	4,682	2,046	433	21.2	667	32.6
Harrisonburg City	16.2	5,066	2,755	8,507	6,681	1,826	964	52.8	1,485	81.3
Fairfax County	15.8	118,944	59,121	319,748	201,414	118,334	20,692	17.5	31,866	26.9
Winchester City	15.8	2,536	1,428	5,292	4,816	476	500	105.0	770	161.7
Arlington County	15.2	24,100	11,150	82,689	32,807	49,882	3,902	7.8	6,010	12.0
Galax City	13.5	553	320	981	1,309	–328	112	—	173	—
Loudoun County	12.6	25,467	13,886	83,383	74,325	9,058	4,860	53.7	7,485	82.6
Fredericksburg City	11.0	1,763	960	7,233	3,957	3,276	336	10.3	518	15.8
Stafford County	9.5	7,253	4,247	27,820	31,997	–4,177	1,487	—	2,289	—
Falls Church City	9.1	771	393	5,147	2,051	3,096	137	4.4	212	6.8
Culpeper County	8.9	2,614	1,430	8,457	11,743	–3,286	501	—	771	—

Sources: 2010 Census Summary File, Virginia State Board of Elections, impreMedia/Latino Decisions Weekly Tracking Poll (Week 11), and 2012 Latino Election Eve Poll margin is 51.4 percent under the 77 percent Hispanic turnout prediction. Recalling immigration-policy saliency and Latinos' assessments of candidates' statements about immigration policy, the difference of Hispanic influence between the presidential and Senate races does not necessarily suggest any differences in enthusiasm for Obama versus Kaine. Instead, this difference is likely attributable to preferences among non-Latino Virginia voters.

In addition to margins and Hispanic influence statewide, tables 3 and 4 show the variables plugged into the calculus of statewide Latino impact for fifteen of Virginia's high-density Hispanic localities (where the Hispanic population is over 8 percent of the locality total). The Old Dominion is one of the states covered by Section 5 of the Voting Rights Act, which stipulates that changes in policy that affect voting in the commonwealth are subject to federal review or "preclearance" (U.S. Department of Justice 2013). However, in the past decade many local Virginia jurisdictions have applied for, and been awarded, "bailout" status from the U.S. District Court for the District of Columbia. The nearly thirty jurisdictions that have been "bailed out" from the preclearance provisions include the cities of Bedford, Fairfax, Manassas Park, Salem, Williamsburg, and Winchester, along with the counties of Augusta, Bedford, Botetourt, Carroll, Craig, Culpeper, Essex, Fairfax, Grayson, Greene, James City, King George, Middlesex, Page, Prince William, Pulaski, Rappahannock, Roanoke, Rockingham, Shenandoah, Warren, Washington, and Wythe (U.S. Department of Justice 2013). Six of these jurisdictions are localities with growing Hispanic populations and are places in which they might wield influence on electoral outcomes. Degrees of Hispanic influence on the presidential and Senate contests vary significantly in these localities. In the presidential race, under the 50 percent turnout assumption, Latinos in the large and urban Fairfax County accounted for 18 percent of Obama's margin, and accounted for Obama's entire margin in the small city of Winchester (table 3). Latinos' estimated contribution to Tim Kaine's margin of victory in the high-density Hispanic localities is, like contributions at the state level, somewhat more muted under both the 50 percent and 77 percent Hispanic-turnout assumptions.

A look at the localities in which Latinos did not contribute as much to Kaine's margin of victory suggests that Kaine's higher levels of support, compared to President Obama, were, again, more a product of non-Hispanic support even in Virginia's potentially high-influence localities. We should note, nonetheless, that future Latino influence on elections is not based solely on the population of Hispanic eligible voters. As more cities and counties experience rapid rates of growth in that population, mechanisms like Section 5 VRA "bailouts" are potential sources for further debates of Latino influence on elections.

Lessons from Virginia's Latino Electorate

Through their positions on immigration policy and the rights of immigrants, Democrats' and Republicans' vastly different visions for incorporating an evidently evolving Virginia electorate made the choice to paint Virginia red or blue in 2012 an easy one for Virginia's electorate. That evolving electorate, led by a rapidly growing Latino population with a good deal of experience with the effects of local immigration policy debates, played a decisive role in the presidential and Senate contests in Virginia. Beyond the influence of Virginia's Latino votes in 2012, the characteristics of the *virginiano* electorate—heterogeneity and rapid growth—suggest a few important lessons for the future of national and local elections in states in which Latinos are new to the political scene.

In future election cycles, as we witnessed in 2012, Virginia will continue to be an important state in which to study questions related to the consequences of an increasingly heterogeneous U.S. Hispanic electorate for Latino voter outreach, mobilization, and turnout. As much as Virginia Hispanics' demographic profile is analytically important to the study of electoral politics, the implications of this rapidly growing demographic will also be important to students of group identity formation, group consciousness, and political incorporation.

Looking to the future of electoral politics in Virginia, the Virginia Hispanic electorate's profile offers a more pluralistic portrait of Hispanic voters' attitudes and orientations compared to states in which a single national-origin group might dominate political discourse and attract the attention of candidates in national elections seeking to build broad coalitions of support. To be sure, immigration politics—and strong immigration policy rhetoric in particular—had the effect of unifying Virginia's Latinos (who vary significantly from one another in socioeconomic, citizenship, and nation/origin dimensions) firmly behind Democrats in 2012. Virginia's already divided electorate, the feature of ideological divisions in the state that kept it in the swing-state column in 2012, may be followed by division in the commonwealth's Hispanic electorate. Immigration-policy saliency was high in Virginia and in other states, but relative to Hispanic support for President Obama and Democrat candidates in eight other U.S. Senate races in Latino influence states, Virginia Hispanics' two-to-one support for President Obama, and nearly three-to-one support for Tim Kaine, was modest in comparison to Latino support for Democrats in the ten other states represented in the 2012 Latino Election Eve Poll. Only Florida's Latino voters were less enthusiastic about President Obama's reelection (58 percent supported Obama, 40 percent supported Romney) than Virginia Hispanics.

As if gaining Hispanic electoral support were not already difficult enough for statewide and presidential candidates, Virginia's Latino voters demand that campaign messages be a degree or two more fine-tuned. Fortunately for both Democrats and Republicans seeking Virginia statewide office and the presidency in 2012, the daunting task of tailoring political messages to each and every national-origin group of Hispanics was conveniently mitigated by a single policy that unified the Virginia Hispanic electorate: Immigration.

Even without the immigration debate at center stage, we can likely look forward to more and more culturally competent appeals to Latino voters—appeals that use messaging that recognizes the heterogeneity of the group. This is an area in which Virginia, North Carolina, and other states experiencing rapid growth among their Hispanic populations in the early twenty-first century will be the bellwethers of Latino political influence in U.S. electoral politics. While we may continue to look to national advocacy organizations, Hispanic-oriented and Spanish-language media, and Hispanics in state legislatures nationwide to determine the tone and scope of Hispanic policy agendas, and for understanding how electoral coalitions and political incorporation are working, our attention should also turn to parts of the United States with increasingly heterogeneous Hispanic populations.

The contributions of Virginia Hispanics to the margins of victory for President Obama and now Senator Kaine present us with evidence of how the decisiveness of the Latino vote in 2012 is especially meaningful in the swing state of Virginia. Because of such a small margin of victory for Obama in particular, the small but rapidly growing Virginia Latino electorate makes Virginia a potential bellwether in future elections. Hispanics are indeed on a trajectory to transform the Virginia electorate, and political elites—like Tim Kaine, who on election night declared "¡Somos virginianos, todos!" or "We are all Virginians!"—are taking note.

NOTE

1. Hispanic linked fate here refers to the degree to which Latinos, especially nonimmigrant Latinos, believe their own economic and political interests are linked to the interests of all Hispanic co-ethnics. Immigration policy preferences among all U.S. Hispanics reflect this belief.

REFERENCES

Aranda-Yanoc, Edgar. 2013. Author's interview with Edgar Aranda-Yanoc, chair of the Board of Directors of the Virginia Coalition of Latino Organizations (VACOLAO), February 16. Falls Church, Virginia.

Bowler, Shaun, and Gary M. Segura. 2011. *The Future Is Ours: Minority Politics, Political Behavior, and the Multiracial Era of American Politics.* Los Angeles: Sage/CQ Press.

Clapp, Susan A. 2011. "Hispanics in Virginia." Demographics and Workforce Group, Weldon Cooper Center for Public Service, University of Virginia, Charlottesville, VA. Available at coopercenter.org.

Dawson, Michael C. 1995. *Behind the Mule: Race and Class in African-American Politics*. Princeton, NJ: Princeton University Press.

de la Garza, Rodolfo, and Louis DeSipio. 1992. *From Rhetoric to Reality: Latino Politics in the 1988 Elections*. Boulder, CO: Westview Press.

————, eds. 1997. *Awash in the Mainstream: Latino Politics in the 1996 Elections*. Boulder, CO: Westview Press.

————, eds. 2005. *Muted Voices: Latinos and the 2000 Elections*. Lanham, MD: Rowman and Littlefield.

García, F. Chris, ed. 1997. *Pursuing Power: Latinos and the Political System*. Notre Dame, IN: University of Notre Dame Press.

Park, Annabel, and Eric Byler. 2009. *9500 Liberty*. Documentary film.

Pew Research Hispanic Center. 2012. "Mapping the 2012 Latino Electorate." Available at pewhispanic.org.

Sanchez, Gabriel R. 2006. "The Role of Group Consciousness in Political Participation among Latinos in the United States." *American Politics Research* 34, no. 4: 427–50.

U.S. Census Bureau. 2010. 2010 Census Summary File 2. Available at census.gov.

U.S. Department of Justice (DOJ). 2013. Section 4 of the Voting Rights Act. Available at justice.gov.

Virginia State Board of Elections. 2012. "November 6, 2012 General Election Results." Available at voterinfo.sbe.virginia.gov.

Weldon Cooper Center for Public Service. 2013. "2020 Population Projections by Ethnicity and Race for Virginia and Its PDCs and Member Localities." Available at coopercenter.org/demographics.

BETINA CUTAIA WILKINSON

North Carolina Latinos

An Emerging, Influential Electorate in the South

LATINOS IN NORTH CAROLINA HAVE ESTABLISHED A RELATIVELY NEW PRESENCE in the state, yet their extensive growth in numbers and political clout has provided them with national recognition. During the late twentieth century, North Carolina was the leading immigrant destination site. From 1980 to 2000, the size of the state's Latino population increased considerably, with the Raleigh-Durham region experiencing a 1,180 percent growth rate (Suro and Singer 2002, 5). The surge of Latinos continued in the twenty-first century with the Latino population increasing by 111 percent from 2000 to 2010 (DeFrancesco Soto 2012). In general, the size of the Latino population in the Tar Heel State has skyrocketed from 1.2 percent of the state's total population in 1990 to 8.4 percent in 2010, making Latinos in this state the eleventh largest Latino population in the United States (U.S. Census Bureau 2000, 2010). Similar to the Latino population in the state of Virginia, the emerging Latino presence in North Carolina has amplified the size and influence of the state's Latino electorate. The number of Latinos registered to vote increased more than tenfold from 2004 to 2012 (Motel and Patten 2012). In the 2008 presidential election, Latino voters were very influential in their swing state (Barreto, Collingwood, and Manzano 2010). Further, the young Latino electorate in North Carolina, like the one in Virginia, has played and continues to play a vital role in the nation's comprehensive immigration policy dialogue. In this chapter, I examine North Carolina Latinos' electoral preferences and strength in the 2012 presidential election as well as their commitment to the Democratic Party. I begin with a description of the state's Latino population and then highlight the Latino electorate's 2012 voting behavior and policy preferences, comparing Catholic Latinos with Born Again Christian Latinos. The chapter concludes with a brief description of the pivotal races in the state. The emerging themes in this chapter are that the 2012 election clearly manifests North Carolina Latinos' burgeoning strength in and out of the voting booth in addition to their consistent commitment to the Democratic Party, often regardless of their religious affiliation.

The Growth of the Latino Population in North Carolina

Latinos in North Carolina began to manifest their presence in the Tar Heel State in the late twentieth century. While there are several explanations for Latinos' recent immigration to North Carolina, the immigration literature would attribute it to three major motives. First, new trade policies such as the 1994 National American Free Trade Agreement (NAFTA) diminished employment opportunities for those in the state's textile, furniture, and clothing industries, yet expanded the demand for jobs in other industries such as poultry and meat food processing, foreign-owned car manufacturing, and high-tech research. This change in industry resulted in a demand for unskilled labor, with several of these industries actively recruiting Mexicans and Central Americans to migrate to the United States and work in their factories and plants (Torres 2000; Duchon and Murphy 2001; Marrow 2011, 10–13). Today, a significant portion of Latinos reside in small towns, primarily due to a high demand for workers in food-processing plants as well as on tobacco, cotton, peach, and vegetable farms (see Marrow 2011; Gill 2012; DePriest 2012; N.C. Dept. Agriculture 2014; North Carolina in the Global Economy 2013). According to the latest Census results, there are more than twenty-five small cities and towns throughout the state with Latino populations exceeding 20 percent. While these areas may be smaller in population size than other metropolitan areas, Latino residents are often the backbone of these towns. Without them, some areas would dwindle in size (Chesser 2012). Still, several urban regions have recently experienced a large influx of Latinos due to greater employment opportunities, and the chance both to be reunited with family and to gain a better quality of life. Based on the latest U.S. Census data, Winston-Salem has the largest Latino population, with Latinos making up 14.7 percent of the city's populace. Durham (14.2 percent), Charlotte (13 percent), and Raleigh (11.4 percent) trail Winston-Salem in the size of the Latino population (Chesser 2012; U.S. Census Bureau 2010).

Two other motives for Latinos' decision to settle in North Carolina include sheer survival and practical concerns. Given the ongoing (though lessening) economic crisis in Mexico, many with and without legal status sought a better life in the southern part of the United States (Massey, Durand, and Malone 2002). Many of these Latino immigrants have settled in small rural towns, though large numbers have chosen to reside in larger Southern metropolitan areas as well. The last reason for Latinos' attraction to North Carolina is for practical issues such as access to driver's licenses, reduced employment competition, low housing costs, and low crime rates. Since undocumented immigrants were able to obtain a driver's license before 2006, North Carolina experienced a large influx of Latino newcomers during this time (Perez 2008). This driver's license policy is no longer in effect today. Latinos were also attracted to the South, including states like North Carolina, since it was a new immigrant destination with little to no Latino competition for jobs. In addition, the rural locations that many were migrating to had more affordable housing and lower crime rates than many traditional Latino areas in the Southwest (Marrow 2005, 781–82; Marrow 2011).

The Demographic Profile of North Carolina Latinos

The demographic characteristics of Latino residents in the Tar Heel State somewhat parallel those of the national Latino population (as reflected in the Census Bureau's 2010 data). Though most Latinos in North Carolina are native-born (52 percent), as compared to the national population (63 percent), the number of foreign-born Latinos in the state (48 percent) is greater than the national average. Like the U.S. Latino population, the most dominant national origin of Latinos is Mexican (61 percent). Latinos in North Carolina are also quite young, and slightly younger than the national Latino population since the median age is twenty-four years. The median personal earnings of Latinos sixteen years and older in the state is $17,500, slightly lower than the median earnings of U.S. Latinos, $20,000. Also, similar to the national average for earnings of all U.S. workers (including those who are full-time, year-round workers), native-born Latinos earn slightly more than foreign-born Latinos in North Carolina (U.S. Census Bureau 2010; Pew Research Hispanic Center 2011).

Latinos' Brewing Political Influence

North Carolina Latinos' demographic profile and compelling growth in numbers translate into their escalating electoral strength. While Latinos make up less than 3 percent of the state's registered voters, the number of Latinos registered to vote has increased more than tenfold from 10,000 in 2004 to 113,000 in November 2012 (Motel and Patten 2012). Further, the Latino vote grew by 117 percent from 2000 to 2010 (Barreto and Segura 2012a). This surge is due in part to Latinos' aging and increasing eligibility to vote. Approximately 37 percent of Latinos between the ages of eighteen and twenty-nine were eligible to vote in 2012. The share of eligible Latinos in this age range was in fact higher than that of Latinos of *any* other age category. What is more, the percentage of eligible Latino voters ages eighteen to twenty-nine is strikingly larger than the percentage of whites (18.6 percent), blacks (24.2 percent), and Asian Americans (27.9 percent) of the same age category. These statistics reveal not only that the face of the Latino vote is younger and more potent than that of other racial/ethnic groups but also that the future electoral results in North Carolina will be greatly shaped by Latino voters (Motel and Patten 2012; DeFrancesco Soto 2012).

How do these statistics then shape the importance placed on the 2012 Latino vote in North Carolina? In 2008, President Obama won the popular vote in this state by a very slight margin, 14,177 votes. This was the first time that a Democratic presidential candidate won in the Tar Heel State since 1976, and Latinos played a pivotal role in Obama's victory (DeFrancesco Soto 2012). With a close victory in 2008, a Democratic governor, *and* a supportive and growing Latino electorate, it is not surprising that President Obama chose to hold the 2012 Democratic National Convention in Charlotte, North Carolina. The convention spotlighted Latinos, with Los Angeles mayor Antonio Villaraigosa as the convention's chairman; numerous Latino political and community leaders, including an undocumented immigrant (Benita Veliz); and San Antonio mayor Julian Castro as the convention's keynote speaker (Becerra 2012; Foley 2012; Miles 2012). Further, campaigns, political scientists, and voters throughout the nation placed a spotlight on the Latino electorate in the Tar Heel State, since pollsters and political scientists prognosticated months before the election that the presidential race in this state was very competitive (with the electoral share of the votes for Obama and Romney within three percentage points of each other). The closer the election became, the greater the importance placed on Latinos, a small yet influential 2.9 percent of the North Carolina electorate capable of swaying the election results in favor of Obama or Romney (Barreto 2011; DeFrancesco Soto 2012; Barreto and Segura 2012a; Barreto and Segura 2012b).

North Carolina Latinos and the 2012 Election

North Carolina was a battleground state in 2012, and Latinos played a pivotal role in the election results. In the next few paragraphs, I provide a systematic discussion of North Carolina Latinos' voting behavior in the 2012 election using data from the impreMedia/Latino Decisions 2012 Latino Election Eve Poll. I begin by describing the significance placed on North Carolina leading up to the 2012 election, highlight Latino residents' preference for the presidential candidate, and discuss the factors that structured their vote choice. Emphasis is placed on differences in voting behavior and attitudes between Catholics and Born Again Christians for several reasons. Recent studies have given increasing significance to the extent that religion shapes Latinos' voting behavior and alliance with the Republican Party (de la Garza and Cortina 2007; Kelly and Morgan 2008; McKenzie and Rouse 2013; Ralls 2013). Furthermore, while some Catholic and Born Again Latinos' conservative stances on social policies may prompt them to identify more with Republicans, Catholic and religiously unaffiliated Latinos expressed stronger support for Obama than evangelical Protestant Latinos months before the 2012 election (see Leal et al. 2005; de la Garza and Cortina 2007; Pew Research Center 2012). Thus it is fruitful and timely to assess North Carolina Latinos' political behavior and views.[1]

North Carolina has had the reputation of being a swing state for quite some time. President Obama won the state by the skin of his teeth in 2008, and his campaign actually never left the state after the 2008 election. For several years afterwards, the campaign maintained an office near the capitol with numerous volunteers and staffers. Yet unlike in several other swing states, Romney and Obama did not spend a lot of time in North Carolina themselves as the 2012 election neared. Each candidate only made five trips to the state throughout the entire election season. Obama's last visit to North Carolina was for the Democratic National Convention in September. Nonetheless, the war between the two candidates was primarily on the ground and in the air. Romney spent about $45 million on pro-Romney ads, while Obama spent $24.2 million (Christensen 2012). In the days leading up to the election, the Obama campaign had influential leaders such as Bill Clinton, Jill Biden, and Michelle Obama visit Democratic-leaning cities in the state. While North Carolina polls leading up to the election revealed that Obama and Romney were neck and neck, some attributed Obama's diminishing concentration on North Carolina to Democratic governor Beverly Perdue's reputation and recent decision to retire. Some considered her a vulnerable Democrat for the 2012 election due to her bleak poll numbers and ongoing criminal cases associated with fundraising for her 2008 race (Frank 2012). Another possible motive for Obama's direct engagement of North Carolina voters late in the campaign was potential voters' deep concern for the state's high unemployment rate, 9.6 percent, the fifth highest in the United States. Poll data of North Carolina voters (regardless of race or ethnicity) leading up to the election revealed that the majority of voters deemed the economy the most important issue facing the country, and economic concerns may have depressed some voters' commitment to Obama. Mitt Romney narrowly won the Tar Heel State with only 51 percent of the vote and approximately 96,000 more votes than Obama (Christensen 2012).

Though President Obama did not win the North Carolina popular vote in the 2012 presidential election, the close election results illustrate the significance of the Latino vote. As figure 1 reveals, 71.5 percent of Latinos voted for President Obama, while only 27.5 percent favored Mitt Romney.[2] Interestingly, Catholic Latinos expressed a stronger commitment to Obama than Latinos in general, with a striking 76.1 percent favoring Obama over Romney as the presidential candidate. When juxtaposing Catholic Latinos' presidential vote with those of Born Again Christians, I find that the majority of all religious groups state that they will/have voted for Obama, though Catholics were more fervent supporters of Obama than the others (Leal et al. 2005). When examining Latinos' presidential vote choice by nativity, I find that native-born and foreign-born Latinos did not differ in their support for Obama, since more than 70 percent of both groups supported the incumbent president. Still, these results provide evidence that North Carolina Latinos were firmly committed to reelecting President Obama regardless of their nativity and somewhat their religion.

Throughout North Carolina, Obama also won in counties with a significant portion of Latinos. In Forsyth County, including Winston-Salem, a city with the largest Latino population in the state, President Obama won with 53.2 percent of the vote. In Mecklenburg County, containing Charlotte, the city where the Democratic National Convention was hosted, Obama obtained 60.8 percent of the vote. Further, in Durham County, with one of the highest percentages of Latinos by county (13.5 percent), Obama won with 75.9 percent of the vote (*Charlotte Observer* 2012).

Immigration and Outreach: Explaining North Carolina Latinos' Commitment to Obama

Latinos' fervent support for Obama does not come as a surprise. About one-third of Latinos (33.2 percent) asserted that they were voting in the upcoming election to support the Democratic candidate, and 40 percent stated that they were voting to support the Latino community. These results reveal that North Carolina Latinos do not want to be overlooked, are united, engaged in politics, and want to exercise their right to vote. What is striking is that nearly *86 percent* of Latinos who stated that they

Figure 1. North Carolina Vote for President

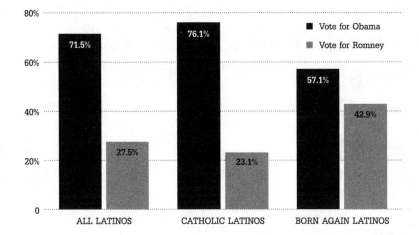

were voting to help the Latino community affirmed that they voted or will vote for Barack Obama. Clearly, Latinos in North Carolina perceived that Obama had the interests of their ethnic group in mind. What is more, the issue of immigration and Democrats' outreach played key roles in shaping President Obama's success among Latinos in the Tar Heel State.

Immigration is a topic of deep concern to Latinos and was certainly a determinant of Latinos' presidential vote choice.[3] As figure 2 illustrates, the economy/jobs, education, and health care trail immigration as the policy topic that Latinos deem as most critical to their community, which politicians should address.[4] While the economy and job growth were of major importance to Latinos (40.1 percent) given that many were affected by the recent economic downturn, immigration was still slightly more critical. This does not come as a surprise since approximately 65 percent of Latino respondents stated that they know someone who is an undocumented immigrant. When comparing Catholic Latinos with their Born Again Christian counterparts, both groups placed less importance on immigration than jobs and the economy, though the difference in importance indicated by Catholics is smaller (immigration: 36.8 percent to jobs/economy: 37.7 percent) than that of Born Again Christians (immigration: 30.8 percent to jobs/economy: 38.8 percent).

Latinos' deep concern about immigration is often portrayed by North Carolina organizations led by Latino youth. These organizations raise awareness of sociopolitical injustices experienced by immigrants, and motivate changes to immigration legislation. For instance, El Cambio, a grassroots organization consisting mostly of

Figure 2. North Carolina: Most Important Issue Facing the Latino Community

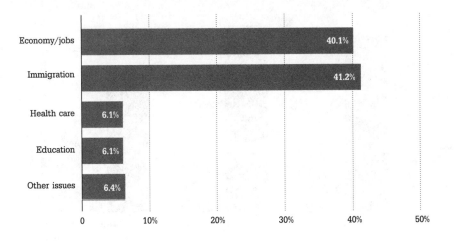

undocumented youth based in Yadkin County, has been very active in organizing and participating in rallies to promote awareness of undocumented adults' struggles with deportations, racial profiling, and being able to afford higher education (El Cambio NC n.d.). The NC Dream Team is a Raleigh-based organization led by undocumented youth that focuses on passing the DREAM Act and developing an immigrant-rights movement in the state. Besides participating in protests and rallies to raise awareness of social inequalities, the NC Dream Team organizes trainings to instruct individuals on how to release friends and family from jail and how to prevent deportations of loved ones who are in an immigration detention center (NC Dream Team n.d.). El Cambio and the NC Dream Team have also worked together to achieve their goals. In early 2012, members of both organizations helped obtain the release of Uriel Alberto, an undocumented youth who openly protested North Carolina's immigration policies, by forming an online petition for his release and joining him in a hunger strike to protest anti-immigration laws (Forbes 2012). Currently, El Cambio and the NC Dream Team are working with other political organizations throughout the state to halt mass deportations and provide a path to citizenship for the 11 million undocumented immigrants in the United States in light of President Obama's and the Senate's bipartisan effort to reform immigration (Paz 2013). Hence, North Carolina Latinos are deeply concerned about immigration, painting a clear picture of the significant struggles of the undocumented and remaining devoted to reforming current immigration policies.

Given Latinos' solid concern for, and commitment to, immigration reform, it comes as no surprise that their attitudes toward Obama's and Romney's proposed immigration plans were quite distinct. Figure 3 displays Latinos' response to each candidate's plan.[5] Months before the election, Mitt Romney expressed his opinion that undocumented immigrants should not be given the opportunity to work in the United States and should therefore self-deport. This plan was not popular among North Carolina Latinos, with 57.4 percent stating that this proposal made them less enthusiastic about Romney. On the other hand, President Obama announced over the summer of 2012 that the Department of Homeland Security would stop deporting undocumented immigrant youth who attend college or serve in the military, and would provide them with a renewable work permit. Latinos expressed stronger support for this program, with 53 percent asserting that this plan made them more enthusiastic about Obama. Still, these programs did not result in considerably positive or negative feelings toward the candidates. Approximately 22 percent of Latinos claimed that Romney's proposal had no effect on their attitudes toward him, and 31.1 percent of Latinos stated that Obama's plan had no effect on how they regarded Obama. A possible explanation for the later finding is that some Latinos had firm perceptions of Obama—negative or positive—that were not going to be altered based on an impromptu program, which some regarded as a political ploy to win the Latino vote. (Remember, under President Obama's first term, more immigrants were deported than during a term of any other president in U.S. history). As to differences in religion, I find that Catholic and Born Again Latinos' feelings toward Obama's and Romney's plans largely mirror the views of the general population. These results reveal that North Carolina Latinos, regardless of religion, greatly value immigration reform, and that the Republican Party should adopt less conservative immigration policies if they seek to attract the Latino vote in the Tar Heel State.

Months and days leading up to the 2012 presidential election, outreach to the Latino community in North Carolina was significant. Given that the number of Latino registered voters declined from 2008 to 2010 and many moved from one neighborhood to another for better economic opportunities, get-out-the-vote initiatives by the Democratic Party, left-leaning Latino organizations, and even undocumented immigrants began earlier than usual (Thompson 2012). Voto Latino, a group designed to empower Latinos, was very active before and during the Democratic National Convention in registering Latino youths to vote (Van Brussel 2012). Bilingual volunteers from the organization Democracy North Carolina, and youth advocacy groups such as El Cambio, Latin America Coalition, and El Pueblo participated in voter-registration drives to register Latinos in various public locations, including Latino Credit Union branches throughout the state (Frank and Christensen 2012). The mobilization efforts of the Latino youth groups can be defined as proactive (to reduce the barriers of engagement and heighten Latinos' political participation) as well as reactive (in response to Latinos' perception that they are politically threatened by legislation or political rhetoric) (see Ramírez 2013). Not

Figure 3. North Carolina: Candidates on Immigration, Effect on Latino Voters

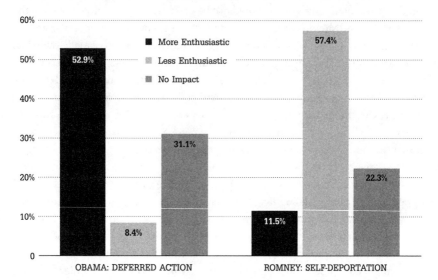

only did the groups seek to register and encourage Latinos to vote, but they also sought to inform the community about comprehensive immigration reform and the negative impact of restrictive immigration legislation (e.g., Arizona's SB 1070) and voter ID laws. These youth advocacy groups provided individuals with new reasons as to why Latinos' votes in the upcoming election were so essential.

The Democratic and Republican National Conventions also reached out to the Latino population. The fact that the Democratic National Convention was held in the city of Charlotte weeks before the election made it easier for party representatives and affiliates to reach out to the Latino community before, during, and after the convention. The Republican Party did reach out to Latino voters, though not to the extent that Democrats did. Both the Democratic and Republican National Conventions attempted to make Latinos feel welcome, with Latino speakers such as Marco Rubio, Susana Martinez, Julian Castro, Antonio Villaraigosa, and Benita Veliz. The conventions' invitations to Latino speakers increased some Latinos' favorable inclinations toward the parties, though more Latinos asserted that the Latino speakers increased the favorability of the Democratic Party than the Republican Party (Barreto 2012).

The aforementioned outreach efforts influenced North Carolina Latinos' presidential vote choice, and carried over to Latinos' perception of the presidential candidates. Latino impreMedia/Decisions poll data indicate that 57 percent of Latinos in North Carolina affirmed that they were contacted by Democrats, while only 8.6 percent were contacted by Republicans. The consequences of these efforts—or lack thereof—are illustrated in Latinos' perception of how much Obama and Romney cared about the Latino community. Figure 4 presents North Carolina Latinos' perception of how much they believed Obama and Romney cared about them.[6] Nearly 65 percent of Latinos perceived that Barack Obama truly cared for Latinos, and only 14.7 percent sensed that Romney truly cared about them. What is more, there is variation between Christians and all Latinos as well as among distinct groups of Latino Christians. While 66.1 percent of Catholics thought that Obama cared about them, a large number of Born Again Christians, 46.2 percent, believed the same. When it comes to Romney, 59.1 percent of Catholic Latinos and 49.8 percent of Born Again Christian Latinos thought that Romney did not care too much about them. Further, more than 10 percent of the general Latino population, Catholics and Born Again Christians, believed that Romney was hostile. Similar to the significance placed on immigration, Latinos did not greatly diverge by religion as to how much they believed the candidates cared about them. Further, Democrats and Obama did a better job of welcoming *all* Latinos in North Carolina in comparison to Romney and Republicans.

Pivotal House Races in North Carolina

The importance of the Latino vote was also illustrated in several House races in districts with emerging Latino populations. The narrowness of these races may

Figure 4. North Carolina: Effect of Candidate Latino Outreach on Voters' Perceptions (percent)

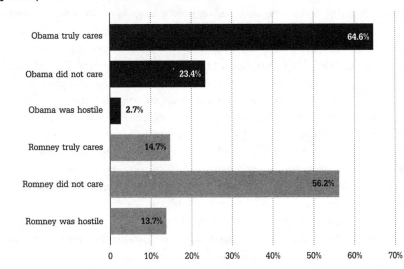

have increased Latinos' turnout rate in their district, in addition to shaping their presidential vote choice. Overall, Republicans picked up three new seats in the House of Representatives after the 2012 election (Sullivan 2012).

One of the most highly competitive races took place in the 8th District (located east of Charlotte and south of the Piedmont Triad area, including Mecklenburg County) with a Latino population of 12.2 percent (Gutierrez-Gunter and Hall 2012). Here, Democratic incumbent Larry Kissell was defeated by Republican newcomer Richard Hudson, 54 to 45 percent of the vote. While Kissell represented this district for two consecutive terms, he was regarded as a weak candidate. Before the election, state Republican leaders led efforts to change the boundaries of the district, resulting in the addition of heavily Republican counties along with the removal of several Democratic regions. Kissell also labeled himself a conservative Democrat who was against the president's proposed health-care reform and who was not going to endorse Obama for his second term. This lack of support as well as his failure to attend the Democratic National Convention in Charlotte—approximately fifteen miles from his district—angered several Democrats and influenced numerous African American supporters to discontinue endorsing Kissell several months before the election. Meanwhile, Hudson was deemed by many to be a fresh, effective Republican candidate who was committed to improving the economic growth of a district greatly affected by a rising unemployment rate (Ordonez 2012; Lyttle 2012).

The congressional race in the 9th District (located in the southwestern part of the state, including Mecklenburg County and Union County, and with a Latino population of 10 percent) was also quite contentious (Gutierrez-Gunter and Hall 2012). After serving the congressional district for eighteen years, Republican Sue Myrick decided to retire. The open seat spurred a heated race between Democrat Jennifer Roberts and Republican Robert Pittenger, which eventually led to Pittenger's narrow victory over Roberts, 52 to 46 percent. Their differences in background, values, and records were highly emphasized throughout the campaigns. While Roberts cast Pittenger as a political insider who sought a position in Washington to serve his interests and those of his friends and business colleagues, Pittenger portrayed Roberts as a big-government liberal who raised taxes. The rivals were deeply divided on several policy issues. In the end, Pittenger outspent Roberts six to one, spending 3 million dollars and making this race the most expensive congressional race in the state's history (Morrill 2012; Dunn 2012).

The election in the 7th District was also close, though it received less attention than the two aforementioned. This district includes a significant portion of the southeastern part of the state, including Wilmington, some parts of Raleigh, and Cumberland County, with a Latino population of 10 percent (Gutierrez-Gunter and Hall 2012). Democratic representative Mike McIntyre defeated state senator David

Rouzer to serve the district for his ninth term. The Republican-leaning district gave McIntyre 50.1 percent of the vote while his contender, Rouzer, won 49.9 percent (Sullivan 2012; Politico 2012).

When it comes to the densely populated urban areas with large black and booming Latino populations, several Democratic representatives had a firm hold on their seats in heavily Democratic districts. Representative Mel Watt of District 12 (including several portions of Charlotte, Winston-Salem, and Greensboro) won more than 80 percent of the vote for a seat that he has been holding since 1992. Democrat David Price of the 4th District was reelected with nearly 75 percent of the vote. Price's district, one he has been representing for nearly twenty-five years, is located largely in the middle of the state and encompasses most of the cities of Durham, Raleigh, and Fayetteville, including the "Research Triangle" area where both the University of North Carolina at Chapel Hill and Duke University lie. The 1st Congressional District (located in the northeastern part of the state) was won again, with 75 percent of the vote, by Democratic representative G. K. Butterfield, who has been representing this district since 2004 (U.S. House of Representatives n.d.; Politico n.d.). These results are not surprising given that, as previously argued by Barreto and Gross, Latinos' and African Americans' combined electoral influence is greater than the sum of the individual groups' electoral influence considered separately.

Conclusion

Though some were surprised by the 2012 presidential and state election results in North Carolina, Latino voters in the swing state strongly revealed their electoral strength and commitment to the Democratic Party. Mitt Romney won the presidential election in North Carolina by a narrow margin. A Republican governor, Pat McCrory, was elected into office for the first time in twenty years. Republicans picked up three new seats in the House of Representatives. In May 2012, Amendment 1, a constitutional amendment declaring that marriage between a man and a woman is the only domestic union that the state will recognize, was approved (Gordon 2012). Notwithstanding, the fastest-growing electorate in the state, Latinos, was vital to the success of the Democratic Party. Latinos clearly perceived that Democrats reached out to and cared for them more than Republicans. Young immigrant Latinos participated in get-out-the-vote initiatives and advocated in favor of Democratic candidates they perceived as more favorably inclined toward their concerns about immigration reform, racial profiling, and civil rights. The importance of the Latino vote was also illustrated in several contested House races in districts with large black and emerging Latino populations. In districts with the largest Latino populations, such as the

12th and the 4th, Democratic incumbents were overwhelmingly supported by their constituents. A combination of Latinos' consistent support of Democrats in state and national elections with their growth (from 0.2 percent of the registered voters in 2004 to 1.7 percent in 2012 according to the Pew Research Hispanic Center) and their commitment to the Democratic Party *regardless* of religion strongly illustrates that Latinos are a key constituent for Democrats' success in North Carolina. What is more, as the Latino electorate expands, the North Carolina voting population that currently leans to the right will change, and Latinos will have greater opportunities to steer politicians' agendas in their favor.

NOTES

1. In the Latino Decisions poll, 61.2 percent of North Carolina Latinos identify as Catholic, and 13.5 percent identify as Born Again.

2. Presidential vote choice for Obama is measured as 0 = other and 1= vote for Barack Obama. Presidential vote choice for Romney is measured as 0 = other and 1= vote for Mitt Romney.

3. This statement is supported by results from an estimated ordered logistical model with a dichotomous dependent variable (1=Obama as the presidential vote choice, 1=Romney as the presidential vote choice) controlling for the effects of attitudes toward Obama's deferred-action program, being contacted by Democrats, native status, religion, education, household income, and gender.

4. The most important issues facing the Latino community were measured as 1=Create more jobs/fix the economy; 2=Immigration reform/DREAM Act; 3=Health care; 4=Education reform/schools; 5=War in Afghanistan/War on terror/Foreign policy; 6=Housing/mortgages; 7=Gas prices/energy/oil; 8=Race relations/discrimination against Latinos; 9=Address Taxes; 10=Global warming/environment; 11=Something else; 88=Don't know; 99=Refused.

5. Response to Obama's homeland security policy is measured as 1=More enthusiastic about Obama; 2=Less enthusiastic about Obama; 3=Have no effect; 88=It depends/Don't know; 99=Refused. Response to Romney's homeland security policy is measured as 1=More enthusiastic about Romney; 2=Less enthusiastic about Romney; 3=Have no effect; 88=It depends/Don't know; 99=Refused.

6. Perception of Obama's Latino outreach is measured as 0=Obama truly cares about the Latino community; 1=Didn't care too much; 2=Was being hostile; 8=Don't know; 9=Refused. Perception of Romney's Latino outreach is measured as 0=Romney truly cares about the Latino community; 1=Didn't care too much; 2=Was being hostile; 8=Don't know; 9=Refused.

REFERENCES

Barreto, Matt A. 2011. "Where Latino Votes Will Matter in 2012." *Latino Decisions*, March 31. Available at latinodecisions.com.

———. 2012. "Who Out-Latino'd Who? Assessing the RNC and DNC Conventions Latino Outreach." *Latino Decisions*, September 12. Available at latinodecisions.com.

Barreto, Matt A., Loren Collingwood, and Sylvia Manzano. 2010. "A New Measure of Group Influence in Presidential Elections: Assessing Latino Influence in 2008." *Political Research Quarterly* 63, no. 4: 908–21.

Barreto, Matt A., and Gary M. Segura. 2012a. "ImpreMedia/Latino Decisions 2012 Latino Election Eve Poll." *Latino Decisions*, November 7. Available at latinodecisions.com.

———. 2012b. "Projecting Latino Electoral Influence in 2012." *Latino Decisions*, April 5. Available at latinodecisions.com.

Becerra, Hector. 2012. "Illegal Immigrant Makes History, Addresses Democratic Convention." *Los Angeles Times*, September 5.

Charlotte Observer. 2012. "2012 Election Results: Full North Carolina Returns, Maps." Available at charlotteobserver.com.

Chesser, John. 2012. "Hispanics in N.C.: Big Numbers in Small Towns." August 15. Available at ui.uncc.edu.

Christensen, Rob. 2012. "Romney Puts N.C. Back in the Red Column." *NewsObserver.com*, November 7.

DeFrancesco Soto, Victoria M. 2012. "Latino Vote Pivotal in North Carolina." *Latino Decisions*, September 27. Available at latinodecisions.com.

DePriest, Joe. 2012. "Former Migrant Expands His Cleveland County Farm." *Charlotte Observer*, July 31. Available at charlotteobserver.com.

de la Garza, Rodolfo, and Jeronimo Cortina. 2007. "Are Latinos Republicans but Just Don't Know It? The Latino Vote in the 2000 and 2004 Presidential Elections." *American Politics Research* 35, no. 2: 202–23.

Duchon, Deborah A., and Arthur D. Murphy. 2001. "Introduction: From Patrones and Caciquesto Good Ole Boys." In *Latino Workers in the Contemporary South*, ed. Arthur D. Murphy, Colleen Blanchard, and Jennifer A. Hill, 1–9. Athens: University of Georgia Press.

Dunn, Andrew. 2012. "9th Congressional District: Pittenger Defeats Roberts." *Charlotte Observer*, November 7. Available at charlotteobserver.com.

El Cambio NC. N.d. Available at elcambio.webs.com/aboutus.htm.

Foley, Elise. 2012. "Democratic National Convention Draws Record Number of Latino Delegates." *Huffington Post*, September 3. Available at huffingtonpost.com.

Forbes, David. 2012. "Undocumented Youth Arrested at NC Legislature on Hunger Strike." *Mountain Express*, March 6. Available at mountainx.com.

Frank, John. 2012. "Gov. Bev Perdue Will Not Run for Re-Election." *News Observer*, January 26. Available at newsobserver.com.

Frank, John, and Rob Christensen. 2012. "Latino Voter Registration Drive Kicks Off This Week." *News Observer*, September 23. Available at newsobserver.com.

Gill, Hannah. 2012. "Latinos in North Carolina: A Growing Part of the State's Economic and Social Landscape." *Immigration Policy Center*. Available at immigrationpolicy.org.

Gordon, Michael. 2012. "Amendment One: N.C. Voters Approve Measure to Block Same-Sex Marriage." *Charlotte Observer*, May 9. Available at charlotteobserver.com.

Gutierrez-Gunter, Isela, and Bob Hall. 2012. "A Snapshot of Latino Voters in North Carolina." *Democracy North Carolina*. Available at democracy-nc.org.

Kelly, Nathan, and Jana Morgan. 2008. "Religious Traditionalism and Latino Politics in the United States." *American Politics Research* 36, no. 2: 236–63.

Leal, David, Matt A. Barreto, Jongho Lee, and Rodolfo O. de la Garza. 2005. "The Latino Vote in the 2004 Election." *PS: Political Science & Politics* 38: 41–49.

Lopez, Mark Hugo, and Mark Taylor. 2012. "Latinos and the 2012 Election." *Pew Research Hispanic Center*, November 7. Available at pewhispanic.org.

Lyttle, Steve. 2012. "Early Results: McCrory Wins; Hudson Ousts Kissell from Congress." *Charlotte Observer*, November 6. Available at charlotteobserver.com.

Marrow, Helen B. 2005. "New Destinations and Immigrant Incorporation." *Perspectives on Politics* 3, no. 4: 781–99.

———. 2011. *New Destination Dreaming: Immigration, Race, and Legal Status in the Rural American South*. Stanford, CA: Stanford University Press.

Massey, Douglas, Jorge Durand, and Nolan J. Malone. 2002. *Beyond Smoke and Mirrors: Mexican Immigration in an Era of Economic Integration*. New York: Russell Sage Foundation.

McKenzie, Brian D., and Stella M. Rouse. 2013. "Shades of Faith: Religious Foundations of Political Attitudes among African Americans, Latinos, and Whites." *American Journal of Political Science* 57, no. 1: 218–35.

Miles, Kathleen. 2012. "Antonio Villaraigosa, DNC Chairman 2012, Says GOP Platform 'Looks Like the Platform of 1812' (VIDEO)." *Huffington Post*, September 4. Available at huffingtonpost.com.

Morrill, Jim. 2012. "Decision 2012: 9th District Foes Spar on Ethics." *Charlotte Observer*, October 16. Available at charlotteobserver.com.

Motel, Seth, and Eileen Patten. 2012. "Latinos in the 2012 Election: North Carolina." *Pew Research Hispanic Center*, November 5. Available at pewhispanic.org.

———. 2013. "Statistical Portrait of Hispanics in the United States, 2011." *Pew Research Hispanic Center*, February 15. Available at pewhispanic.org.

NC Dream Team. N.d. Available at ncdreamteam.org.

North Carolina Department of Agriculture and Consumer Services. 2014. "Agricultural Overview–Commodities." Available at ncagr.gov.

———. 2013. "Agricultural Statistics—Summary of Commodities by County." Available at ncagr. gov.

North Carolina in the Global Economy. 2013. "Hog Farming." Available at soc.duke.edu.

Ordonez, Franco. 2012. "8th Congressional District: Hudson Defeats Incumbent Kissell." *Charlotte Observer*, November 7. Available at charlotteobserver.com.

Paz, Adrian Romero. 2013. "Se unen en favor de la reforma: En Piedmont comienzan a organizarse tras el anuncio del gobierno federal." *Que Pasa Noticias Greensboro/Winston-Salem*. Available at greensboro.quepasanoticias.com.

Perez, Jorge. 2008. "License Rule Hurt Car Sales." *Charlotte Observer*, January 30. Available at newsobserver.com.

Pew Research Center. 2012. "Latinos, Religion and Campaign 2012." *Pew Forum on Religion and Public Life*. Available at pewforum.org .

Pew Research Hispanic Center. 2011. "Demographic Profile of Hispanics in North Carolina, 2010." Available at pewhispanic.org.

Politico. 2012. "2012 North Carolina House Results." Available at politico.com.

Ralls, Steve. 2013. "Immigration Equality-LD Poll: Latino Voters Overwhelming Support Inclusion of Gay Families in Immigration Reform." *Latino Decisions*, March 8. Available at latinodecisions.com.

Ramírez, Ricardo. 2013. *Mobilizing Opportunities: The Evolving Latino Electorate and the Future of American Politics*. Charlottesville: University of Virginia Press.

Sorg, Lisa. 2012. "Uriel Alberto Released from Wake County Jail." *Triangulator*, March 15. Available at indyweek.com.

Sullivan, Sean. 2012. "Democratic Rep. Mike McIntyre Defeats Republican David Rouzer in North Carolina." *Washington Post*, November 29.

Suro, Roberto, and Audrey Singer. 2002. "Latino Growth in Metropolitan America: Changing Patterns, New Locations." The Brookings Institution, Center on Urban and Metropolitan Policy, and the Pew Hispanic Center. Available at brookings.edu.

Swartz, Deven. 2012. "Uriel Alberto Immigration Hearing Canceled, to Be Released on Bond." *Fox 8 News*, March 14. Available on myfox8.com.

Thompson, Krissah. 2012. "Economy Blamed for Decline in Voter Registration among Hispanics, Blacks." *Washington Post*, May 5.

Torres, Cruz C. 2000. "Emerging Latino Communities: A New Challenge for the Rural South." Southern Rural Development Center Newsletter, no. 12: 1–8.U.S. Census Bureau. 2001. "The Hispanic Population: Census 2000 Brief." Available at census.gov.

———. 2010. "American Fact Finder." Available at census.gov.

U.S. House of Representatives. N.d. Available at house.gov.

Van Brussel, Joe. 2012. "Rosario Dawson at DNC on 'Voto Latino' and Engaging Youth in Politics." *Huffington Post*, September 9. Available at huffingtonpost.com.

CASEY A. KLOFSTAD

Florida's Latino Electorate in the 2012 Election

IN TWO IMPORTANT WAYS, FLORIDA IS AN OUTLIER COMPARED TO MANY OF the other states covered in this volume. First, Florida is a relative bystander in the debate on immigration reform. Florida does not share a border with Mexico, and Latinos living in Florida are also much less likely to know an undocumented immigrant compared to Latinos in other states. Second, due to Florida's large Cuban American population, Florida's Latino community is more supportive of the Republican Party compared to its counterparts in other states.

Importantly, however, in looking at the 2012 election these differences between Latinos in Florida and other states are not as large as they might appear at face value. While Florida is seemingly removed from the front lines of the immigration debate, as was the case in other states Florida's Latino community was highly supportive of the Democratic Party's approach to immigration reform, and staunchly opposed to the Republicans'. Likewise, while Cuban Americans shift Florida Latino partisanship towards the Republican Party, Florida's Latino electorate as a whole is still a stronghold for Democrats.

In this chapter, I first assess the growing influence of Latinos in the State of Florida. Next, using survey data collected by Latino Decisions on the eve of the

2012 election from likely Latino voters in eleven battleground states, I compare the policy preferences of Latinos in Florida to those in other states. Finally, I use the impreMedia/Latino Decisions data, and data collected by Latino Decisions and America's Voice in September 2012 from registered Latino voters, to examine Latino voter turnout and vote choice in the State of Florida. It is important to underscore that these data are not representative of all Latinos in the state. Instead they are representative of Latinos who are likely to vote. As such, any inferences made from these data only apply to this subset of Florida's Latino community.

The analyses presented here were conducted with Stata/MP (version 11.2 for Windows). Unless indicated otherwise, the results presented in this chapter are weighted to account for discrepancies between the demographics of the survey sample frames and the demographics of the Latino population. These weights were provided by Latino Decisions. All of the results presented exclude "don't know" and "refused to answer" responses. Missing values are excluded from the analyses using listwise deletion.

Florida's Growing and Changing Latino Electorate

As in other parts of the United States, Florida's Latino community is growing. Data from the United States Census indicate that the percentage of Floridians of Hispanic or Latino origin grew from 12.2 percent in the year 1990 to 16.8 percent in the year 2000, an increase of over 4 percentage points. This trend of population growth increased in magnitude over the first decade of the twenty-first century. In 2010 Latinos constituted 22.5 percent of Florida's population (Ennis et al. 2011), an increase of close to 6 percentage points from the year 2000. Census estimates reported by the Florida Office of Economic and Demographic Research (n.d.) indicate even more rapid growth in Florida's Latino community in the future, which is projected to rise to 46.5 percent of the state's population in the year 2020, an increase of 24 percentage points from the year 2010.

Concomitantly, the Latino electorate in Florida has also grown. Florida Division of Elections (n.d.) records show that Latinos grew from approximately 1.5 percent of registered voters in the year 1994 to approximately 9 percent in the year 2000, an increase of 7.5 percentage points. These figures are estimates because 1994 and 2000 registration records in the State of Florida were broken down by three racial categories: white, black, and "other." In 2012, state records show that individuals who identified as Hispanic, of any race, made up 13 percent of registered voters in Florida, an increase of 4 percentage points from the 2000 election. This suggests that while Latino voter registration in Florida is still growing, the rate of growth may have decreased since the early 2000s. That said, estimates show that Latinos were between 16.5 and 19.2 percent of eligible voters in the state in 2012 (Barreto and Segura 2012; Barreto 2012), which suggests continued steady growth in Florida's Latino electorate.

A critical component of this increase in Latino political clout in Florida is the growth of the Puerto Rican community in cities such as Tampa and Orlando (National Public Radio 2012; Smith 2012). Traditionally, Florida is synonymous with Cuban Americans. According to the 2010 Census, they are the largest Latino community in the state (29 percent), and more Cuban Americans live in Florida than in any other state (Ennis et al. 2011). However, Puerto Ricans are a growing constituency within Florida. Florida has the second-largest Puerto Rican population in the country next to New York (Ennis et al. 2011), and data from the 2010 Census show that they are the second-largest Latino community in the state (20 percent). This demographic shift has the potential to transform Florida's electorate. Importantly, Puerto Rican migrants are citizens and immediately have the right to vote, making them a potentially powerful political force in the state. Likewise (as I discuss below), unlike Cuban Americans who tend to be Republican-leaning, Puerto Ricans are more Democratic-leaning. If the trend of increased Puerto Rican migration to Florida continues, this could lead to a more stable advantage for the Democratic Party in this critical swing state.

Partisanship of Latinos in Florida

The partisanship of Florida's Latino community is out of step with Latinos in other parts of the United States. The impreMedia/Latino Decisions poll asked respondents: "Generally speaking, do you think of yourself as a Republican, a Democrat, an Independent, or something else?" As shown in table 1, while a plurality of Florida's Latinos identify as Democrats, they are also more likely to identify as Republicans compared to Latinos in other parts of the country. More specifically, if responses to the partisanship question are coded, whereby 1 = Democrat, 2 = Independent, and 3 = Republican, the mean response in Florida is significantly closer to the Republican side of the spectrum compared to other states (Florida: $\bar{x}$ = 1.87, other states $\bar{x}$ = 1.47; $t = 12.84_{5246}$, $p < 0.01$). As alluded to in the previous section, Latinos as a group in Florida are more right-leaning because of the large Cuban American community in the state (table 1). On the Democrat-Independent-Republican scale described above, among Latinos in Florida Cuban Americans are significantly more likely to identify as Republicans than Puerto Ricans (Cuban Americans: $\bar{x}$ = 2.27, Puerto Ricans: $\bar{x}$ = 1.62; $t = 5.97_{289}$, $p < 0.01$).

A multitude of reasons exist for why Cuban Americans are partisan outliers

Table 1. Latino Partisan Identification

	By State		In Florida	
	Florida	All others	Cuban Americans	Puerto Ricans
Democrat	43%	66%	27%	53%
Independent	27%	21%	19%	32%
Republican	30%	13%	54%	15%

Source: impreMedia/Latino Decisions (November 2012).
Note: Results exclude respondents who replied "something else" or "don't know," and those who refused to answer the question.

among other Latinos (Bishin and Klofstad 2012; Eckstein 2006). Arguably at the top of the list is the fact that earlier émigrés can be stereotyped as political refugees who fled the island in response to Fidel Castro's communist revolution. Moreover, the Cuban American community in Florida also believes that Democrats have failed in their attempts at foreign policy regarding Cuba, from John F. Kennedy's Bay of Pigs invasion on forward. In sum, the community has developed antipathy towards left-leaning politics in general and the Democratic Party in particular.

The story of Cuban Americans' affinity for the Republican Party is more than just Fidel Castro, however. For example, early Cuban immigrants were typically of higher socioeconomic status and faced less discrimination than other immigrant groups, which contributes to their Republican leanings. In contrast, more recent Cuban immigrants—from the 1980 Mariel Boatlift on—are better described as economic refugees of much more meager means than their predecessors. This newer cohort of Cuban immigrants is more likely to be motivated by the desire for greater financial opportunities in the United States, and less by the desire to flee political persecution. They also are more likely than earlier Cuban immigrants to have strong ties to friends and family who are still on the island, and consequently are in favor of loosening restrictions on travel and sending remittances to Cuba. Taken together, more recent Cuban immigrants are more moderate in their political preferences.

Clearly there has been a shift in the demographics of Florida's Cuban American community. However, it is less clear to what degree this shift has influenced the Cuban American electorate. On one hand, as it is costly to naturalize, this newer cohort of more moderate Cuban immigrants is less likely to obtain citizenship and the right to vote. On the other hand, however, there is some evidence that native-born Cuban Americans are more moderate in terms of their partisanship and views on Cuban foreign policy (Bishin and Klofstad 2012). Likewise, competing 2012 exit polls conducted in Florida have led to a debate over whether President Obama actually won the Cuban American vote (Bishin 2012; Crowley Political Report 2012a, 2012b; Tamayo 2012). This debate aside, for now it is clear that the Cuban American community in Florida leans farther to the right compared to other Latinos (table 1). Only future elections will tell whether changes in the demographics of the Cuban American community will lead to a shift in the political preferences of Florida's Latino electorate.

Policy Issues in the 2012 Election

As with all voters, in this "Great Recession" the economy was the most important issue on the minds of Florida's Latino community during the 2012 election. The impreMedia/Latino Decisions respondents were asked: "Thinking about the 2012 election, what are the most important issues facing the Latino/Hispanic community that our politicians should address?" In total, 51 percent of Latinos in Florida identified the economy as the most important issue they considered during the election. By comparison, Latinos in other states were less likely (45 percent) to list the economy as their most important issue. This significant difference between Florida and the rest of the country ($t_{5423} = 2.65$, $p = 0.01$) is likely due to the fact that Florida has been one of the hardest-hit states in the recession. To wit, the unemployment rate among Latinos in Florida was higher than the national average during the 2012 election (Gómez 2012).

Given the importance of the economy in the 2012 election, how did Florida's Latino community perceive the economic policies of the Obama and Romney campaigns? Respondents to the impreMedia/Latino Decisions poll were asked whether the best approach to deficit reduction is "cutting existing programs, raising taxes on the wealthy, or some combination of the two." If one codes responses to this question whereby 1 = "raising taxes," 2 = "some combination," and 3 = "cutting existing programs," the average in Florida is significantly closer to the more conservative end of the scale compared to the average across other states (Florida: $\bar{x} = 1.82$, other states $\bar{x} = 1.73$; $t_{5159} = 3.18$, $p < 0.01$). This being said, the substantive difference between these means is quite small. Likewise, a plurality of Florida's Latinos (49 percent) desired a combination of spending cuts and raising taxes on the wealthy, the path endorsed by Obama during the campaign. This figure is comparable to 47 percent in other states polled by impreMedia/Latino Decisions. Consequently, while Latinos in Florida are more right-leaning than those in other states, their opinions on the economy are not wildly out of step with the wider Latino community in the United States.

While the economy was at the forefront of issues that concerned Florida's Latino community during the 2012 election, immigration was their second most important issue. Florida is relatively isolated, geographically, from the frontline of the immigration debate. Likewise, the impreMedia/Latino Decisions poll shows that Florida's

Latinos are less likely than those in other states to know an undocumented immigrant (Florida: 48 percent, other states: 65 percent; t_{5560} = 7.70, p < 0.01). Nonetheless, the impreMedia/Latino Decisions data also show that Latinos in Florida were just as likely as Latinos in other states to list immigration as their second issue of concern during the 2012 election (Florida: 26 percent, other states: 25 percent; t_{5423} = 0.61, p = 0.54). This suggests that there is a sense of "linked fate" (Dawson 1995) in the Latino community when it comes to immigration policy. Even those who are seemingly less affected by this issue have similar attitudes to those who are.

With this in mind, how did Latinos in Florida perceive the immigration policies put forth by the Obama and Romney campaigns? Respondents to the impreMedia/Latino Decisions survey were randomly assigned to report how enthusiastic the Obama or Romney immigration platforms made them. The question about Obama made reference to his policy "to stop the deportation of any undocumented immigrant youth." The question about Romney made reference to his policy whereby "undocumented immigrants are not allowed to work here in the United States" and should "self-deport." As shown in figure 1, if one codes the policy questions whereby 1 = "less enthusiastic," 2 = "have no effect," and 3 = "more enthusiastic," Latinos in Florida were significantly more enthused by Obama's approach to immigration reform than Romney's (Obama: $\bar{x}$ = 2.38, Romney: $\bar{x}$ = 1.57; t_{609} = 14.58, p < 0.01). This disparity in the perceptions of the two candidates likely played a role in Obama wining the State of Florida in 2012.

That said, however, there may be some hope for Republicans in Florida if they change their approach to immigration reform. The impreMedia/Latino Decisions poll asked respondents how likely they would be to vote Republican if the party "took a leadership role in supporting comprehensive immigration reform, with an eventual pathway to citizenship." In total, 13 percent of Latinos in Florida reported that this policy shift would increase their likelihood of voting Republican, compared to 7 percent in another states. Moreover, if one codes the responses to this question whereby 1 = "less likely," 2 = "no effect," and 3 = "more likely," the mean response given in Florida is more favorable towards the Republicans compared to other states (Florida: $\bar{x}$ = 1.57, other states $\bar{x}$ = 1.43; t_{2696} = 3.51, p < 0.01). While this hypothetical increase in support for Republicans is not overly large, in a swing state like Florida even small shifts in the electorate can have a large influence (Obama beat Romney in Florida by only 74,309 votes, less than 1 percentage point).

Finally, while the economy and immigration were the most important issues for Latinos in Florida during the 2012 election, health care was also a salient part of the election. Data from the impreMedia/Latino Decisions poll show that this was the fourth most important policy issue mentioned by Florida's Latino community (6 percent) behind education (7 percent), immigration (26 percent), and the economy

Figure 1. Overall Impressions of the 2012 Obama and Romney Campaigns

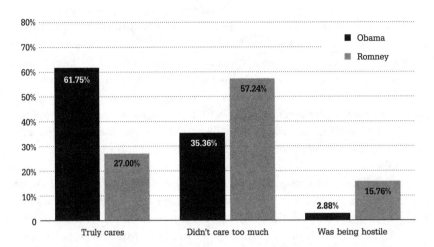

Note: Data are from Latinos in Florida polled by impreMedia/Latino Decisions (November 2012).

(51 percent). Poll respondents were asked whether the Affordable Care Act ("Obamacare") should be left to stand or be repealed. Latinos in Florida were more likely to support repeal than their counterparts in other states (Florida: 41 percent, other states: 28 percent; t_{2507} = 4.69, p < 0.01). They were also more likely to report in the impreMedia/Latino Decisions poll that individuals should be responsible for their own health care instead of the government (Florida: 35 percent, other states: 27 percent; t_{2618} = 2.88, p < 0.01). Importantly, however, a majority of Florida's Latinos were supportive of maintaining the Affordable Care Act (59 percent), and in favor of government playing a role in providing health care (65 percent). Again, while Florida's Latinos are more right-leaning than Latinos in other states, they still support the Democratic Party overall.

Campaign Outreach to the Latino Community during the 2012 Election

Data collected by the *Washington Post* (n.d.) show that the Obama and Romney campaigns visited Florida 115 times over the course of the election, second only to the state of Ohio. Many of these visits were held along the "I-4 Corridor" that stretches from Tampa to Orlando, an area of increased growth in Florida's Puerto Rican community.

In an effort to win back Republican gains made with Latino voters during the

George W. Bush era, the GOP made a number of unprecedented moves to court Florida's Latino voters, including placing a Hispanic outreach director in the state, and heavy use of Spanish-language television and radio advertisements, many of which focused on blaming President Obama for the high unemployment rate among Latinos (Dade 2012; Llorente 2012; Rama 2012). Arguably the more memorable of these advertisements was "Nosotros" ("Us"), a Spanish-language television advertisement narrated by Governor Mitt Romney's son Craig, who became fluent in Spanish during his time as a Mormon missionary in Chile (Killingsworth 2012; Llorente 2012).

Eager to build upon their gains made among Latinos voters since the 2008 election, the Democratic Party also made heavy use of Spanish-language television and radio advertising in Florida, much of which blamed Republicans for cuts in government programs favored by the Latino community (Dade 2012; Llorente 2012; Rama 2012). One of the most notable of these advertisements featured the endorsement of prominent Univisión television talk-show host Cristina Saralegui, also known as the "Hispanic Oprah" (Bolstad 2012). After the 2008 election, Democrats also worked to register over 70,000 Florida Latinos to vote (Llorente 2012). In response to pressure from the Latino community, in the middle of the 2012 campaign President Obama also directed the Department of Homeland Security to stop the deportation of undocumented immigrants under the age of thirty (Bolstad 2012; Cohen 2012; Foley 2012).

These unprecedented outreach efforts by both parties were effective in grabbing the attention of Florida's Latino community. Respondents to the impreMedia/Latino Decisions poll were asked: "Were you contacted by the Democrats, Republicans, both parties, or by representatives of community organizations?" Latinos living in Florida were significantly more likely to be contacted by these groups during the campaign compared to their counterparts in other states (Florida: 37 percent, other states: 31 percent; $t_{5675} = 3.49$, $p < 0.01$).

While the campaigns were effective at getting their messages out, how were these contacts perceived? Figure 2 presents the general impression Florida's Latino community had of the outreach efforts made to them by the Obama and Romney campaigns. The impreMedia/Latino Decisions respondents were asked whether each candidate was "someone who truly cares about the Hispanic/Latino community, that he didn't care too much about Hispanic/Latinos, or that [he] was hostile towards Hispanic/Latinos." The efforts of the Obama campaign were perceived far more favorably than those of the Romney campaign. More specifically, if one codes the two survey questions whereby 1 = "truly cares," 2 = "not too much," and 3 = "hostile," Latinos' impression of the Obama campaign was significantly more favorable than their impression of the Romney campaign (Obama: unweighted $\bar{x} = 1.46$, Romney unweighted: $\bar{x} = 1.83$; $t_{649} = 9.17$, $p < 0.01$). This difference of means test was unweighted

Figure 2. Enthusiasm for Obama and Romney in 2012 over Their Immigration Policies

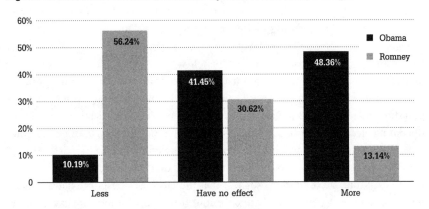

Note: Data are from Latinos in Florida polled by impreMedia/Latino Decisions (November 2012).

because Stata/MP cannot compute a weighted paired t-test. However, the weighted means are comparable to the unweighted means (Obama weighted: $\bar{x}$ = 1.41, Romney weighted: $\bar{x}$ = 1.89). As discussed below, these diametrically opposed perceptions of the two campaigns are likely linked to the perception that the Republican Party is out of touch with the political preferences of Florida's Latino community.

Voter Turnout

As ordered by Republican governor Rick Scott in the spring of 2012, the Florida Secretary of State's office ordered county election officials to compare voter-registration records to state and federal records on citizenship status. This action was pejoratively referred to as a "purge" of the voting rolls. In the summer of 2012 it was reported (Ross 2012) that around 180,000 of the 11.3 million registered voters (less than 2 percent) in the State of Florida were flagged as possible noncitizens, 58 percent of whom were Latinos, and 79 percent of whom were registered as either Democrats or "no-party-affiliation." Of that list of 180,000, county election officials were notified to make contact with approximately 2,700 possible noncitizens on the registration rolls (.02 percent of the state's registered voters). As the most populous county in the state, Miami-Dade received around two-thirds of those notices. Of those, the *Miami Herald* (Caputo and Madan 2012) reported that only thirteen registered voters had identified themselves as noncitizens, and of those only two were found to have voted in past elections.

Given the relatively small number of individuals purged from Florida's voter rolls leading up to the 2012 election, the direct influence of this policy on voter turnout was negligible. However, it was possible that this policy would have a much larger indirect effect by intimidating Latinos from turning out. Indeed, the Latino Decisions/America's Voice poll shows that 72 percent of Florida's Latino registered voters were somewhat or very concerned that "people who are legally eligible to vote could be wrongly removed from the voter list." However, this fear over the purge did not reduce Latinos' enthusiasm to vote. Data from the Latino Decisions/America's Voice poll show that 71 percent of Latinos in Florida were very enthusiastic to vote in the upcoming election. Likewise, when asked in the Latino Decisions/America's Voice poll how enthusiastic they felt about voting in 2012 compared to the historic 2008 election, 58 percent of Latinos in Florida reported that they were more enthusiastic in 2012. All told, these findings suggest that the Florida voter purge had neither a direct nor indirect influence on Latino turnout. This said, an important caveat is that the Latino Decisions/America's Voice data were collected from registered voters. As such, it could be that unregistered Latinos were intimidated from registering and turning out by the purge. This proposition cannot be tested with the Latino Decisions/America's Voice data.

This aside, the high level of enthusiasm Latinos had leading into the 2012 election is reflected in turnout figures. Florida is one of many states that have implemented early voting. The early voting period in Florida, shortened by the Republican majority in the statehouse from fourteen days in 2008 to eight in 2012, ran from October 11 to November 3. When asked in the impreMedia/Latino Decisions poll whether they had already voted early, 52 percent reported that they had, a significantly higher rate compared to the 42 percent early-vote rate of Latinos in other states (t_{5791} = 5.05, p < 0.01). Exit poll estimates suggest that Latino turnout increased from 15 percent of Florida's voters in 2008 to 17 percent in 2012 (Weiner 2012).

Vote Choice

In line with findings presented earlier in this chapter (table 1), data from the impreMedia/Latino Decisions poll (table 2) show that Latinos in Florida were more supportive of the Republican Party compared to Latinos in other states. Republican candidates won significantly more votes from Latinos in Florida for president (Florida: 41 percent, all other states: 21 percent; t_{5160} = 10.92, p < 0.01) and House of Representatives (Florida: 42 percent, all other states: 21 percent; t_{5044} = 11.22, p < 0.01). Likewise, in the race for U.S. Senate, for example, Connie Mack won a larger share of Florida's Latino vote compared to Jeff Flake in Arizona (Mack: 40 percent, Flake: 17 percent; t_{1059} = 7.66, p < 0.01).

Table 2. 2012 Latino Vote Share by State

	President		U.S. House		U.S. Senate	
	Florida	All others	Florida	All others	Florida	Arizona
Democrat	59%	79%	58%	79%	60%	83%
Republican	41%	21%	42%	21%	40%	17%

Source: impreMedia/Latino Decisions (November 2012).
Note: Results exclude respondents who replied "don't know," and respondents who refused to answer the question.

This said, despite the influence of the more conservative preferences of Florida's Cuban American electorate, Florida's Latinos as a whole broke heavily for the Democratic Party in 2012. The data in table 2 show that a strong majority of Florida's Latinos voted Democrat for the president, House, and Senate. Likewise, exit polls show that while President Obama lost votes in many major demographic groups in Florida, including men, partisan Independents, and whites, he picked up 3 percentage points among Latinos between 2008 and 2012 (an increase from 57 percent to 60 percent). Given that his margin of victory in the state was less than 1 percentage point, and given the state's sizable prize of 29 electoral votes, one can argue that the Latino vote in Florida played a critical role in reelecting the president. Moreover, Obama's success with Florida Latinos in the past two presidential election cycles is a drastic change from 2004, when George W. Bush won 56 percent of Florida's Latino vote according to exit polls.

Conclusion

Florida is an outlier in the Latino community. The state's Latinos are relatively isolated from the immigration debate, and lean farther to the right politically compared to Latinos in other states. Despite these differences, however, during the 2012 election Florida's Latinos were not wildly out of step with their counterparts in the rest of the country. As in other states, immigration policy is highly salient among Florida's Latinos, and they are far more supportive of the Democrats' approach to immigration reform. In this same vein, while Cuban Americans pull Florida's Latinos to the right, the community overall is still highly supportive of the Democratic Party. This support was a critical component of President Obama winning reelection in 2012.

This is recent history. What does the future portend for Florida's Latino community? If current trends hold, the community will continue to grow in size and political clout. Current trends also suggest that due to Puerto Rican migration to the state, and trends toward ideological moderation in the Cuban American community

(Bishin and Klofstad 2012), Florida's Latino voters could give an increasing advantage to Democratic candidates. One possible exception to these trends, however, is the wild card of immigration reform. The data presented here suggest that some Latinos in Florida could be persuaded to vote Republican if the party takes a lead in reforming immigration policy, provided they create a path to citizenship for the undocumented. The question is whether the Republican Party will heed this advice. The state's native son, Cuban American senator Marco Rubio could play a critical role in this process should the Republican Party pursue a new approach to immigration reform.

All told, in the past Latinos could have been described as a sleeping political giant. As evidenced in Florida in 2012, the sleeper has awakened. It is incumbent on both political parties to recognize this, and to pay earnest attention to the preferences of this constituency. Doing so is not only good governance, but also good politics—as seen by the increasingly strong performance of the Democratic Party in Florida over the past eight years.

NOTE

Special thanks to Ben Bishin for his invaluable insights on the Cuban American community in Florida, and Marc Caputo of the *Miami Herald* for his extensive expertise in Florida politics.

REFERENCES

Barreto, Matt A. 2012. "Where Latino Votes Will Matter in 2012." March 31. Available at latinodecisions.com.

Barreto, Matt A., and Gary M. Segura. 2012. "Projecting Latino Electoral Influence in 2012: What Percent of the Latino Vote Candidates Need to Win Each State." April 5. Available at latinodecisions.com.

Bishin, Benjamin G. 2012. "Did Little Havana Just Go Blue?" *The Monkey Cage*, November 11. Available at themonkeycage.org.

Bishin, Benjamin G., and Casey A. Klofstad. 2012. "The Political Incorporation of Cuban Americans: Why Won't Little Havana Turn Blue?" *Political Research Quarterly* 65: 588–601.

Bolstad, Erika. 2012. "Cristina Saralegui Says She'll Endorse President Barack Obama." *Miami Herald*, June 17.

Caputo, Marc, and Monique O. Madan. 2012. "Investigation of Two Noncitizen Voters May Bolster Scott's Fight with Feds." *Miami Herald*, June 2.

Cohen, Tom. 2012. "Obama Administration to Stop Deporting Some Young Illegal Immigrants." *CNN*, June 16. Available at cnn.com.

Crowley Political Report. 2012a. "Florida, Cuban Voters, the Media and What Went Wrong." *Crowley Political Report*, November 16. Available at crowleypoliticalreport.com.

———. 2012b. "Sergio Bendixen Disagrees with Our Poll Analysis." *Crowley Political Report*,

November 19. Available at crowleypoliticalreport.com.

Dade, Corey. 2012. "Latino Voters: Seen, but Will They Be Heard, in 2012?" *National Public Radio*, May 16. Available at npr.org.

Dawson, Michael C. 1995. *Behind the Mule: Race and Class in African-American Politics.* Princeton, NJ: Princeton University Press.

Eckstein, Susan. 2006. "Cuban Émigrés and the American Dream." *Perspectives on Politics* 4: 297–307.

Ennis, Sharon R., Merays Ríos Vargas, and Nora G. Albert. 2011. "The Hispanic Population: 2010." United States Census Bureau. Available at census.gov.

Florida Division of Elections. N.d. "Voter Registration Statistics by Election." Available at election. dos.state.fl.us.

Florida Office of Economic and Demographic Research. N.d. "Population Projections by Age, Sex, Race, and Hispanic Origin for Florida and Its Counties, 2015–2040, with Estimates for 2012." Available at edr.state.fl.us.

Foley, Elise. 2012. "Obama Administration to Stop Deporting Younger Undocumented Immigrants and Grant Work Permits." *Huffington Post*, June 15. Available at huffingtonpost.com.

Gómez, Serafin. 2012. "Unemployment Jumps to 11 Percent among Latinos, Report Says." *Fox News Latino*, June 1. Available at latino.foxnews.com.

Killingsworth, Sylvia. 2012. "Can Romney Speak Spanish?" *New Yorker*, January 14.

Llorente, Elizabeth. 2012. "New Romney Ad in Florida Kicks Race for Latino Vote into High Gear." *Fox News Latino*, January 11. Available at latino.foxnews.com.

National Public Radio. 2012. "Influx of Puerto Ricans Changes Florida's Voter Calculus." *National Public Radio*, June 27. Available at npr.org.

Rama, Padmananda. 2012. "In Swing States, Obama Campaign Begins Push for Another Latino Vote Landslide." *National Public Radio*, April 19. Available at npr.org.

Ross, Janell. 2012. "Florida Voter Purge Will Continue, Defying Federal Warning." *Huffington Post*, June 2. Available at huffingtonpost.com.

Smith, Adam C. 2012. "Puerto Rico a Force in Florida Voting." *Tampa Bay Times*, March 17.

Tamayo, Juan O. 2012. "Did Obama or Romney Win the Cuban-American Vote?" *Miami Herald*, November 12.

Washington Post. N.d. "Presidential Campaign Stops: Who's Going Where." Available at washingtonpost.com.

Weiner, Rachel. "Florida Exit Polls: Obama Wins Hispanics, Loses Whites." *Washington Post*, November 6.

DAVID F. DAMORE

It's the Economy Stupid? Not So Fast

The Impact of the Latino Vote on the 2012
Presidential Election in Nevada

PERHAPS NO STATE BETTER CAPTURES THE DEMOGRAPHIC AND GEOGRAPHIC
shifts that are reshaping the American political landscape than Nevada. Fueled by
rapid growth in its Latino population over the last two decades, the Silver State has
been transformed from a rarely contested, sparsely populated, rural outpost into a
highly urbanized and ethnically diverse state that has commanded outsized attention
in recent electoral cycles.

As a consequence of these changes, Nevada, particularly at the presidential level,
is increasingly trending towards the Democratic Party, as evidenced by the fact that
Barack Obama is the first Democratic presidential candidate to win a majority of the
Nevada vote in consecutive elections in nearly fifty years.[1] Yet, from the perspective
of traditional political-science research that emphasizes economic conditions for
explaining presidential-election outcomes (e.g., Fiorina 1981; Hibbs 2000), Nevada
should hardly have been competitive, let alone a state that Obama carried by almost
7 percent. After all, throughout 2012 Nevada led the nation in unemployment and
bankruptcies and was not far behind in foreclosures.

Indeed, the inability of Mitt Romney to capture the state's 6 Electoral College
votes despite Nevada's economic ills may be the most telling indicator of the electoral

implications of the country's changing political geography and demography. Quite simply, even in a state that was ground zero for the Great Recession, the toxicity of Romney's rhetoric on immigration and his campaign's failure to engage Nevada's Latino community in a constructive manner undercut his prospects in a state where Latino voters were pivotal in determining the outcome.[2] In this regard, Nevada provides a powerful case study of the linkages between the Latino vote, immigration, and Republicans' inability to win a presidential election that are detailed in the chapter by Hastings in this volume.

To assess these dynamics, I analyze the impact of the Latino vote on the 2012 election in Nevada. The chapter begins with a profile of Nevada's Latino population and recent efforts to mobilize Latino electoral participation. This is followed by an overview of the 2012 electoral context in Nevada, and then a discussion of the fall campaign, with particular attention devoted to the role of immigration policy in shaping the behavior and policy preferences of Latino voters. Section four presents an examination of individual-level variation in the Latino vote using data from the Nevada subsample of the impreMedia/Latino Decisions 2012 Latino Election Eve Poll. The chapter concludes with a discussion of the consequences of increased political engagement by Nevada's Latino community.

Mobilizing the Latino Electorate

In the last two decades, Nevada has been the fastest growing state in the country, posting population gains of 66 percent during the 1990s and 35 percent during the first decade of the twenty-first century. Much of this growth was fueled by an explosion in the state's Latino community, which increased from 10.4 percent of the population in 1990, to 19.7 percent in 2000, to 26 percent in 2010. There has also been substantial growth in the state's Asian and Pacific Islander and African American communities, which constitute 7.8 percent and 8.1 percent of Nevada's population respectively. In addition to becoming a highly diverse state, Nevada has become one of the country's most urban states, as nearly 90 percent of all Nevadans live in just two counties.

As a consequence, and as detailed in tables 1 and 2, Nevada has three distinct regions, known colloquially as "The Three Nevadas": the north (Washoe County), Southern Nevada (Clark County), and the rurals (the remainder of the state). Demographically, Clark County emerged as majority-minority, with Latinos constituting nearly 30 percent of the county's population. In contrast, while Washoe County and rural Nevada have growing Latino populations, both remain overwhelmingly white. These demographic differences correspond to significant political differences.

Table 1. The Three Nevadas: Demographics, 2010

County	Population	% of Population	Latinos	% Latino	Nonwhite	% Nonwhite
Clark	1,951,269	72.3%	567,819	29.1%	1,014,660	52.0%
Washoe	421,407	15.6%	93,552	22.2%	143,278	34.0%
All Other Counties	327,875	12.1%	62,599	19.2%	96,657	29.4%
Total	2,700,552	—	723,990	26.5%	1,254,595	45.9%

Source: Data from "Nevada Quick Facts from the US Census," http://quickfacts.census.gov/qfd/states/32000.html.

Table 2. The Three Nevadas: Voter Registration, 2012

County	Registered	% of Registered	Democrats– Republicans	% Democratic	% Republican	% Other*
Clark	851,804	67.7%	+127,471	45.8%	30.9%	23.3%
Washoe	241,459	19.2%	−1,169	37.5%	38.0%	24.5%
All Other Counties	164,358	13.1%	−36,115	27.9%	49.9%	22.2%
Total	1,257,621	—	+90,187	41.9%	34.7%	23.4%

Source: Data from Nevada Secretary of State's "Voter Registration Statistics October 2012 (Close of Voter Registration–General Election Active Voters by County and Party," http://www.nvsos.gov/.

*Includes nonpartisans and minor party registrants.

Specifically, as the data in table 2 indicate, Clark County is strongly Democratic. At the time of the 2012 election, the county had 127,000 more Democrats than Republicans. In contrast, Republicans dominate the rural counties, while Washoe County is more or less evenly split between Democrats and Republicans.

There are two additional points from tables 1 and 2 meriting discussion. First, better than one in five Nevadans is registered as either a nonpartisan or with a minor party, and the preferences of these voters ebb and flow within the national political context. Second, while just 62 percent of age-eligible Nevadans were registered to vote in 2012, both Washoe County and the rural counties have registration rates that exceed their population shares, while registration in Clark County lags behind its share of the population. Much of this difference stems from the larger share of residents who are under the age of eighteen in Clark as compared to Washoe and the rural counties. In particular, while Clark County is home to 78 percent of the state's Latino population, just 37 percent of Nevada's Latinos are age-eligible to vote.

Nationally, the 2010 reelection of U.S. Senate majority leader Harry Reid demonstrated the importance of the Latino vote in Nevada. However, the seeds for Reid's 2010 reelection had been sown a decade previously when the Nevada Democratic Party's Latino outreach efforts began—a notable outlier to the lack of attention that the political parties have historically devoted to Latinos. The intensity of these efforts increased significantly after the poor Democratic showings in the 2002 and 2004 elections. In particular, after ascending to the top Democratic leadership position in the U.S. Senate in 2005, Reid began rebuilding the state party organization (see Damore 2011). Central to this overhaul was proactively engaging the state's Latino community in hopes of encouraging long-term political participation.[3]

In addition to Reid's capacity to steer substantial resources to the state party organization and attract top talent, the ability of the Democrats to mobilize the Latino community was aided by three factors. First, because the bulk of the state's Latino population is concentrated in east Las Vegas, the Democrats' outreach efforts benefited from economy of scale. Second—in contrast to much of the country, where the influence of organized labor is waning—because of the nature of Southern Nevada's economy, organized labor in Nevada has remained resilient.

Specifically, the Service Employees International Union (SEIU) Local 1107 and the Culinary Workers Local 226, both of which have substantial Latino member-ship, have developed sophisticated political arms that are engaged in proactive mobilization, largely to the benefit of Democratic candidates. These entities were particularly engaged in the 2012 cycle given Republican efforts throughout the country to curtail unionization and union political activity. Lastly, these combined investments produced a cadre of Latino political activists who have begun to create an autonomous Latino political infrastructure.

To be sure, there are well-established Latino organizations in Nevada that have been active in the state's politics, such as the Latin Chamber of Commerce and His-panics in Politics, as well as chapters of national organizations such as the National Council of La Raza. However, the new generation of grassroots organizations, such as Mi Familia Vota, is particularly adept at using social media to engage younger Latinos in politics. To this end, an analysis of the final pre-election voter-registration file for Clark County conducted by the Ramirez Group (a Southern Nevada public relations firm) found a 37 percent increase in registered voters with Latino surnames between March and October, many of whom were young, first-time voters.

The ascension of the Nevada Democratic Party was also facilitated by the downfall of the state GOP. Racked by infighting, continuous leadership turnover, and an inability to execute the most basic functions of a state party organization (e.g., raising money, registering voters, or maintaining an updated voter database), cycle by cycle the Nevada Republican Party deteriorated until (as is discussed below) it imploded in 2012. Given such internal upheaval, the state party devoted little effort to engaging the state's Latino community. And while the Republicans' minority status in the Nevada legislature precluded the party from implementing immigration enforcement policies akin to those in Arizona (Support Our Law Enforcement and

Safe Neighborhoods Act) or Utah (Illegal Immigration Enforcement Act), in 2011 GOP state legislators introduced bills requiring law enforcement agencies to verify the immigration status of individuals taken into custody, and obligating the attorney general's office to create an agreement with the United States attorney general to enforce federal immigration laws.[4]

Far and away, however, it was Sharron Angle's 2010 U.S. Senate campaign that openly fomented enmity between Nevada Republicans and the state's Latino community. A staple of her extensive advertising buys were spots featuring dark-complected and threatening youths and labeling Harry Reid as "the best friend an illegal alien ever had" because of his opposition to Arizona's immigration enforcement law and support for policies that "gave special tax breaks to illegal aliens" and put "Americans' safety and jobs at risk" (see Damore 2011). To add insult to injury, when Angle was asked by a Las Vegas–area high school student about the racial undertones in her immigration spots, at a meeting of the Hispanic Student Union, she responded by saying, "I don't know that all of you are Latino. Some of you look a little more Asian to me," before adding, "I've been called the first Asian legislator in our Nevada State Assembly." As Gross and Barreto note at the beginning of this volume, Angle's efforts, and those of outside groups seeking to suppress the Latino vote, had the opposite effect, as 2010 Latino turnout in Nevada was the highest in the country, and 90 percent of these voters supported Reid.

Commensurate with the combined resources of Nevada Democrats, organized labor, and various community groups devoted to engaging Latinos in the electoral process, the Latino share of the electorate increased gradually from 2000 to 2012. Exit polls suggest that in 2000 Latinos constituted 12 percent of the vote. However, in 2012, the Latino share of the electorate was 18 percent.[5] Moreover, and as discussed below, the increased turnout among Latino voters (and these voters' propensity to vote Democratic) is the single biggest cause for Nevada's Democratic shift.

Obama's Nevada Headwinds

Despite the Democrats organizational strength in Nevada and the increased mobilization of Latino voters into the Democratic Party, the state's economic conditions were a major obstacle to President Obama's prospects of winning Nevada. Indeed, during the previous four years, no state was as adversely affected by the Great Recession as Nevada.

The decrease in conventions and tourism activity, coupled with less gambling among those who did visit the state, meant huge decreases in the state's general revenue fund, which is highly dependent upon gaming and hospitality. The housing meltdown that battered much of the West during Obama's first term hit Nevada particularly hard, resulting in a sharp rise in foreclosures. This was accompanied by a collapse in home equity values that left two-thirds of all homeowners owing more on their homes than they were worth, and steep increases in the state's unemployment rate (particularly in the construction sector) that spiked at 14 percent in October 2010. With so many Nevadans out of work, consumer spending tanked and led to further economic constriction, all of which cut into the other pillar of Nevada's tax base: sales tax. The situation was so dire that after leading the country in population growth for nineteen straight years, Nevada's population (for the first time since the 1920s) contracted in 2009 and 2010.

Needless to say, few Nevadans were optimistic about the state's future heading into the 2012 electoral cycle. Moreover, because the state often fails to apply for available federal grants and is notoriously tight-fisted in appropriating state funds to programs (e.g., education, social services, and health care) that can induce federal money, Nevada is at the bottom in securing per capita federal dollars despite being an electorally competitive state that is represented by the U.S. Senate majority leader (Hudak 2013). In addition, many of the Obama administration's programs that sought to fix the beleaguered housing market in states like Nevada were ineffective because so few Nevadans could meet their requirements.[6] As a consequence, there were few opportunities for the president to claim credit for alleviating the state's economic woes.

Two inopportune comments by Obama added to his problems. In February 2009, while taking aim at excessive spending by bailed-out bank executives, the president lectured that "You can't get corporate jets, you can't go take a trip to Las Vegas or go down to the Super Bowl on the taxpayers' dime." A year later, President Obama again invoked Las Vegas in a less than flattering manner by suggesting at a New Hampshire town hall meeting, "When times are tough, you tighten your belts. You don't go buying a boat when you can barely pay your mortgage. You don't blow a bunch of cash on Vegas when you're trying to save for college." Both comments were given ample attention by the state's media outlets and became a standard GOP talking point throughout the 2012 election cycle. Then Las Vegas mayor, Democrat Oscar Goodman, took such umbrage at the president's remarks that he refused to greet Obama at the airport when the president visited Las Vegas.

The Fall Campaign

Still, heading into the fall, both Romney and Obama were optimistic about their chances in Nevada and responded accordingly. Both campaigns flooded the state's airwaves with campaign spots and Nevada was a frequent stop on both campaigns' itineraries.[7] For Obama, the state's demography and proven Democratic campaign infrastructure, not to mention a hefty voter registration advantage (see table 2), buoyed his chances. For Romney, Nevada's economic conditions provided his campaign with ready-made attacks on Obama. However, given the Democratic registration advantage, Romney's path to victory in Nevada was a narrow one that necessitated not just a strong Republican turnout (particularly in the state's rural counties and among his LDS base) but also cutting Obama's margins among minority voters and winning the vast majority of the state's large number of nonpartisan voters.

Yet, even though the Romney campaign was optimistic about Nevada, not one poll showed Mitt Romney leading President Obama.[8] Moreover, because Romney's victory in the February Nevada caucus had been secured by strong LDS turnout, his campaign had not developed much organization in the state. To make matters worse, unlike Obama, who had the assistance of arguably the country's best state party, Romney had to contend with a party that was taken over by supporters of Ron Paul and those who openly opposed his candidacy.[9]

To circumvent the state party, Romney's campaign created a separate entity called "Team Nevada" that sought to coordinate Romney's efforts with those of U.S. Senate candidate Dean Heller and incumbent House member Joe Heck, who was running for reelection in Nevada's 3rd District. To match the Democrats' get-out-the-vote efforts, "Team Nevada" took advantage of Romney's deep ties in the LDS community by busing in an army of well-intentioned (albeit not particularly skilled) volunteers from neighboring states in the campaign's final weeks. While the Republican effort was much stronger than four years previously when John McCain invested little in the state, "Team Nevada" was no match for the coordinated efforts of the Obama campaign, the battle-tested Nevada Democratic Party, and allied labor and grassroots organizations. The disparity between the campaigns was particularly glaring when it came to engaging the Latino electorate. For instance, despite spending upwards of $30 million on ad buys in Nevada, Romney devoted few resources to Spanish-language advertising.[10] And, while Obama had twenty-five field offices in Nevada, with seventeen offices located in Nevada's largest city, Las Vegas (32 percent Latino), and the state's third largest city, North Las Vegas (39 percent Latino), of Mitt Romney's eleven field offices in Nevada, only two were located in Las Vegas and none in North Las Vegas. Romney's east Las Vegas office that focused on outreach to Southern Nevada's Latino community opened less than a month before early voting began and when, according to the October 6-State Battleground Poll, just 5 percent of Latino voters were undecided.

Consistent with these differences, according to the Election Eve Poll, two-thirds of respondents reported being contacted by the Democrats while just 44 percent

Figure 1. Policy Preferences of Nevada Latino Voters for Selective Issues, 2012 (percent)

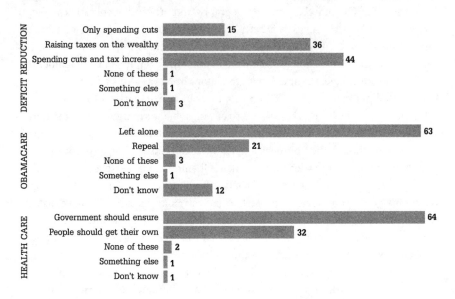

Note: Data from the Nevada subsample of the impreMedia/Latino Decisions Election Eve Poll.

reported being contacted by the Republicans. Equally as problematic for Romney, though, were the policies that he and the GOP were pushing. Specifically, the data presented in figure 1, which summarize (respectively) Nevada Latinos' preferences for deficit reduction, repealing the Patient Protection and Affordable Care Act (i.e., Obamacare), and the role of government in providing access to health care, suggest little convergence with the Republican agenda. In terms of deficit reduction, just 15 percent supported a solution that relies exclusively on spending cuts, while 36 percent favored closing the deficit by raising taxes on the wealthy, and 44 percent preferred a mix of spending cuts and tax increases, the position Obama advocated during the campaign. The Patient Protection and Affordable Care Act was overwhelmingly popular among Latino voters, as 63 percent indicated that they want the law left as is and only 12 percent favored its repeal. Lastly, twice as many Latino voters supported a role for the federal government in ensuring universal access to health insurance as compared to making individuals responsible for obtaining health insurance.

A common Republican refrain throughout the 2012 election cycle was that Latinos are a "natural constituency" for the GOP given the party's economic messages and its family-values agenda (e.g., opposition to abortion and gay marriage). In Nevada, there is little evidence to support these claims. Figure 2 summarizes the

Figure 2. Perceptions of the Most Important Problem Facing the Latino Community among Nevada Latino Voters, 2012

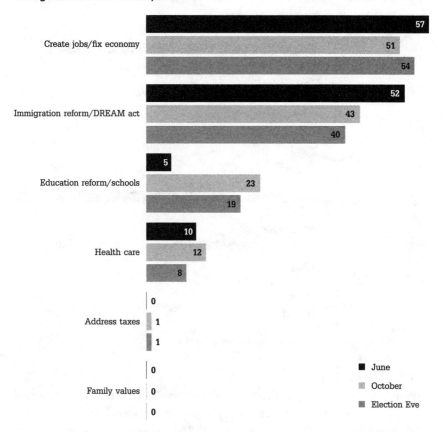

Note: Data from the Nevada subsamples for the June Latino Decision/America's Voice 5-State Battleground Poll, the October Latino Decision/America's Voice 6-State Battleground Poll, and the impreMedia/Latino Decisions Election Eve Poll. Percentages do not equal 100 percent because some issues were excluded from the figure due to space.

responses to an open-ended question from Latino Decisions' polling from June, October, and Election Eve assessing the issues that were the most important for the Latino community. Not surprisingly, economic issues and job creation were consistently the primary concern, followed by immigration reform and passage of the DREAM Act, while issues championed by the GOP, such as family values (1 percent) and taxes (0 percent), had little traction among Latinos in Nevada.

So while Romney's messaging attacked Obama on the economy, it was the candidates' positions on immigration that would loom large. For many Latinos immigration was an issue of great personal importance, as 67 percent of respondents

Figure 3. Impact of Immigration-Related Issues on Enthusiasm for Obama and Romney and Perceptions of Obama's and Romney's Attitudes toward the Latino Community among Nevada Latino Voters, 2012 (percent)

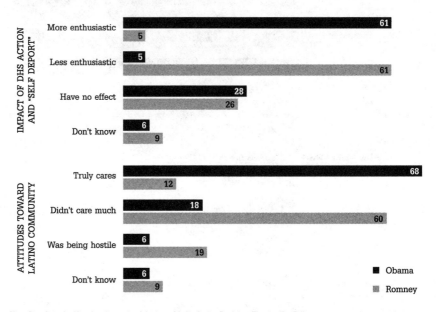

Note: Data from the Nevada subsample of the impreMedia/Latino Decisions Election Eve Poll.

reported knowing a family member, friend, or coworker who was undocumented. Similarly, the October Battleground Survey found that 53 percent knew someone who would benefit from passage of the DREAM Act. The data presented in figure 3 nicely capture these differences. The top panel juxtaposes the impact on voter enthusiasm in response to Obama's decision in June to stop the Department of Homeland Security (DHS) from deporting undocumented youth who attend college or serve in the military and provide them with a renewable work permit, and Romney's statement that immigrants who cannot legally work in the United States should "self-deport."[11] Obama's DHS action was quite popular, as 61 percent indicated that the decision made them more enthusiastic about Obama. In contrast, the same share responded that Romney's advocacy for "self-deportation" made them less enthusiastic about his candidacy. As a consequence (and as detailed in the bottom panel of figure 3), nearly four out of five Latino voters in Nevada saw Romney as either uncaring or hostile to the Latino community. Just 12 percent responded that Romney truly cares about the Latino community. In contrast, 68 percent of voters perceived Obama as caring, with 18 percent responding that the president does not care too much, and only 6 percent felt that Obama was hostile.

The extended time it took for Romney to secure his party's nomination provided him with little opportunity to moderate what had become a whole litany of positions on immigration that were perceived by most Latinos as antagonistic to their community.[12] Romney's lurch to the right during the nomination campaign is even more puzzling given that outside of the Latino community, immigration was not a policy priority for most Americans, including the majority of Republicans.[13] Moreover, most polling showed support for positions much less restrictive than Romney's. By misreading the political terrain so badly, Romney significantly weakened his general election prospects in states such as Nevada.

In contrast, President Obama's deferred-action decision was a political masterstroke. As Hastings notes in chapter 3, it allowed the president to sharpen the immigration contrast with Romney by embracing a policy that already enjoyed broad support among not just Latinos, but the public more generally. The decision also shifted attention away from Obama's deportation record and inaction on comprehensive immigration reform during his first term. In response, between June and October the share of the Nevada Latinos who reported being "very enthusiastic" about voting in 2012 increased by 8 percent, and those responding that they were more enthusiastic about voting in 2012 as compared to 2008 increased by 19 percent. As if that were not enough, at a late September campaign rally in east Las Vegas that drew 11,000 people, the popular Mexican pop-rock band Maná performed and offered its support for the president's reelection. Two days later, a few hundred mostly non-Latinos attended a rally at a suburban casino ballroom featuring Romney surrogate Marco Rubio.

Contours of the 2012 Latino Vote in Nevada

Moving into November, no observers of Nevada politics expected Romney to win the majority of Latino votes given that more than four times as many Latinos in Nevada are Democrats as opposed to Republicans (see figure 4). However, because of the incongruence between the GOP's platform and the policy priorities of the Latino community, as well as Romney's hard-line positions on immigration and his campaign's poor outreach efforts, any hopes of cutting into Obama's margin of support had all but evaporated. In the end, Obama won 80 percent of the Latino vote as compared to 17 percent for Romney. Moreover, as figure 4 details, Obama dominated every subgroup except for those identifying as Republican. And even among Romney's co-partisans, 27 percent defected to Obama.

Figure 4. Variation in the Presidential Vote among Nevada Latinos, 2012 (percent)

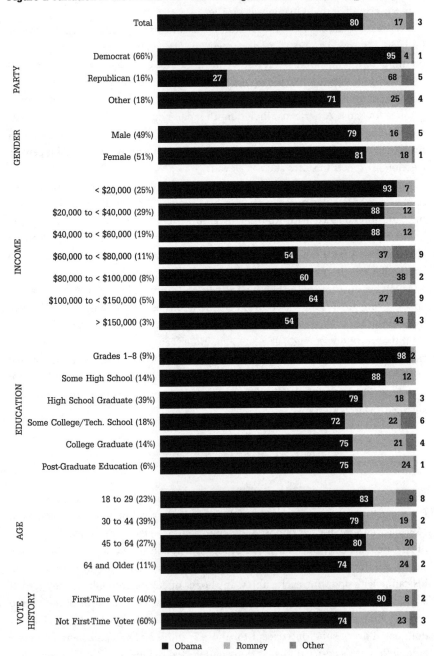

Note: Data from the Nevada subsample of the impreMedia/Latino Decisions Election Eve Poll.

Of particular note is the near-equivalent support for Obama among male and female Latinos. Whereas the June and October Latino Decisions' battleground polls for Nevada suggested a small gender gap, this did not come to fruition in November. The vote distributions for income and education highlight the president's overwhelming support among lower-income and less-educated Latinos. Perhaps the one bit of good news for the GOP can be found in the vote distributions disaggregated by income.[14] While Obama won every income category, his margin decreased among those with incomes greater than $60,000. Unfortunately for the Republicans, just 27 percent of the Latino electorate had household incomes above that level, and even among the highest earning Latinos, Romney failed to win a majority. Romney's vote share also increased slightly among those with some education beyond high school.

Figure 4 also suggests troubling long-term prospects for the Republican Party in Nevada. Latinos who were twenty-nine years old or younger were the least supportive of Romney among all age groups. Moreover, not only did these voters constitute nearly a quarter of the Latino electorate, these voters were the least likely age group to identify themselves as Republicans. The patterns are even more lopsided for first-time voters, who accounted for 40 percent of the 2012 Latino turnout in Nevada. These voters supported President Obama at a 90 percent clip and were more than nine times more likely to identify as Democrats than as Republicans.

The magnitude of Romney's defeat in the Latino community was so complete that it nearly matched that of Sharron Angle's two years previously in her campaign against Harry Reid (Barreto 2010; Damore 2011). Thus, in successive elections, Latino voters had been decisive in delivering two key contests in Nevada for the Democrats. The Latino vote also came in for the Democrats in 2008, but its impact went unnoticed because of the historical nature of Obama's victory, which included a 12 percent win in Nevada. Not so in 2010 or 2012, when the net Latino Democratic vote was greater than either Reid's or Obama's margin of victory.

Discussion and Conclusion

Writing prior to the 2012 election, Bowler and Segura (2012, 3) argued, "Minority voters are a critical part of the Democratic coalition. Without minority voters reflecting these dramatic pro-Democratic distributions, Democrats do not win national elections." No context better captures these dynamics than Nevada, where the gradual increase in both the size of the Latino electorate and its support for Democratic candidates has shifted the state from Republican-leaning to Democratic-leaning. As such, Nevada exemplifies trends that are already transforming the Mountain West into a swing region where the electoral outcomes in once isolated states now exert significant influence on the national partisan balance (Teixeira 2012).

In light of Bowler and Segura's thesis, and with the addition of the 2012 data point, the question remains, given the demographic trajectory in states like Nevada, is this shift immutable? Certainly, as Barreto, Manzano, and Segura note in this volume's concluding chapter, it is difficult to think that if Republicans continue to advocate policies that are so far out of step with the preferences of minority voters (particularly Latinos) and promote candidates as tone-deaf on immigration as Mitt Romney, that the party will fare any better in future elections. Moreover, as Nevada's Latino community (particularly the immense and strongly Democratic under-thirty demographic) become more engaged in politics, the GOP's window of opportunity, and by extension its ability to compete in Nevada, may be rapidly closing.

Yet, even as bad as 2012 was for the GOP at the top of the ticket, the Republican candidate for the U.S. Senate, Dean Heller, won a narrow plurality victory over scandal-plagued Democrat Shelley Berkley.[15] And, while the state sent its first African American representative to the House, Steven Horsford, who was elected to the newly created majority-minority 4th District, Republican Joe Heck easily defeated his Democratic opponent in the swing 3rd District, where Latino voters may hold the balance of power (Segura 2013).

More generally, one of the most interesting findings of the 2012 Latino Election Eve Poll is that while 40 percent of Latino voters in Nevada indicated that they were motivated to turn out to support Democrats (13 percent voted to support the Republicans), a near equal share (39 percent) responded that they voted to support the Latino community. Thus, the degree to which partisan and community identification diverge presents an opening for Republicans. Nationally, the most obvious action that the GOP can take to build goodwill would be to play a constructive role in the passage of comprehensive immigration reform that includes a pathway to citizenship for undocumented immigrants. The Election Eve Poll reported that a third of Nevada Latinos indicated that, if this were done, they would be more likely to vote Republican in the future.

Since the election, it appears that some of this message has been received. The Nevada Republican Party was one of the first state party organizations to support a pathway to citizenship for unauthorized immigrants. There has also been a noticeable shift in tone from U.S. Senator Dean Heller. While serving in the House of Representatives, Heller cosponsored legislation to make English the country's official language, supported amending Section 1 of the 14th Amendment to end "birthright citizenship," and opposed the DREAM Act and President Obama's DHS directive by declaring that "I don't support amnesty." As part of his latest rebranding,

Heller presents himself as "very pragmatic" and speaks about the need for inclusion and a "more humanitarian approach" on immigration (Demirjian 2012). To this end, Heller was one of fourteen Republicans who voted for S.744 (the Border Security, Economic Opportunity, and Immigration Modernization Act) in June 2013.

It is also worth noting that, to date, the ability of the Latino vote to determine winners and losers has largely been limited to statewide federal elections. In contrast, the influence of the Latino community in state and local politics remains a work in progress. To be sure, the number of Latinos elected to public office in Nevada has increased in recent election cycles. However, much of the increase has been aided by term limits and confined to the election of Latinos from heavily concentrated Latino districts to the Nevada legislature. Presently, there are no Latinos serving on the powerful Clark County Commission or the Board of Regents of the University of Nevada, and there are only two Latinos serving on the city councils for the state's three largest cities, Las Vegas, Henderson, and North Las Vegas. And while Nevada has recently elected two Latinos to statewide office, Republican governor Brian Sandoval and Democratic attorney general Catherine Cortez Masto, neither has made ethnicity a central component of their political identities, and Sandoval won with little support from the Latino community.

Still, the growth of the Latino community coupled with the 2011 reapportionment and redistricting (see Damore 2013) means that Latinos are positioned to affect electoral outcomes up and down the ballot. Thus, as Latino participation continues to increase, office-seeking politicians of all stripes will need to be responsive to Latino interests if they hope to win and hold office. Moreover, the continued development of a political infrastructure that is separate from the Nevada Democratic Party and organized labor is producing a new generation of Latino leaders who are giving policy structure to their community's interests and needs. This was most evident during Immigrant Lobbying Day midway through the 2013 session of the Nevada legislature. Hearing rooms in Carson City and in Las Vegas were filled with the faces of the Latino community (many of whom had traveled overnight the vast distance from Southern Nevada), there to testify and lobby for funding for English Language Learners, driver's license permits for undocumented immigrants, and a resolution urging Congress to pass comprehensive immigration reform, which the state senate passed unanimously on the spot.

As for President Obama, Nevada will always loom large in his political legacy. Not only did the state deliver for him in both 2008 and 2012, but it is his partnership with Harry Reid that produced the signature legislative accomplishments of his first term, including the American Recovery and Reinvestment Act (2009), the Patient Protection and Affordable Care Act (2010), the "Dodd-Frank" Wall Street Reform and Consumer Protection Act (2010), the Don't Ask Don't Tell Repeal Act (2010), and the Budget Control Act (2011). And in his second term, it will once again be Reid who will navigate Obama's policy priorities through Congress.

Obama's affinity for Nevada also extends to its diverse population. Late in October, after a long day of campaigning, and near midnight, Obama made an unannounced visit to the back of the house at the Bellagio. There he greeted kitchen workers and room cleaners by telling them that "You are what makes Las Vegas run, you are what makes the Strip run, and all of you represent the dignity of work" (Spillman 2012). Later, Obama advisor David Plouffe noted that the stop had been one of the president's favorites, offering, "For him that was the people he's fighting for. He loves stuff like that. That was a unique one" (Baker 2012). Thus, it was no surprise that late in January 2013, the president selected Las Vegas as the backdrop for his remarks outlining his administration's comprehensive immigration reform principles. Part victory rally, part policy speech, the event was a clear thank-you to the state's Latino and organized-labor communities and a down payment on promises to be fulfilled in a second Obama term.

NOTES

1. Bill Clinton carried Nevada with plurality wins in 1992 (37 percent) and 1996 (46 percent).

2. Barreto (2013) estimates that without taking into consideration the Latino vote, President Obama would have lost Nevada to Mitt Romney by 4 percentage points, and as Gross and Barreto note in their chapter of this volume, Nevada appeared in 90 percent of the statistical simulations assessing Latino Electoral College voting power.

3. See the chapter by Ramírez and NALEO Educational Fund in this volume for a discussion of the different forms of political mobilization.

4. Also in 2010, a proposed ballot initiative entitled "Nevada Immigration Verification," which sought "to discourage and deter the unlawful entry and presence of aliens and economic activity of persons unlawfully present in the United States," was challenged in court by the American Civil Liberties Union and a coalition of local businesses. The initiative proposal was subsequently withdrawn.

5. Although exit polls are problematic for determining the preferences of Latino voters (see Segura 2012), they provide the only over-time estimates of the Latino vote share in Nevada.

6. These include the Home Affordable Mortgage Program, the Home Affordable Foreclosure Alternative, the Home Affordable Refinance Program and its progeny, the Neighborhood Stabilization Program, and the Hardest-Hit Fund—many of which the president personally promoted during his frequent visits to Nevada during his first term.

7. According to data collected by the *Washington Post*, the candidates, their running mates, and spouses visited the state thirty-four times between June and Election Day. The candidates spent a combined $55 million to air 97,379 advertisements in the state. Nevada was also the recipient of significant campaign activity by independent groups emboldened by the post–*Citizens United v. Federal Election Commission* campaign-finance landscape.

8. Because of the difficulties that pollsters have estimating the size of Nevada's Latino

electorate and sampling a representative cross-section of Latino voters, most public polling conducted in Nevada underestimates Democratic support and/or overestimates support for Republican candidates (see Damore 2012).

9. The Paul supporters, who controlled twenty-two of Nevada's twenty-eight delegates to the Republican National Convention, not only refused to support Romney, they sought changes to Republican Party rules that would have placed Paul's name in nomination. In response, the delegation was seated at the back of the hall and was lodged miles from the convention site, despite having been promised top accommodations from party officials in exchange for agreeing to move the date of the Nevada caucus back to allow Florida to hold its nominating event before Nevada. In the end, only five delegates voted for Romney. There were five delegates who abstained, one delegate whose vote was not announced, and seventeen delegates who cast votes for Paul in violation of party rules. Much of the delegation also skipped Nevada governor Brian Sandoval's address at the convention.

10. Jones (2012) reports that on two of the largest Spanish-language television stations in Las Vegas, 63 percent of ad messaging supported President Obama (49 percent by the Obama campaign and 14 percent by SEIU) compared to 37 percent for Mitt Romney. Moreover, just 4 percent of the total Republican messaging was purchased directly from the Romney campaign.

11. Note that for these questions, the sample was split in half, so that 200 respondents were asked the Obama DHS question and 200 respondents were asked the Romney "self-deport" question.

12. Among other positions, Romney pledged to end deferred action, veto the DREAM Act, build a fence along the U.S.-Mexico border, oppose education benefits for unauthorized immigrants and their children, and end visa caps for spouses and minor children of legal immigrants.

13. For instance, in 2008, 35 percent of Nevada Republican presidential-caucus goers cited "illegal immigration" as the most important issue facing the country. In 2012, the share of GOP caucus goers who felt that way was 4 percent.

14. Note that 20 percent of the sample either did not know or refused to report their household income.

15. Data from the 2012 Latino Election Eve Poll indicate no surge in support for Heller among Latinos, as both Heller and Romney secured 17 percent of the Latino vote. Berkley, however, ran well behind Obama across all segments of the electorate as she received 84,000 fewer votes than the president (in contrast, Heller's vote total was 6,000 less than Romney's). Most of the Obama voters who deserted Berkley opted to roll off (1 percent), support minor party candidates (4.9 percent), or cast a "none of the above" vote (4.5 percent) (see Damore, Waters, and Bowler 2012) instead of countenancing a vote for Heller. Among Latinos, Berkley won 69 percent of the vote, which resulted in a net decrease in the aggregate vote relative to Obama of around 2 percent. Given that Berkley's margin of defeat was 1.2 percent, the fall-off in Latino support relative to Obama may have made the difference.

REFERENCES

Baker, Peter. 2012. "A President's Last Race, Win or Lose." *New York Times*, November 4.

Barreto, Matt. 2010. "Proving the Exit Polls Wrong—Harry Reid Did Win over 90% of the Latino Vote." *Latino Decisions Blog*. Available at latinodecisions.com.

————. 2013. "Comprehensive Immigration Reform and Winning the Latino Vote." *Latino Decisions Blog*. Available at latinodecisions.com.

Bowler, Shaun, and Gary M. Segura. 2012. *The Future Is Ours*. Los Angeles: SAGE/CQ Press.

Damore, David F. 2011. "Reid vs. Angle in Nevada's Senate Race: Harry Houdini Escapes the Wave." In *Cases in Congressional Campaigns: Storming the Hill*, 2nd ed., edited by David Dulio and Randall Adkins. New York: Routledge, 32–53.

————. 2012. "Nevada's Odd Numbers: The Complexity of Polling the Silver State." *Latino Decisions Blog*. Available at latinodecisions.com.

————. 2013. "Swimming against the Tide: Partisan Gridlock and the 2011 Nevada Redistricting." In *The Political Battle over Congressional Redistricting*, ed. William J. Miller and Jeremy D. Walling. Lanham, MD: Lexington Books, 67–86.

Damore, David F., Mallory M. Waters, and Shaun Bowler. 2012. "Unhappy, Uninformed, or Uninterested? Understanding 'None of the Above' Voting." *Political Research Quarterly* 65, no. 4 (December): 895–907.

Demirjian, Karoun. 2012. "For Dean Heller, a 'Fresh Start' in Senate Comes at Frenetic Pace." *Las Vegas Sun*, December 12.

Fiorina, Morris P. 1981. *Retrospective Voting in American National Elections*. New Haven, CT: Yale University Press.

Hibbs, Douglas A., Jr. 2000. "Bread and Peace Voting in U.S. Presidential Elections." *Public Choice* 104, nos. 1–2: 149–80.

Hudak, John. 2013. "Why Nevada Falls Short on Federal Funding." *Las Vegas Sun*, March 17.

Jones, Jay. 2012. "A Clamor for Air Time in the Silver State." *Columbia Journalism Review*, September 27. Available at cjr.org.

Segura, Gary M. 2012. "How the Exit Polls Misrepresent Latino Voters, and Badly." *Latino Decisions Blog*. Available at latinodecisions.com.

————. 2013. "The Political Calculus of Immigration Reform: What Republicans and Democrats Stand to Gain or Lose in the Upcoming Debate." *Latino Decisions Blog*. Available at latinodecisions.com.

Spillman, Benjamin. 2012. "Political Eye: President Makes Time for Culinary Workers." *Las Vegas Review-Journal*, October 29.

Teixeira, Ruy, ed. 2012. *America's New Swing Region*. Washington, DC: Brookings Institution Press.

MATT A. BARRETO, SYLVIA MANZANO, and GARY SEGURA

Looking to 2014 and Beyond

THE AUTHORS OF THIS BOOK HAVE MADE CLEAR THAT THE 2012 ELECTION WAS a defining moment for Latino politics. With President Obama receiving a record level of support (75 percent), Latinos proved to be decisive to the election outcome—reflecting the potential of this segment of the wider electorate. The election season also saw both parties featuring Latinos in highly visible roles at conventions. This included Mayor Castro from San Antonio speaking during prime time at the Democratic Convention and Governor Martinez from New Mexico speaking on the Republican national stage. The undeniable influence of the Latino electorate continued after the election as well, as Latinos remained at the center of national discussions regarding a potentially enduring coalition of minority voters, the future of party politics, and the prospect of the passage of immigration reform.

This book provides a comprehensive discussion of the 2012 election with a specific focus on how the Latino electorate contributed. We organized the book around key themes and attempted to provide a balanced discussion of national trends from the campaigns and state-level dynamics to give readers a full view of the various ways in which Latinos made 2012 an election to remember. The authors use the data exceedingly well to write the story of Latinos and the 2012 race.

This concluding chapter builds on the primary themes of this volume by projecting into the future of Latino electoral politics in the United States. Demographics were crucial to the 2012 race, as the population growth over the past decade is what fueled Latino influence in the election. We therefore begin our discussion of future influence for Latinos with the demographic profile leading up to 2012 and how the youthfulness of the population will increase Latino electoral influence into the future. Given that immigration was a dominant theme of the 2012 race (and consequently a major focus of this book), this conclusion transitions into a discussion of how immigration policy will likely color the ways in which Latinos will engage in the electoral system in the near future. Here we draw from more recent Latino Decisions survey data to provide readers with a sense of how Latino voters reacted to discussions of comprehensive immigration reform following the 2012 election and how passage of immigration reform policy could directly impact Latino views of each party and their future voting behavior.

We close by continuing the approach of state-level analysis with the states of Texas and Arizona—two states that are at the heart of discussions regarding the electoral map in the United States and where Latinos are poised to be a deciding factor in future electoral outcomes. In both cases, lack of mobilization has led to a vast, untapped Latino electorate that, if properly engaged, will increase competitiveness for the electoral votes coming from Arizona and Texas.

Continued Growth, Expanding Electoral Influence

New data from the November 2012 U.S. Census Current Population Survey (CPS) reveal a major shift in the U.S. voting population, with the number of white, non-Hispanic voters declining by more than 2 million from 2008 to 2012. In contrast, the number of Latino, African American, and Asian American voters increased by a combined 3.7 million in just four years. During the run-up to the 2012 election, many notable pollsters and pundits failed to observe the changing demographics of the American electorate, with some, such as Gallup, forecasting that as many as 80 percent of all voters would be white, after which noted political scientist Alan Abramowitz predicted that "Gallup's likely voter sample appears to be substantially under-representing non-white voters," two weeks before election day. Building on the analysis by Abramowitz, Latino Decisions posted a lengthy report in October 2012 focused on how most polls were missing the growing Latino electorate. Now that the Census has released its official estimates, the data are clear. The Latino, black, and Asian electorates are growing at a historic pace, and for the first time in history the raw number of white votes declined from one election to the next. These changes are not unique to 2012, but part of a larger and irreversible trend in American politics in which the electorate is becoming increasingly diverse.

From 2008 to 2012, the total number of votes cast among white non-Hispanics changed from 100,042,000 to 98,041,000, a net drop of 2 million votes. In contrast, the number of Latino voters increased from 9,745,000 in 2008 to 11,188,000 in 2012, a net increase of 1.4 million, and African American votes increased even more, by nearly 1.7 million. Asian American voters, who received considerable notice in 2012 for the first time, grew by over half a million, from 3,357,000 to 3,904,000. In total, nearly 3.7 million more minority votes were cast in 2012, while white votes dropped by 2 million.

The changes are even more dramatic comparing 2004 to 2012. Although white votes increased slightly from 2004 to 2008, across eight years from 2004 to 2012, the number of whites voting declined by 1.5 million. During the same time period, the number of black voters grew by almost 3.8 million, while the number of Latino voters grew by 3.6 million. Asian Americans added 1.1 million voters, and combined, there were a staggering 8.5 million more minority voters in 2012 than in 2004. In short, while white voters are declining (a group Republicans won in both 2008 and 2012 by an average 57 to 41 percent in both years), minority voters are growing by over 8 million (a group that Obama won in both 2008 and 2012 by an average 81 to 19 percent in both years). Demographics emerged as the backdrop of the 2012 election and will remain so moving forward.

The trends identified in the November 2012 U.S. Census CPS will continue for some time to come and continue to have major electoral implications. This trend is driven largely by the comparatively young age of Latinos, blacks, and Asians, which ensures that the minority population will only continue to increase as part of the eligible-to-vote and voting population. As of 2012, the median age of the white, non-Hispanic population was 42.3, while the median age for Asian Americans was about nine years younger at 33.2, blacks were over eleven years younger than whites at 30.9, and Latinos were about fifteen years younger at a median age of 27.6. What's more, the Census reported in 2012 that for the first time ever, a majority of all babies born in the United States were nonwhite.

As reflected in figure 1, the population dynamics are sure to change the American electorate beyond 2012 as the number of Latino, black, and Asian voters continues to grow at a pace much faster than for whites, who are likely to continue facing declines in their voting-eligible population for years to come. While the figure illustrates that all three nonwhite populations are growing more quickly than whites, Latinos are clearly leading the pack. Somewhere near 2050 we will begin to discuss the prospect of Latinos overtaking whites as the largest racial and ethnic population in the country!

Figure 1. Racial Composition of the American Electorate, 1976–2024

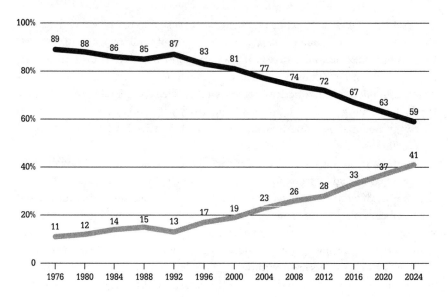

The 2012 election was truly a defining moment in Latino politics. As documented in this volume, Latino voters were decisive for the first time in a presidential race. Barack Obama defeated Mitt Romney by 4.96 million votes, and according to the Latino Decisions analysis of the election returns and Latino voting data, Latinos provided Obama with a 5.8 million vote margin. If the Republicans could have won 40 percent of the Latino vote in 2012, that would have erased 3.6 million net votes—or 72 percent of the 4.96 million they lost by. This provides some reason for optimism for Republicans. One of the dominant themes present across the states covered in this volume is that Republican candidates don't need to win the Latino vote completely; they just need to stop alienating Latino voters to the degree that they have in the past.

Although Latinos are not the only demographic group to whom Republicans need to improve their showing, they represent the single largest bloc of voters who are movable. An estimated 11.2 million Latinos cast a ballot in 2012 according to the Census, and more than 12.5 million are likely to cast a vote in 2016, further increasing the share of all voters who are Latino nationally and in key states. In 2004, George W. Bush won around 40 percent of the Latino vote and was able to carry states with large and growing Latino electorates like New Mexico, Nevada, Colorado, Florida, and Virginia—all states that Obama won in 2008 and again in 2012. The polling data today suggest that Marco Rubio most of all, but Jeb Bush and Paul Ryan as well, can equal or eclipse the 40 percent mark among Latinos if they provide leadership on immigration reform to get a bill signed into law. However they remain far from the 40 percent mark right now.

The Continued Influence of Immigration Policy

This book emphasizes the impact that immigration policy had on the 2012 race, and our more recent polling strongly suggests that immigration will continue to influence Latino voting behavior in upcoming races. As congressional debates have slowly moved through both houses, immigration-policy salience among Latinos has increased over time. As reflected in table 1, the percentage of Latinos who indicated that immigration policy was the most important issue that the president and Congress should address jumped to 58 percent in February of this year, and it stayed well above 50 percent in June—both higher than what was observed during the 2012 race.

With the prospect of comprehensive immigration policy becoming a reality, following the outcome of the 2012 presidential election, where Latinos proved to be a critical component of the winning coalition, Latino Decisions, like many others, began analyzing the potential electoral implications associated with this policy eventually passing. For example, in a June 2013 survey we found that a large number (34 percent) of Latino voters indicate that they are open to voting for the Republican Party if they take a leadership role in advancing comprehensive immigration reform (CIR). Though very promising for GOP hopes of improving their standing with the Latino electorate, there are two important caveats to this finding. First, this question specifically states that the law would include a *pathway to citizenship*, a divisive issue among the Republican members of Congress. Second, the law would have to pass, as our data indicate that Latino voters will not reward members of the GOP for trying to pass a bill if other elements of their party work to block it.

Table 1. For Latinos, Immigration is a Priority

		November 2012	February 2013	June 2013
What are the most important issues that the President and Congress should address?	Immigration	35%	58%	55%
	Economy/Jobs	58%	38%	35%
	Education	20%	19%	15%
	Health Care	14%	15%	14%

Source: Latino Decisions/America's Voice, June 2013 (*n* = 500).

To analyze whether the conventional wisdom is right that the GOP House caucus has little incentive to pass comprehensive immigration reform because most Republican House members represent districts that are overwhelmingly white, we identified twenty-four marginal Republican-held districts (as well as twenty-eight similarly situated Democratic districts) where Latino voters could decide outcomes in 2014 and beyond.[1]

Our analysis utilizes the America's Voice/Latino Decisions Midterm Battleground Districts Survey, which sampled 400 registered Latino voters who voted in the 2010 midterm election (a subgroup that we label Midterm Voters and who tend to be better informed and more conservative than the broader Latino electorate), and another 400 registered Latino voters who did not vote in the 2010 midterm but did vote in the 2012 presidential election (e.g., Presidential Surge Voters).[2] In general, the survey indicated that both the policies and processes being pursued by House Republicans have little or no resonance among Latino voters who are positioned to determine winners and losers in districts held by vulnerable Republican House members.

In terms of policy, 60 percent of Midterm Voters and 57 percent of Presidential Surge Voters view immigration as the most important issue that the president and Congress should address. These voters are also paying attention to the immigration debate, as 86 percent of the Midterm Voter sample and 75 percent of the Presidential Surge sample indicated that they had either heard or read news about the immigration reforms Congress is considering. Not surprisingly, failure by the House Republicans to pass immigration reform that includes a pathway to citizenship results in decreased approval of House Republicans. Even if House Republicans were to pass the KIDS Act, which would provide a path to citizenship only for DREAMers, just 28 percent of Midterm Voters and 26 percent of Presidential Surge Voters indicated that they would either be much more likely or somewhat more likely to support Republicans. In contrast, 65 percent of Midterm Voters and 68 percent of Presidential Surge Votes residing in GOP -held battleground districts responded that such an outcome would make them either somewhat or much less likely to support Republicans. In short, the half-a-loaf approach being offered by some House Republicans does little to improve the party's standing with Latino voters living in marginal Republican districts.

This survey also revealed that these voters have little appetite for how House Republicans are addressing immigration reform. Most notably, nearly twice as many Midterm (60 percent to 32 percent) and Presidential Surge Voters (59 percent to 31 percent) think that House Speaker John Boehner should let members of Congress vote on comprehensive immigration legislation instead of putting the vote on hold until a majority of House Republicans agree to support the bill. Not surprisingly, if

Speaker Boehner does not allow immigration legislation to move forward, the vast majority of Latino voters residing in tier one and tier two GOP -held House districts are likely to view Republicans in Congress either somewhat or much less favorably (72 percent for Midterm Voters and 79 percent for Presidential Surge Voters). These voters also see Republican efforts to make border security a prerequisite before a pathway to citizenship can be put in place as a means to block immigration reform (64 percent for Midterm Voters and 85 percent for Presidential Surge Voters) instead of as a legitimate concern (29 percent/25 percent).

To be sure, as the data presented here indicate, the present trajectory of immigration reform in the House of Representatives does not bode well for the twenty-four Republicans representing marginal districts where Latinos can determine outcomes in the 2014 midterm election. Indeed, as the situation presently stands, Democrats in Congress and President Obama enjoy a better than two-to-one favorability to unfavorability rating among both Midterm and Presidential Surge Voters, while Republicans in Congress have a net unfavorability of 35 and 37 points respectively among Midterm Voters and Presidential Surge Voters. As a consequence, 58 percent of Midterm Voters and 64 percent of Presidential Surge Voters indicated that they will either vote for the Democratic House candidate or are likely to do so, as compared to only 19 percent of Midterm Voters and 18 percent of Presidential Surge Voters who indicated that they will vote for, or are likely to vote for the Republican House candidate. Depending upon how the immigration debate unfolds, Latino voters can tilt the outcome in 2014 in a manner that determines which party controls the House of Representatives in 2015.

Although more speculative at this point, our initial polls focused on the 2016 presidential race suggest that similar to what could happen in 2014, the GOP may need the boost that passage of CIR may provide from Latino voters to give them a realistic shot at winning that race. For example, when respondents to an America's Voice/Latino Decisions 2016 Presidential Survey (conducted in July 2013) were asked who they would support if the 2016 presidential election were today, no more than 28 percent supported Rubio, no more than 25 percent supported Ryan, and no more than 30 percent supported Bush. However, consistent with our findings for the 2014 congressional election, these candidates would get a significant boost if they took a progressive stance on CIR. For example, when responding to a prompt noting Rubio's efforts to pass a law that includes a path to citizenship for undocumented immigrants, a robust 54 percent of Latino voters said they would be likely to vote for Republican Senator Marco Rubio, including 50 percent of Latinos who voted for Obama in 2012. However, without being provided this prompt, Rubio failed to reach even 30 percent among Latino voters. This is similar to what we find for the other potential GOP candidates. Even former vice-presidential candidate Paul Ryan (who was part of the 2012 self-deportation disaster) stands to gain from a shift in immigration policy among Latino voters. Therefore, while each candidate has much to gain from the immigration issue, each GOP hopeful will fail to improve on the historic defeat among Latino voters in 2012 if they distance themselves from the immigration bill and House Republicans are perceived to block the passage of CIR.

On the Democratic side, Hillary Clinton is the runaway favorite among Latinos, and she would take anywhere from 66 percent to 74 percent of the Latino vote if the election were held today. Vice President Joe Biden does not fare as well as Clinton, though he still commands 30 to 40 point leads over Republican rivals. Thus, Republicans need some momentum with Latino voters, and Latino voters seem to be consistently saying that passing a comprehensive immigration reform bill is the way forward.

When Will Arizona and Texas Turn Blue?

The Latino electorate demonstrated electoral influence in 2012 and is poised to impact the 2014 and 2016 races. Demonstrating their continued power, two of the most important Electoral College battles on the horizon directly involve Latino voters. Both Arizona and Texas are states with large and increasing Latino populations that have been solidly Republican, but they are projected to eventually shift toward the Democrats due to the same demographic patterns that have been discussed in great detail in this book. This projection warrants a discussion of the nuances associated with Latino and immigration politics in the states of Texas and Arizona. With continued growth in Latino voting-eligible population and increased mobilization, Latinos will heighten the competition for these electoral votes.

LATINO POLITICS IN THE STATE OF ARIZONA

Arizona is a state that has already become part of the federal electoral discussion, due in large part to Latino growth among the voting-eligible population. Latinos currently make up 30 percent of Arizona's population, representing a significantly larger share than the national average of 17 percent. The projected growth of the Latino population in Arizona also outpaces national averages, as Latinos will constitute an estimated 44 percent of the population by 2050, eclipsing the white, non-Hispanic proportion in the state. Arizona and Mexico are inextricably tied due to their common history and the 370-mile-long border they share. Many Hispanics are, of course, native to the region, which explains the pronounced presence of Latinos in the state (91 percent are Mexican-origin) relative to national trends. Similar to the national numbers reported earlier in this chapter, population growth trajectories by race/ethnicity differ due to sharp age differences between whites and Hispanics. Latinos in Arizona are very young compared to whites, as over half of Arizona's Hispanic population is less than thirty years of age, with a median age of twenty-five. Among White Arizonans, the median age is forty-five, and over 40 percent are age fifty or older. There is no question that Arizona's demographic destiny includes an ever-increasing share of minorities, and Latinos could ultimately make up the largest single ethnic group in the state.

By 2014 Arizona's eligible electorate will be 25 percent Latino. In congressional elections, the impact stands to be most notable in Congressional Districts 1, 2, and 9, where the share of registered Latino voters eclipsed the very narrow margins of victory for Democratic candidates in 2012. If new Latino voters cast their ballots in ways similar to their co-ethnic counterparts already participating, these three districts will move from being competitive swing districts to solidly blue and safe Democratic districts.

The demographic power of Latinos remains significant even when we isolate eligible voters, with substantial room for growth. Currently 43 percent of American citizens under eighteen years old are Hispanic in Arizona. Beyond this large number of newly eligible voters, the Hispanic electorate stands to grow significantly in Arizona due to current participation rates not reaching their full potential. Voter engagement has not moved in tandem with population growth; during the 2012 general election, only 52 percent of Latinos eligible (citizen voting age population [CVAP]) to register to vote in Arizona were registered, and only 40 percent of the Latino voting-eligible population cast a ballot. Registered voter participation was significantly higher; 78 percent of registered Arizona Hispanics voted in 2012. These numbers clearly indicate that with increased voter mobilization specific to Latinos, the state's Latino population could have a marked impact on national elections.

To illustrate the influence increased Latino registration and turnout could have in Arizona, we explore the outcome of the 2012 race at both current rates of turnout for Latinos and higher rates. Consistent with the national trend, the impreMedia/Latino Decisions 2012 Latino Election Eve Poll found that Arizona's Latino population cast 79 percent of their ballots for President Obama and only 20 percent for Romney. While overwhelmingly supportive of Obama, at 17 percent of the statewide electorate, the Latino vote was not enough to provide a Democratic victory. Mitt Romney comfortably carried Arizona by a 10-point margin, beating President Obama by a net 212,382 votes.

The Latino participation gap is significant in the state, and it had major consequences for the 2012 race, as more than half (60 percent) of the eligible Latino population did not vote in 2012. Table 2 re-estimates the presidential-race outcome

Table 2. Re-estimating Arizona's Presidential Race

	Romney	Obama	Win Margin
Actual	1,143,051	930,669	212,382
Eligible Latino nonvoter (589k at 20/79 split)	117,800	465,310	
Total	*1,260,851*	*1,395,979*	*135,128*

Source: Arizona Secretary of State, impreMedia/Latino Decisions 2012 Election Eve Poll.

if the additional 589,000 voting-eligible Latinos in Arizona had turned out. Based on the Arizona Election Eve Poll, we estimate the Latino vote split at 20 percent for Romney and 79 percent for Obama. Under those conditions President Obama would have carried the state, picking up 11 more electoral votes. Arizona's U.S. Senate race was much closer than the presidential contest. Republican Jeff Flake beat Democratic candidate Richard Carmona by only a 4 point margin. Latino voters supported the co-ethnic candidate at a rate of 83 percent. Carmona needed less than 100,000 additional votes to win. Just a portion of the nonparticipating voting-eligible Latinos in the state could have delivered them. Latino voters have the capacity to make any statewide contest competitive. At this point, Latinos make up 23 percent of Arizona's entire eligible electorate. The fact that they vote in a cohesive manner makes their collective impact more potent, whereby the Latino vote margin could be decisive in close elections.

The growth in Latino registration and turnout from 2008 provides some reason for optimism that Latinos could actualize their overall electoral potential in this critical swing state down the line. Specifically, there were 106,000 more Latinos registered to vote in Arizona in 2012, and 109,000 more Latinos cast a ballot in the state compared to 2008. These figures are indicative of the fact that population size and composition on their own do not spur voter mobilization or competitive elections. Still, they provide evidence of growing political influence that should not be dismissed in Arizona.

Presidential and high-profile statewide contests dominate the headlines, but they do not always capture incremental political changes that can build to a crescendo over a few election cycles. For example, during the last election cycle, Democrats won five of nine congressional seats despite Republicans having a registration advantage in six congressional districts. This would not be possible without Latino voters in Arizona who voted solidly Democrat in the past election. The 2012 election also saw Arizona Democrats pick up eight seats in the state legislature, ending the GOP supermajority in Phoenix.

Immigration policy has a more prominent role in Latino politics in Arizona than it does in other states (according to data collected by Latino Decisions). Of course, this is not surprising given the spate of policy, practices, and rhetoric detrimental to Latinos and immigrants that have flourished under the leadership of elected officials like Governor Jan Brewer and Sheriff Joe Arpaio over the past few years. Last November, a plurality of Latino voters (41 percent) said that the reason they voted was to support the Latino community. Arizona Latinos felt more strongly about group interests compared to the national average, and relative to their peers in western states. Similarly, 48 percent of Arizona's Latino electorate cited immigration as the most important issue in the 2012 election, compared to the national Latino average of 35 percent. Immigration will continue to play a dominant role in Latino political behavior in the coming elections in Arizona.

Hispanic voters in Arizona have absorbed the brunt of the harsh political environment state Republicans have crafted around immigration and Latino identity issues (e.g., language policy, ethnic studies, and voting rights). It is perfectly reasonable that this electorate places a high priority on the issues that have been thrust upon them in many ways. In spite of it all, the Arizona Latino electorate remains willing to support GOP candidates if the party passes comprehensive immigration reform inclusive of a pathway to citizenship. In fact Arizona Hispanic voters are more inclined to support Republicans under that condition than their counterparts in any other state. Given the current and growing influence of Hispanic voters in state legislative, congressional, and statewide races, the party would be wise to take them up on the offer.

LATINO POLITICS IN THE STATE OF TEXAS

Nowhere is the tremendous untapped electoral potential of the Latino electorate more visible than in the state of Texas. Hispanics currently constitute 38.2 percent of all Texans, which equates to approximately 10 million out of 26 million residents in the state. Symbolic of just how important Texas is to Latino politics nationally, nearly 20 percent of all Latinos who live in the United States make their home in Texas. It is no surprise that the state is among those with a majority-minority population. Reflective of the national population projections discussed throughout this book, by the end of the decade a plurality of the state of Texas (42 percent) will be Hispanic, and by 2040 the majority of Texans will be of Hispanic origin. These trends are a product of 1,254 miles of border and centuries of history that Mexico and Texas share. This relationship has led to 88 percent of Texas Hispanics, or Tejanos, being of Mexican origin.

The role of sharp age-distribution differences between Latinos and non-Latinos in population projections has been emphasized across several chapters of this volume, and the same holds true for Texas. Half of Hispanic Texans are under the age of thirty, as opposed to only 35 percent of non-Hispanic whites. Only 18 percent of Hispanic Texans are over age fifty compared to 38 percent of whites. Put another way, half of all Texans under the age of eighteen are Hispanic, while 64 percent of Texans over fifty are non-Hispanic whites. One key demographic factor that makes Texas unique compared to most other states is that the vast majority of Texas Hispanics are American citizens (77 percent), where 70 percent are U.S. born and 7 percent are naturalized citizens. Among the small share of foreign-born Texas Hispanics, 65 percent have resided in the United States over fifteen years. In short, Hispanics have well-established roots in Texas and a high proportion of eligible voters within their community.

The Hispanic share of the total active Texas electorate (those who cast a ballot) is more than twice the national average. One out of four registered voters in Texas is Hispanic, compared to only 9 percent at the national level. In the 2012 election, 22 percent of all votes in Texas were cast by Hispanic voters, compared to only 8 percent nationally. Although these numbers appear positive at first glance, Texas Hispanics have turnout rates that rank among the lowest in the nation. The participation gap is especially large and persistent in Texas.

Considering the eligible electorate (those over age eighteen who are American citizens), we find that a stunning 61 percent of Hispanic Texans eligible to vote did not participate in the 2012 presidential election. As depicted in figure 2, that is a 22-point turnout difference from their white counterparts in the state. State and Census Bureau estimates place the nonvoting but eligible Hispanic population at around 2.9 million, a striking number by any measure. The large proportion of unengaged Hispanics is part of what keeps Texas from being politically competitive. If Hispanic voter mobilization efforts were successful in the state, Texas would be as competitive as Florida in statewide contests, including presidential elections.

The most obvious explanation for the low turnout rate of Latinos in Texas is that Hispanic voters in Texas are the most undermobilized in the country. As discussed in more detail in the Ramírez and NALEO chapter, during the 2012 election, only 25 percent of Hispanic voters in Texas reported being contacted by campaigns or organizations encouraging them to vote. The national average was 31 percent, and in Colorado, contact rates were highest at 59 percent. All other states in the West with similar Hispanic demography registered higher mobilization rates than Texas. Increasing national Hispanic voter-turnout rates requires mobilizing Texas and California, where half of all Hispanic Americans reside. Among those who did vote, Hispanic Texans reveal a strong sense of community motivation that rivals partisan attachments. Among Latinos in Texas who voted, 34 percent said they voted to support the Latino community, while 35 percent voted to support Democrats, and 20 percent to support the Republican Party. In a state with little mobilization from

Figure 2. 2012 Eligible Voter Participation

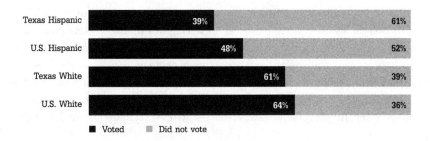

Source: U.S. Census Bureau, November 2012 CPS Report

either party, this makes sense. A third of those who vote do so out of concern for their own group interests, not to advance one party over another.

One of the dominant themes in this book is the importance of immigration to Hispanic voters in 2012, and Texas was no exception. Over half of Latino Texans said that the president's decision on deferred action (DACA) made them more enthusiastic about supporting him. On the other hand, 55 percent of Hispanic Texans said that Romney's reference to self-deportation as a solution to immigration policy made them less enthused about his candidacy. When asked about the current immigration debate, 36 percent of Texas Hispanic voters indicated they would be more inclined to support future Republican candidates if the party advanced comprehensive immigration reform, including a pathway to citizenship. Texas Latinos rate above the national average on this point, displaying more willingness to vote for GOP candidates compared to Latinos in several other states.

Up to this point, Texas has avoided a signature piece of legislation or anti-immigrant pied piper to divide the electorate along ethnic and party lines. Should the GOP take this direction, they will find themselves in a very difficult position as the scenarios we illustrated suggest. Republicans in California, Nevada, New Mexico, Colorado, and increasingly in Arizona, have seen how such antagonism can increase Hispanic turnout and Democratic vote share. Hispanic voters are American citizens; they do not directly benefit from deferred action or a pathway to citizenship. But, we also know that Hispanic voters are strongly motivated by factors important to their community (a third are voting for reasons unrelated to either party), which includes undocumented immigrants. In fact, 58 percent of Hispanic Texan voters know someone who is an undocumented immigrant. It makes sense that such strong responses emerge when candidates and parties take clear positions on immigration.

Over the last two decades, Texas has become more Republican and more Hispanic, a trend that differs substantially from other locales where we have seen a rise in Latino population leading to an increase in Democratic partisans. It is true that the Republican Party has been very successful in winning all statewide offices and picking up seats in the state legislature during this time frame. However, those gains were made in spite of Hispanic votes, not because of them. Outside of George W. Bush's two presidential elections, GOP presidential candidates have struggled to gain above 30 percent of the state Hispanic vote. The most recent contests show Hispanic voters trending further away from the state average support for Republican presidential candidates. Despite the fact that 79 percent of Hispanic voters in Texas voted for President Obama, Mitt Romney carried the state by a 16-point margin (57 to 41). Texas is a good example of how increased turnout among Hispanic voters can turn an uncompetitive contest into a tight race. If an additional 2.9 million eligible Hispanics had voted, Romney's victory margin would be less than 1 point.

Based on the Texas Election Eve Poll, we estimate the additional Hispanic vote split at 29 percent for Romney and 70 percent for Obama. Under those conditions, Romney's margin would narrow to a mere 0.4 percent. With 38 electoral votes up for grabs, Texas would alter the tenor and electoral calculus of presidential campaigns. There is no guarantee that an increased Latino turnout would benefit only the Democratic Party, however, as Hispanic voters could help elect a Republican president as well. If Hispanics make up 25 percent of the state electorate (it was 22 percent in 2012), and 40 percent vote for the GOP candidate, the Republican Party would win at huge margins, with 60 percent of the statewide vote. This is precisely what occurred during the two contests where George W. Bush ran for the presidency. On the other hand, if the Hispanic GOP vote drops to the 10 percent range—as it did in Colorado and Arizona in 2012—and Latino turnout increases, then Democrats win with a 2 to 3 point advantage. In either scenario, it is clear that Hispanic voters are critical to election outcomes in Texas.

Latino political influence in Texas is constrained due not only to underperformance in turnout but also to population concentration in specific regions of the state. Hispanics are 80 percent or more of the population in border areas like El Paso, Laredo, and the Rio Grande Valley. Metro counties Travis, Harris, and Bexar are between 40 percent and 60 percent Latino. Suburban counties and the Dallas–Fort Worth area are less Hispanic, despite recent increases in those locales.

Population concentration has implications for representation. In 2012, thirty-four of the current thirty-six representatives from Texas won their elections by margins of 18 points or more. Further, most of the Texas congressional delegation and state legislature do not have significant shares of Hispanic voters in their districts, allowing them to adopt policy positions that are detrimental or contrary to the preferences of most Hispanic Texans with little concern for political consequences on Election Day. For example, not a single Republican representative from Texas voted against Iowa Rep. Steve King's amendment to repeal the deferred action program (DACA), a program that boosted Hispanic support in Texas for President Obama.

The scope of Hispanic voter influence is clearly visible in the policy positions adopted by officeholders accountable to the statewide electorate. Hispanics account for about one out of five voters in general elections; thus moderate positions on immigration issues (for example Governor Perry's support for in-state tuition for undocumented immigrants who graduate from Texas high schools) signal attention to this electorate. Republicans in Congress harm the statewide prospects for their co-partisans when they adopt antagonistic policy and political approaches to immigration distasteful to Hispanic voters. The Republican-controlled state legislature has significant authority over the redistricting process; thus it is unlikely that more Hispanic-influence districts (very likely to support Democrats) will be created for some time. For this reason, measurable increases in Hispanic political impact are likely to surface sooner in statewide elections rather than congressional or state legislative races.

As the Hispanic population and eligible electorate continue to grow in Texas, signals of their political influence will continue to surface. At this point, Hispanic impact on the 2014 election is already evident. A Hispanic Democrat, state senator Leticia Van de Putte, is running for lieutenant governor of Texas, which has put immigration and other Hispanic-themed issues on the table. Republicans have stepped up outreach efforts in the state by way of public events in Hispanic communities featuring Hispanic Republican elected officials and enhanced field operations. Beyond 2014, there are larger trends to consider. For the most part, Hispanic voters throughout the United States are inclined to vote for Democrats, but their propensity for split-ticket voting and support of Republican candidates is well documented. President George W. Bush demonstrated a sincere interest in comprehensive immigration reform and engaged in a respectful dialogue with Hispanic voters. These policy positions and personal overtures were well received by Hispanics in Texas and beyond, making his gains with this segment of the electorate a model for Republican outreach.

This book has captured the vital role Latino voters played in the 2012 election in a comprehensive fashion, discussing both the aggregate and state-focused implications of the growing power of the Latino electorate. Here, we have highlighted the projected influence Latino voters will have on the 2014 and 2016 races (based on Latino Decisions data available at the time of publication), as well as the more long-term influence driven by Latino-fueled demographic changes across the nation. We have focused on the states of Arizona and Texas, two states where there are a large number of Latino voters, but they are not yet fully energized. We hope that the analysis provided here will offer insights to candidates and organizations interested in further mobilizing the Latino vote.

NOTES

1. See Latino Decisions blog post, "How Latino Voters May Decide Control of the U.S. House of Representatives," available at latinodecisions.com.

2. The margins of error for the Midterm Voter and Presidential Surge Voter subsamples are ±4.9% and ±3.5% for the entire sample.

GABRIEL R. SANCHEZ

Appendix
Discussion of the Data Utilized in this Volume

THE 2012 ELECTION WAS A SHOWCASE NOT ONLY OF THE INFLUENCE OF THE Latino electorate, but also of the value of analytics and effective use of survey data. The authors participating in this volume have drawn heavily from the data collected by Latino Decisions during the course of the full election season. This has led to a very cohesive and well-integrated volume, as the data collected for each state are based on the well-respected research design and methodology of Latino Decisions, the leader in Latino public-opinion research. The purpose of this brief appendix is to provide the reader with an overview of the data utilized across this volume, as well as the methodological approach utilized during the data collection process. Because Latino Decisions provides access to the toplines for just about all of our polls, by providing detailed information about the various tools available through Latino Decisions, the reader can essentially dive deeper into the analysis covered across the chapters contained in this text by engaging in their own research.

Latino Decisions is the leader in Latino political opinion research. Founded by professors of political science (and contributors to this volume) Dr. Gary M. Segura and Dr. Matt Barreto, the firm leverages a unique combination of analytical expertise and cultural competencies that are unparalleled in the industry. The Latino Decisions team is comprised exclusively of credentialed research scientists with established publication records, rigorous methodological training, and experience with large-scale collaborative research projects. Latino Decisions employs professional insights and specialized technical skills to produce the most accurate information about Latino political attitudes, experiences, and engagement. The authors participating in this volume have drawn heavily from the data collected by Latino Decisions during the course of the full 2012 election season, which means that the research in this book makes use of the best available data for this purpose. Rather than each chapter containing the methodology of the polls utilized, this chapter focuses on the general methodology Latino Decisions employs in our polls, with a specific discussion of the data sets used by authors in the volume.

Although Latino Decisions is capable of providing a diverse range of services, most frequently our clients are interested in voter behavior. Accordingly, our surveys employ rigorous social-science standards and precise information about Latino demographics to make sure our respondents reflect the Latino electorate accurately. Consequently, our authors and the larger public can be confident in the accuracy of our survey results. Sound methodology and appropriate protocols are essential to a survey's validity; here we highlight the most important aspects to our approach that make Latino Decisions "the gold standard in Latino American political polling," and this volume the most well-informed discussion of the role of Latino voters in the 2012 election.

Latino Decisions conducts surveys of Latinos in the United States, many times focusing specifically on Latino registered voters. In our Latino registered-voters surveys, such as those used in this volume, we poll respondents who self-identify as Latino or Hispanic and who are registered to vote in a given state or nationwide. Our national polls, such as the Election Eve Survey, are always based on fifty-state national sampling proportionate to the Latino population.

Our samples are drawn randomly from the most recent publicly available list of registered voters in the given state or nationwide, and based on Hispanic households (as identified by different commercial vendors), which are then merged with third-party data to secure telephone numbers; both landline and cell-phone numbers are included. The inclusion of cell-phone numbers is critical due to the increasing number of households that have become cell-phone-only across the nation.

One important starting point for identifying Hispanic households is to screen for Hispanic surnames using the Census Bureau list of 12,000 commonly occurring Spanish surnames. However, Latino Decisions does not rely on a Spanish-surname-only sampling approach as this would potentially exclude a large segment of the Latino electorate who lack a Spanish surname (consider former New Mexico governor Bill Richardson as an example). Beyond the surname list, additional non-Spanish-surname Hispanic households are identified by commercial market data and U.S. Census official population statistics at the census block level to more precisely identify Hispanic households in the sample.

Voter-registration status and Hispanic identification are verified upon contact with respondents, who confirm if they are registered to vote and of Hispanic/Latino descent. A wide variety of Census and academic research reports suggest 90 percent of all Latinos in the United States have a Spanish surname, and using a registered-voter list is far superior to a simple random digit dialing (RDD) of Spanish-surname households because a large percentage of Latinos are *not* registered to vote, yet many will say they are registered to vote in RDD samples, resulting in a high percentage of non-registrants in the sample. Latino Decisions (and most reputable pollsters) avoid this simple error by using the registered-voter list as a starting point. This step was particularly vital in this project, as the authors are utilizing the Latino Decisions surveys in this volume to make inferences about Latino *voters*.

Latino Decisions samples with whatever method a particular client prefers, built on the premise of obtaining the most accurate and representative sample possible. These samples have sometimes been simplistically identified as "surname" samples, but in fact, the samples we purchase do contain an appropriate percentage of respondents with non-Spanish surnames, since we also use commercially available markers of Hispanicity. Typically the number of Hispanics with non-Spanish surnames hovers around 10 percent nationally, but in some states such as New Mexico it can be as high as 20 percent. Hispanic households are typically identified first through the use of Spanish-surname lists, identified by the U.S. Census, but this is not the only identifier of Hispanic households. Additional market-based, geographic, and consumer data are routinely collected and merged into voter files to identify potential Hispanic households, as well as to include non-Spanish-surname households in heavily Hispanic Census tracts. Thus, Hispanic households are identified by a wide range of techniques, of which the surname list is a starting point.

One of the most important aspects of the Latino Decisions methodological approach is that surveying is conducted by fully bilingual interviewers. Respondents are greeted in both English and Spanish, and surveys are conducted in either English or Spanish, at the discretion of the respondent. Up to five callbacks are scheduled for each record. The survey instrument is created by Dr. Matt Barreto and Dr. Gary Segura, often in consultation with other Latino political scientists affiliated with Latino Decisions, and translated into Spanish. The survey is administered under the direction of Pacific Marketing Research in Renton, Washington, and performed using a Computer Assisted Telephone Interviewing (CATI) protocol. CATI programming is performed by Pacific Market Research. Our CATI software offers a superior ability to exercise tight control of sample. We can track call histories for every number dialed, ensure that the times when respondents are called are varied (different times of day and on different days) to maximize response rates, and thus achieve a high degree of customization to fit individual project requirements.

The methodological approach and collective experience of Latino Decisions ensures that the data showcased in this volume are simply the best available for a discussion of the role of the Latino voter in the 2012 election. Below we provide a discussion of the specific data sets the authors of the volume make reference to in their chapters.

The impreMedia/Latino Decisions 2012 Latino Election Eve Poll

The 2012 impreMedia/Latino Decisions 2012 Latino Election Eve Poll (or 2012 Latino Election Eve Poll) is the signature Latino Decisions data set from the 2012 election, and consequently it is the dominant source of data for the authors of this chapter. For this poll (in collaboration with impreMedia), Latino Decisions completed 5,600 interviews with Latinos who had already voted or were certain to vote in the November 6, 2012, presidential election. Interviews were conducted via telephone with live callers, all of whom were bilingual, and interviews were completed in the language of preference of the respondent. Overall, 62 percent of interviews for the Latino Election Eve Poll were completed in English and 38 percent in Spanish. Respondents were reached at landline and cell-phone-only households from November 1st through November 5th of 2012, and the interviews averaged twelve minutes in length.

Voters were prescreened based on their vote history in previous presidential elections and date of registration to include a mix of new registrants and first-time voters. Respondents were asked if they had voted early, and if not, if they were 100 percent certain they would vote on November 6th. With any respondent who was not certain, contact was terminated. Using this same methodology in 2010, about 88 percent of the interviewed sample was subsequently confirmed (validated) as having voted, without any meaningful deviation from reported totals.

For eleven individual states, a minimum of 400 interviews were completed to provide state-specific reliable estimates (this was the case for all of the states included in this volume). For the remaining thirty-nine states and the District of Columbia, an additional national sample was completed and then combined with the eleven stand-alone state samples for an overall combined nationally proportionate sample. The national sample of 5,600 is directly proportionate to the Latino voter population nationwide, and it is weighted to reflect the known Census demographics for Latino voters.

The national sample carries an overall margin of error of 1.8 percent. This is adjusted to account for the design effect resulting from twelve unique sample strata of varying size and the post-stratification weighting used to derive the national estimate. California and Florida each had 800 completed interviews, and each carry a margin of error of 3.5 percent. The remaining nine individual states sampled—Arizona, Colorado, Massachusetts, North Carolina, New Mexico, Nevada, Ohio, Texas, and Virginia—all had 400 completed interviews and carry a margin of error of 4.9 percent.

Latino Decisions maintains a webpage dedicated to this data source.[1] Through this webpage, you are able to view the toplines for the full national survey, with breakdowns for key demographic and political variables, as well as examine the state-specific toplines. There is also a link to a set of PowerPoint slides based on this data, which provide a number of interesting figures utilized across this volume. The impreMedia/Latino Decisions 2012 Latino Election Eve Poll is the best data possible to analyze Latino voting patterns during the historic 2012 election. We encourage you to access this page and explore the resources available to analyze the role of Latino voters in the 2012 election.

Latino Decisions/America's Voice Education Fund Latino Vote Map

The Latino Decisions/America's Voice Education Fund Latino Vote Map (or Latino Vote Map) is the backdrop for the Gross and Barreto chapter focused on analyzing the overall impact of the Latino electorate on the outcome of the 2012 election, and it is referenced by several other chapters throughout the volume. The Latino Vote Map was a Latino Decisions/America's Voice Education Fund collaboration created by Matt Barreto and Justin Gross from Latino Decisions to illustrate the dynamic of Latino influence in the presidential election of 2012. This innovative tool is essentially an interactive web applet allowing users to explore what Latino influence looks like visually.[2] Taking real-time weekly polling data from every state for both Latinos and non-Latinos, coupled with the estimated share of all voters who will be Latino, users of the web app can see what happens if Latino turnout is somewhat lower or higher than expected, if the candidates get more or less of the vote support than expected, or both.

For example, if Latino turnout is somewhat lower than expected in Colorado, or Latino voters break more heavily for Romney in Florida, the Latino Vote Map can be adjusted to account for the impact of these nuances. Users can adjust two sliders for Latino vote choice and Latino turnout rate from low to high and watch various states change from red to blue or vice versa. States that never change colors are those with limited Latino influence and are therefore somewhat held constant. States that flip back and forth with just a slight adjustment of the sliders indicate high Latino influence. And ultimately, one can see whether the magic number of 270 is reached by one candidate or another. We encourage the reader to visit the Latino Vote Map web applet and examine different scenarios from the 2012 election, as this visual demonstration provides some intuition for the theoretical and empirical approach we outline below.

The data underlying this map come from the most recently available independent polling results for all fifty states, both for Latinos and for non-Latinos. The creators began by importing state average poll results from Real Clear Politics as well as FiveThirtyEight.com. They then included specific poll results on Latino vote choice from the most recent Latino Decisions polls, or other reputable pollsters, for each state. This database was continually updated on a weekly or daily basis throughout the election season so that the map was always up-to-date with the most recent polling data.

In addition to poll results on candidate vote preference, we also include the share of all voters expected to be Latino in all fifty states. These data come from both U.S. Census reports on the number of Latinos eligible to vote and those registered to vote in each state, as well as from an examination of the current statewide voter files to assess the percentage of all registered voters who are Latino. The map also takes into account historical data on Latino registration and turnout from elections held between 2000 and 2010.

As individuals make their own adjustments to Latino voter turnout or Latino two-party vote choice, all fifty states simultaneously change their most current state-based estimates (so that each state retains a unique model based on current data), and then all fifty states are aggregated to estimate the total electoral votes for each candidate. While this was designed for the historic 2012 election, Latino Decisions will continue to update and utilize the Latino Vote Map technology for future elections to ensure that this important tool is available to continue to measure the influence of Latino voters on the national electorate.

Pre-Election Surveys: Latino Decision/America's Voice Battleground Polls

In addition to the Latino Election Eve Poll, many of the authors from this volume also draw from pre-election surveys conducted by Latino Decisions as well. Latino Decisions collaborated with America's Voice on a series of "battleground polls" that were focused on gauging the political and policy attitudes of Latino voters across key battleground states leading up to the election. As is reflected in the narratives for each state chapter, the value of including these polls is that it allows for analysis of how the attitudes and preferences of Latino voters in these key states fluctuated over time. This significantly improves the richness of each chapter that was able to make use of these data, as it, for example, provides the opportunity to explore whether campaign events influenced voting behavior over the course of the election.

The first wave of these polls was conducted in 2012 from June 12th to the 21st in Arizona, Colorado, Florida, Nevada, and Virginia. The sample size was 400 across each state for a combined total of 2,000 completed surveys. For the full sample there was a margin of error of ±2.1 percent and ±4.9 percent for each individual state. These surveys asked respondents about their projected vote for president, Congress, and the U.S. Senate, along with policy preferences and enthusiasm for voting in 2012. The surveys also asked respondents about their personal connection to undocumented immigrants and approval of President Obama.[3]

The second wave of the Latino Decision/America's Voice Battleground Polls occurred throughout late September and October in 2012. In contrast to the first wave, these polls were conducted independently for each of the six states included—the same five states as the first wave plus New Mexico. As in the first wave, each state had a total of 400 Latino registered voters, with interviews conducted in English or Spanish at the preference of the respondent. The surveys were all consistent in terms of content and averaged twelve minutes in length, with an overall margin of error of 4.9 percent on results that approached a 50/50 split distribution. All respondents confirmed that they were Hispanic or Latino and currently registered to vote across each state. All of the toplines for each state are available on the Latino Decisions webpage under the "Recent Polls" tab, and the link provides the state-by-state crosstabs so that you can view differences in core content across each state.[4]

Latino Decisions is continuously starting new surveys focused on Latino political behavior, some national in scope and some specific to states. Because we provide the crosstabs for all of our surveys and the methodology behind them on our webpage, you can essentially conduct descriptive analysis without actually needing the data. We encourage you to spend some time on the Recent Polls section of the webpage to look at the new data and tools we may have available at the time of publication for this volume.

NOTES

1. This webpage can be found at http://www.latinodecisions.com/2012-election-eve-polls/.
2. Latino Decisions/America's Voice Education Fund Latino Vote Map: www.latinovotemap.org.

3. More information about this first wave is available at http://www.latinodecisions.com/ files/4013/4083/4006/LD_AV_Battleground_Webinar.pdf.

4. Http://www.latinodecisions.com/files/2413/5173/0145/AV_6-state-survey-TOPLINES_-_ FINAL.pdf. The linked document also has the full methodology statement for each state.

Contributors

Evan Bacalao is NALEO's Senior Director of Civic Engagement and leads the NALEO Educational Fund's community-focused efforts, including its naturalization assistance and promotion program, nonpartisan voter-engagement initiatives, leadership in the ya es hora coalition, and its decennial Census outreach campaign. He is a graduate of the University of Southern California.

Matt A. Barreto is a professor in the Political Science Department at the University of Washington, Seattle, and the director of the Washington Institute for the Study of Ethnicity and Race. Barreto is a founding principal of Latino Decisions. He received his PhD in political science from the University of California, Irvine in 2005. He is the author of the book *Ethnic Cues: The Role of Shared Ethnicity in Latino Political Behavior*, published by the University of Michigan Press in 2010.

Tehama Lopez Bunyasi is an assistant professor in the School for Conflict Analysis and Resolution at George Mason University. Her research focuses on race and ethnic politics, public opinion, political behavior, and processes of race-making. Lopez Bunyasi's current book project, *Breaking the Contract: The Political Possibilities of*

Seeing White Privilege, examines how the policy preferences and political behavior of white Americans are shaped by perceptions of racial privilege and exposure to information about racial inequality framed in terms of white racial advantage. In addition to publishing in academic outlets, she has provided political commentary for PBS and the *New York Times*.

David F. Damore is an associate professor in the Political Science Department at the University of Nevada, Las Vegas (UNLV), where he teaches undergraduate and graduate courses in American politics and research methods. He is currently developing two projects. The first examines the impact of Nevada's geography on the state's political and economic development, and the second (coauthored with John Tuman) assesses the causes and consequences of the growth in Nevada's Latino community. In addition to his position at UNLV, Dr. Damore is a nonresident fellow in the Brookings Institution's Governance Studies Program, a key vote advisor to Project Vote Smart, and a senior analyst for Latino Decisions. He regularly comments on Nevada governmental and political issues for local, national, and international media outlets.

Edelmira P. Garcia, Data and Campaigns Manager at NALEO, received her doctoral degree in educational policy studies with a concentration in Latina/o studies from the University of Illinois at Urbana-Champaign. Ms. Garcia is responsible for NALEO's data-driven civic engagement campaigns and direct mobilization strategy implementation and evaluation.

Justin H. Gross is an assistant professor in the Department of Political Science at the University of North Carolina at Chapel Hill. He earned his PhD jointly in statistics and public policy from Carnegie Mellon University. His research focuses on empirical methods (including latent class models, social network analysis, and content analysis). His recent work has centered on the challenge of measuring ideology expressed in text and survey data. Gross serves as chief statistician for Latino Decisions.

A native of Puerto Rico, **Maribel Hastings** is a graduate of the University of Puerto Rico. Before becoming America's Voice senior advisor, she worked for *La Opinión*, the largest Spanish-language daily in the United States. Maribel became *La Opinión's* first Washington, DC, correspondent in 1993. In that capacity, she covered Congress, major political stories, and elections. Previously, she worked for the Associated Press, San Juan, Puerto Rico Bureau. During her career, Maribel has received numerous awards, including the 2007 Media Leadership Award from the American Immigration Lawyers Association (AILA) for her coverage of the immigration debate in the U.S. Senate. She is also a national political commentator for national Spanish-language TV and radio, and publishes a weekly column in the main Spanish-language outlets and news portals in the country.

Casey A. Klofstad is an associate professor of political science at the University of Miami, where he studies the influence of society and biology on political behavior. He is the author of *Civic Talk: Peers, Politics, and the Future of Democracy* (Temple University Press, 2011) and numerous peer-reviewed articles in outlets such as the *American Journal of Political Science, Political Behavior,* and *Public Opinion Quarterly,* among others.

Sylvia Manzano is a principal at Latino Decisions. She holds a PhD in political science from the University of Arizona. Manzano works with clients on strategic planning, survey design, data analysis, demographic research, and focus-group facilitation. Her most recent work includes design and analysis of the 2012 Latino National Election Eve Poll, national studies on Latino stereotypes and ethnic attitudes, and a series of projects that develop strategies to engage Latino voters and promote civic engagement. Manzano's academic research on Latino politics and policy issues has appeared in many academic outlets, including *Political Research Quarterly, State Politics and Policy Quarterly, Politics and Gender,* and *Urban Affairs Review.*

Jason L. Morin is an assistant professor in the Department of Political Science at California State University, Northridge. His research focuses on Latino politics, judicial politics, and representation. His work can be found in various peer-reviewed journals, including *American Politics Research, Political Research Quarterly,* and *Social Science Quarterly.*

Rani Narula-Woods is the Director of National Campaigns and Strategy for NALEO and oversees and manages original research projects and experiments, digital strategy, and data and demographics. Mrs. Narula-Woods is a graduate of Boston University.

Adrian D. Pantoja is a professor in political studies and Chicano studies at Pitzer College and senior analyst for Latino Decisions. His research focuses on Latino politics, immigration, and religion. His work has appeared in numerous books and academic journals, including *Political Research Quarterly, Political Behavior,* and *Social Science Quarterly.*

Robert R. Preuhs is an associate professor in the Political Science Department at Metropolitan State University of Denver. His research focuses on issues of racial/ethnic politics, state politics and policy, and representation. He is the coauthor of *Black-Latino Relations in U.S. National Politics: Beyond Conflict or Cooperation*, as well as author or coauthor of numerous peer-reviewed articles in leading scholarly outlets.

Ricardo Ramírez is an associate professor of political science at the University of Notre Dame and a faculty fellow in the Institute for Latino Studies. He received his PhD in political science from Stanford University. He is the author of *Mobilizing Opportunities: The Evolving Latino Electorate and the Future of American Politics*, published by University of Virginia Press.

Clayton Rosa, Campaigns and Strategy Program Manager at NALEO, is responsible for the development of digital platforms, and assists with the oversight and management of original research. Mr. Rosa received his Master of Public Administration from the University of Southern California and his Bachelor of Arts from McDaniel College.

Gabriel R. Sanchez is an associate professor of political science at the University of New Mexico and the executive director of the Robert Wood Johnson Foundation Center for Health Policy at the University of New Mexico. He is also the director of research for Latino Decisions. Sanchez received his PhD in political science from the University of Arizona, and his research explores the relationship between racial/ethnic identity and political engagement, Latino health policy, and minority legislative behavior. A leading expert on Latino and New Mexico politics, he has provided political commentary to several state, national, and international media outlets, including *NBC Latino*, the *New York Times*, *La Opinion*, the *Economist*, the *Wall Street Journal*, the *Los Angeles Times*, and *National Public Radio*, to name a few.

Shannon Sanchez-Youngman is a doctoral student in political science and a native New Mexican from Albuquerque. She obtained her Bachelor of Science from the University of New Mexico before spending nine years working in the field of women's community health. Shannon's research interests lie in the social determinants of health, particularly how racism impacts Latina women's health.

Gary Segura is a professor of American politics and chair of Chicano/a Studies at Stanford University. He is also cofounder and principal in the polling firm Latino Decisions™. Segura is one of three principal investigators of the 2012 American

National Election Studies, and was one of the principal investigators of the Latino National Survey in 2006. He is a past president of the Midwest Political Science Association and the president-elect of the Western Political Science Association. He is also a past president of El Sector Latino de la Ciencia Política (Latino Caucus in Political Science). In 2010, he was elected a fellow of the American Academy of Arts and Sciences.

D. Xavier Medina Vidal is an assistant professor in the Political Science Department at Virginia Polytechnic Institute and State University (Virginia Tech). Medina Vidal worked as a fiscal analyst for the New Mexico Legislative Finance Committee prior to earning his PhD in political science from the University of California, Riverside. His research focuses on U.S. Hispanic/Latino elite behavior, Spanish-language media, state politics and policymaking, and federalism and subnational politics in Mexico. His work can be found in various peer-reviewed journals, including the *Journal of Legislative Studies, Latin American Politics and Society*, and the *California Journal of Politics and Policy.*

Betina Cutaia Wilkinson is an assistant professor in the Political Science Department at Wake Forest University. Her research interests include race and ethnicity, Latino politics, public opinion, and political behavior. Additionally, Wilkinson has authored and coauthored several peer-reviewed articles on attitudes toward race and immigration in leading scholarly journals.